The Collected Ernie Kurtz

The Collected Ernie Kurtz

Ernest Kurtz

Authors Choice Press
New York Bloomington Shanghai

The Collected Ernie Kurtz

Authors Choice Press
an imprint of iUniverse, Inc.

iUniverse books may be ordered through booksellers or by contacting:

iUniverse
1663 Liberty Drive
Bloomington, IN 47403
www.iuniverse.com
1-800-Authors (1-800-288-4677)

The release which was signed by the original publisher included a
requirement that the following be included on
the copyright page of this new edition:

The first edition of The Collected Ernie Kurtz was published by The Bishop of Books,
Charles Bishop, Jr., 46 Eureka Ave., Wheeling, WV 26003,
in a limited edition of 1,000 copies and is now out-of-print.
The front cover art was done by Bob Ball, 1489
County Road JJ, Neenah, WI 54956.

Cover Design by Bob Ball Computer Graphics, Martins Ferry, Ohio.
Printed by Gilliland Printing, Inc., Arkansas City, Kansas 67005

Originally published by Wheeling WV: Bishop of Books

ISBN: 978-0-595-52099-2

Hindsfoot Foundation Series on Treatment and Recovery

TABLE OF CONTENTS

Dedication and Acknowledgments

To the many friends who by their encouragement and help made this book possible: Charlie Bishop, Bill White, Tom McGovern, Jim Blair; and to my wife, Linda Farris Kurtz, who has encouraged my work in every way; but most especially to our Chocolate Labrador Retriever, Turbo, who would nose my hand from the keyboard for welcome breaks of chase-toy and tummy-scratch.

FOREWORD

Thomas F. McGovern, Ed.D.

Ernie Kurtz has made an outstanding contribution to our understanding of the experience of Alcoholics Anonymous. His writings and lectures over the past twenty years have been characterized by diligent inquiry and thoughtful reflection as he impartially and respectfully examines the birth and growth of Alcoholics Anonymous, seeking to understand the fellowship "on and in it's own terms". He is persistent in his efforts to protect the AA story from distortion and he insists that those who research the fellowship espouse accuracy and objectivity in their work. He is equally insistent that clear distinctions be maintained between Alcoholics Anonymous and a variety of treatment initiatives and, in the same vein, he distinguishes the AA experience from other twelve-step approaches. Above all, Kurtz is impressed by "the varieties of the Alcoholics Anonymous experience", (the possible title of a new book), "with its openness to differences and cherishing of varieties that are given voice in a diversity of meetings and groups."

This collection of Ernie Kurtz's articles compliments his previously published books *Not God: A History of Alcoholics Anonymous* (1978). *Shame and Guilt, Characteristics of the Dependency Cycle: An Historical Perspective for Professionals* (1980) and *The Spirituality of Imperfection* (1992), co-authored with Kathleen Ketcham. Kurtz's first book, "Not God," tells the story of the origins of Alcoholics Anonymous from the early thirties through the death of its co-founder Bill W. in 1971. This work is a classic, unrivaled in its meticulous and detailed capturing of the influences that formed Alcoholics Anonymous and of the spirit that imbues the fellowship as the essential human limitation of alcoholics finds a home in the mutuality of fellow sufferers. *Shame and Guilt* (1980) addresses the healing of the alcoholic's sense of failure as a human being, pointing to the acceptance of the essential limitation inherent in the human condition as a way of addressing guilt and shame.

Kurtz has written that "history and imperfection are my specialties, not necessarily in that order". One can see both influences at work in *The Spirituality of Imperfection* (1992). Kurtz, as historian, consistently identifies the qualities that identify Alcoholics Anonymous as being grounded on an essential spiritual foundation. It is essentially a spirituality of imperfection that is experienced as a willingness to let go, a gratitude that "perceives gift in all reality", a humility that relieves the pain of comparisons, a tolerance that accepts differences without conflict, a forgiveness that invites healing and the being-at-home-ness that is found in accepting one's own story.

The collected pieces in this volume provide refinement and background for the themes covered in the major works. On sees the author at work as he responds to a variety of professional audiences in a labor of love to advance understanding of Alcoholics Anonymous. Kurtz looks at the Alcoholics Anonymous experience from a variety of perspectives. Whether he is examining the origins of the fellowship, its place in American religious history or how others have described it or influenced it, he is always focused on all the available evidence. He is particularly critical of writers and commentators who propose generalizations about AA without the necessary careful qualifications based on content or fact. His narrative, however, is not a dull recitation of factual material. He finds the bridge between AA context and AA practice in the storytelling and conversion narrative of its members.

The identification of the contributions of Carl Jung and William James to Bill W's appreciation of the spiritual dimensions of alcoholism and of sobriety are an outstanding feature of Kurtz's work. Both Jung and James were impressed by the significance of spiritual experiences in the process of conversion and enabled Bill W. to articulate his own spiritual experience. Kurtz is convinced that Jung and James, together with William Duncan Silkworth, were at least as significant as the Oxford Group in fashioning the spiritual orientation of AA. Of particular note is his observation that the storytelling approach of Silkworth was more influential in fashioning the spirituality of AA than the "sharing for witness" approach of the Oxford Group.

Kurtz's treatment of Bill W. is evenhanded and founded on careful research of the available records. His treatment of Bill W's experimentation with LSD provides a deeper appreciation of the humanity of AA's cofounder, as well as of with Bill's willingness to explore every avenue in the service of suffering alcoholics. The rich fabric of the open mindedness and inclusiveness that characterize AA is woven from many threads, and the many colors of human experience are captured in the pattern.

The relationship between AA and various treatment approaches is treated extensively throughout this volume. A rich historical perspective results from Kurtz's treatment of the subject. The deep involvement of AA in the early treatment initiatives of Sister Ignatia is often ignored. Equally unnoticed is the early practice that obligated sponsors to pay for the alcoholics who were being detoxified in hospital units. No argument is advanced that there is an AA brand of treatment or that AA promotes any particular model of alcoholism. In fact, the opposite is true as Kurtz carefully notes the differences between AA, various models of therapy and treatment and, above all, points to AA as a spiritual way of living that promotes sobriety through the agency of the twelve steps.

With characteristic honesty and balance, Kurtz acknowledges that the two realities of AA and treatment have intermingled over time and that their identities have been blurred in the minds of treatment providers, researchers and the public. He insists, however, that AA has always maintained a distinct identity and history with it's own distinctive language, vocabulary where context and content come alive in healing storytelling. Mäkelä, a European commentator on AA, captures the unique character of the AA activity in describing it as "speech events" with an absence of "cross talk."

Paradox and metaphor are present in the language and practice of Alcoholics Anonymous. Kurtz notes the themes of release, gratitude, humility and tolerance that flow from the twelve steps and how these can be viewed other perspectives. Such complexity, however, does not rob the AA experience of its distinctiveness or of its simplicity. AA spirituality, according to Kurtz, can be distinguished from religion because there is no required dogma, no rules that dictate behavior, no institutional authority and no ritual of worship. Yet there is power and direction within the fellowship that gives hope and strength to alcoholics from every walk of life, and from many religious and cultural backgrounds. Kurtz sees mystery and miracles rather than magic as the spiritual force within AA, with the ultimate reality being "a mystery to be lived rather than a problem to be solved".

Writing this foreword has been a challenging and rewarding experience. My personal and professional association with Ernie has involved sharing and storytelling over many years, a most rewarding and enriching experience. Revisiting the pieces he has written over the years is a reminder of the debt of gratitude we owe him as one who has sought to record and faithfully interpret the AA experience through the words and concepts of its founders, its members and, yes, of its commentators too. Ernie, as the historian and researcher, is convinced that quantitative methodology and qualitative sensibility are tools which enable us to mine the rich spiritual core of the AA story. Ernie's life and work are testimony to the value of such an approach.

Thomas F. McGovern, Ed.D.
Dept. of Neuropsychiatry and Behavioral Science
School of Medicine
Texas Tech University
Lubbock, Texas
February 9, 1999

In February of 1992, NIAAA sponsored a conference in Albuquerque, New Mexico, on the topic of "Research on Alcoholics Anonymous: Opportunities and Alternatives." Attendance was by invitation only and was limited to scholars who had published research on A.A. Among attendees were Bill Miller and Barbara McCrady, the conference's conveners, and such scholars and practitioners as Margaret Bean, Linda Beckman, Stephanie Brown, Chad Emrick, Fred Glaser, Nick Heather, and Alan Ogborne. After a brief introduction by Bill Miller, I opened the conference with the following paper, which remains a challenging review of the perils and promise of researching Alcoholics Anonymous.

RESEARCH ON ALCOHOLICS ANONYMOUS:

THE HISTORICAL CONTEXT

Alcoholics Anonymous has been around for almost sixty years; research on Alcoholics Anonymous has been going on for more than fifty years. Yet we still hear mainly about how "inconclusive" are the results of what now number many hundreds of articles. Projects such as this volume seem to verify the law that Mark Keller formulated in 1972: "The investigation of any trait in alcoholics will show that they have either more or less of it." That seems even truer of those alcoholics who are members of Alcoholics Anonymous.[1]

Both Dickens and Goethe suggest that "Those who have no memory have no hope." And so if it is important to see Alcoholics Anonymous over time, it is also important to see *research on Alcoholics Anonymous* over time. For research on A.A. has its own history, and the story of *what*

1

we have learned about Alcoholics Anonymous, and of *how* it was learned, reveals certain patterns that it would be irresponsible to ignore.

One such pattern is the incomplete parallel, over the past half-century, between research on alcoholism and research on Alcoholics Anonymous. The former has emphasized, in turn, the psychological, the sociological, and the biological. The pattern of research into A.A. runs differently: first came the sociological, then the psychological, and now more and more interest is shown in the spiritual. Throughout that pattern, uneven though it may be, we find two recurrent motifs; and it is under those headings of, for want of better terms, *accuracy* and *objectivity*, that this paper is organized.

The First Motif: Accuracy

Most of the earliest research on Alcoholics Anonymous was conducted by sociologists. Their primary method was careful, attentive listening to A.A. members, both within and outside of A.A. meetings, followed by analyses of what they had heard and seen. The names of Robert Freed Bales, Selden Bacon, and others are surely familiar.[2]

The scope of this earliest research was limited, but the questions asked did derive from accurate, exact data. Later researchers, who ask more sophisticated questions, have not always continued that criterion. One example from the conference that engendered these papers. In conversation, a participant mentioned three studies, observing almost parenthetically that they "demonstrated that Alcoholics Anonymous doesn't work." But as Chad Emrick promptly pointed out, the articles in question all studied individuals mandated to A.A. by the courts. "What those articles demonstrate," Emrick observed, "is that *coercing* people into Alcoholics Anonymous does not work."[3]

Another example, more obvious but also more common: whatever the terms used, failure to advert to the A.A. distinction between mere *dryness* and true *sobriety*, between "putting the cork in the bottle" and attaining a degree of *serenity*, signals a very poor understanding of Alcoholics Anonymous. And so claims that "Alcoholics Anonymous emphasizes that drinking is the principal cause of its members' life problems," awaken in the aware reader wonder that an apparently serious student of A.A. seems unfamiliar with the chapter of its book titled "How It Works," wherein may be found the obvious key sentence: "Self-centeredness! That, we think, is the root of our troubles."[4]

Why this confusion? Why the decline of accuracy? Are more recent researchers less careful students? Probably not. A large part of this problem can in fact be laid at the door of Alcoholics Anonymous itself. For especially in recent years, there is a very real sense in which, increasingly, there is no such thing as Alcoholics Anonymous – rather there have developed Varieties of the Alcoholics Anonymous Experience.[5]

Under the impact of alcoholism treatment (through which an increasing number of new A.A. members arrive at the fellowship), shaped also by cultural pressures to widen the concept of addiction, Alcoholics Anonymous, decentralized as it is, now presents itself in a vast variety of groups, of formats, of understandings even of such basic-to-A.A. realities as *serenity*, not to mention spirituality. This can be a difficult point for people like us to accept, people who want to study Alcoholics Anonymous. Even when we study process, we like our phenomenon to hold still. At the very least, we want it to *be* phenomenon rather than a multiplicity of phenomena.[6]

But A.A. doesn't hold still, and increasingly it mutates. Current research suggests that most A.A. members agree that it is no longer possible to assume that every meeting listed in an A.A. meeting-list is an A.A. meeting. To take an example recently offered: "I went to this place where a meeting was listed, in Akron itself, for God's sake, and they began by suggesting we go around the table and tell 'how we had nurtured our inner child today.' Hell! I'm a drunk, so I left: that wasn't the kind of meeting I need to keep me sober."[7]

Note the *kind of* variety addressed here: this point has nothing to do with the different kinds of *subjects* investigated: young or middle-aged or old; also using or not using drugs other than alcohol, legal or illegal; and other such obviously important differences. The point here concerns the varieties of *experiences* available within Alcoholics Anonymous – and the consequent reality that *all* generalizations about Alcoholics Anonymous need careful qualification.[8]

But there is a consolation connected with this caution: Although the *breadth* of A.A.'s varieties is a new phenomenon, the reality of diversity within Alcoholics Anonymous is not merely recent. A.A.'s differences were one reason why it developed in so decentralized a fashion. Early researchers were aware of that, but they fell into the easy (and enduring) trap of researching what was available – studying those A.A.s who welcomed their research. Influenced also by the secularization hypothesis shared by most sociologists of the era, they tended to overlook the Akron birthplace of A.A. and its more Oxford Group-oriented offspring, concentrating their attention on New York A.A. and its derivatives. The affiliations (and so the locations) of those early students also suggest that they found East coast A.A. more convenient to research. Then too, the strong personality and central role of Bill Wilson had much to do with this focus. Although Bill himself to a perhaps surprising extent welcomed diversity and even disagreement, seeing in them a useful spur to the spiritual virtue of *tolerance*, not all members agreed with him, even about that.[9]

Because most of the differences within A.A., then and now, concern "the spiritual," this point will be picked up below, when we examine that aspect of research's history. A final example, however, may helpfully conclude this introduction to the importance – and the difficulty – of *accuracy*. Many recent researchers refer to Alcoholics Anonymous as a "self-help" program. As validly as that term may reflect sociological precision, as useful as it may be to distinguish from help-by-professionals, when the phrase spills over to questionnaires or interview schedules, it implicitly sorts the sample: only relatively recent A.A. adherents accept that term. A majority of those with over ten years sobriety, my research indicates, object to that label, saying: "No, we tried that, self-help, and it didn't work – that's why we're a God-help program."[10]

And so we are brought back to that ungainly topic, "the spiritual." Because "the spiritual" is a delicate if not difficult topic for most academicians, let's approach it from a more familiar and congenial direction: our commitment, as researchers, to objectivity.

The Second Motif: Objectivity

By *objectivity* I mean, first, care that *the kind of questions* asked are *true* to the phenomenon being studied. Recently, ornithologist Robert McFarlane reminded that "Science is the art of phrasing questions and identifying their attendant assumptions."[11] And so in the name of science, let me as a practitioner in the humanities raise some questions about the assumptions that have attended the history of research into Alcoholics Anonymous – questions raised by my research into the way later researchers have used earlier research on A.A.

Why is it that the most richly accurate as well as most objectively balanced recent studies of Alcoholics Anonymous come in dissertation form, from new rather than established scholars – Taylor, Johnson, Vourakis, Smith?[12] Why is it that there are so few references to this literature among the major figures currently publishing in the field? Should not research scholars keep abreast of and make available more widely the newest contributions to knowledge? And why are certain other articles so frequently cited – at times in ways that raise questions about the assumptions attending their citation?

Let me be specific. Many continue to cite Seiden, whose 1955 master's thesis was based on an *n* of 50, to the effect that "the use of A.A. members in research as representative of the total alcoholic population is unwarranted." Given the date, that discovery was a real contribution, meriting mention even if only for historical reasons. But in all the references to it over the most recent 15 years, I have yet to see any mention of one finding that led Seiden to his conclusion: "Whether in terms of amount of ego strength, comparability to psychiatric populations or recovery from alcoholism, the A.A. [members] appear to be psychologically 'healthier,' i.e. deviate less from the theoretically normal (nonalcoholic) personality." Is that totally irrelevant . . . or merely unwelcome at a time when the ruling assumption seems to be that only those inclined to "infantilism," "authoritarianism" and "religiosity" will do well in Alcoholics Anonymous?[13]

5

Another example: Studies of A.A. and spirituality seem bound to cite Robert Kenneth Jones's examination of the "Sectarian Characteristics of Alcoholics Anonymous" (again with an *n* of 50). One wonders how carefully those who cite Jones have read his 1970 article, which blends keen sociological insight with the kind of errors inevitable in an analysis based on however detailed observations of A.A. in just one locality (Merseyside). But the habitual citation of Jones troubles for a deeper reason: the context for his description was the religious situation in England, which – with its established church and categories of "dissenters" – differs from most other cultures in its understanding of *sectarian*; yet Jones is almost always cited without any advertence to that British context. Why? Because the implications of his terminology are congenial?[14]

A final example: the continued citation of Aharan's 1970 criticism that A.A. members "can't express feelings of depression, disillusionment, fear." Aharan worked out of London, Ontario, and so until I moved to the Detroit area, with its convenient bridge and tunnel, I wondered whether a peculiar reticence might characterize Canadian alcoholics. Not so. But in any case, we are talking about citation. And so it is justified to wonder: At how many meetings – and at *what kinds of* meetings – have those who cite Aharan carefully listened? How many sponsors have they interviewed? Even more importantly, have they attended any after-the-meeting gatherings, the importance of which for understanding A.A. has been detailed by Rudy, Denzin, Smith, and others? Given our awareness of the impact of treatment therapies on A.A. practice, Aharan's complaint would seem to invite follow-up study rather than uncritical citation of a two-decade-old generalization that was questionable even when first formulated.[15]

Question: Do we not have some responsibility to evaluate previous research, or at least to place it in some kind of context . . . or is our obligation solely to pile up the names of those who seem to support some point we are making? This is a pragmatically important as well as a methodologically valid question, for the biases that can creep in are not merely benign. We are all familiar, at least in theory, with the Hawthorne and Heisenberg effects: the impact of the observer on the observed.

What, then, are the effects of the condescension some researchers show towards Alcoholics Anonymous? How self-fulfilling, for example, become prophecies about who will do well, and who poorly, in A.A.? Not only can such judgments influence who gets sent to A.A., but do you think for a moment that the newly sober drunk does not have antennae attuned to the referrer's attitudes?

Let's examine another example. After finding that "affiliates who are younger, male, and lower in SES [socio-economic status], have more slips, are in AA a shorter time [and] tend to be less stable," Joseph Boscarino made it the main point of his 1980 article that such individuals should still be referred to A.A., but that "additional efforts should be made to maximize the effectiveness" of such referrals. Most citations of Boscarino refer to his "findings" and ignore his recommendations. Which would seem unfortunate, because a decade after Boscarino, research by Keith Humphreys *et al.* indicated that "it would be unwise . . . to assume that there is a requisite level of education or social stability that must be attained before a client will affiliate with NA or AA." Examining another common assumption, Humphreys's co-authors observed that while it was possible to assume that clients in residential settings were more likely to attend A.A. because they had more severe problems, it was also possible to assume that higher attendance was due to the staff members in such settings more vigorously encouraging clients to such involvement because they themselves were more likely to be "in recovery from substance abuse and to endorse the philosophy of AA/NA." As always, the choice of assumptions lies with the one doing the citing.[16]

A final example of how the failure of respect can shape assumptions that may flaw the interpretation if not the results of research. In 1964, Mindlin reported that those "who had attended A.A. meetings were less likely to describe themselves as isolated, lonely, or socially ill at ease." Two decades later, Ogborne and Glaser (1984) offered her observation as evidence that Alcoholics Anonymous served best those with a developed "capacity to function in group settings." That is one possible reading, but might there not be the barest possibility that A.A. attendance helps some to overcome loneliness and isolation? This latter interpretation is supported not only by Bacon's (1957) comments on A.A.'s "Re-

7

socialization" of the alcoholic, but by Tremper's almost model sensitivity to the which-comes-first question in his 1972 study of "Dependency in Alcoholics."[17]

By this time, I am sure, you sense my own bias on these questions – and so let me speak directly to it, lest my very real animus be misunderstood. I carry no brief for Alcoholics Anonymous. There are many things about and in A.A. that merit questioning, and my sole act of faith here is in the ultimate value of all real research. But the tradition of historical research within which I work holds it to be a fundamental ethic of scholarship that one seeks *first* to understand any phenomenon in and on its own terms; only then can interpretation and criticism worthy of the names result. The ideal is perhaps clearest in the physical sciences . . . to be open-minded in the sense of *respecting* what one studies, whether it be the human genome or Jupiter's moons or the AIDS virus. Such respect is not "bias": it is rather the pre-requisite for accurate study.[18]

When A.A.'s co-founder queried his physician about his "spiritual experience" in Towns Hospital in December of 1934, what if Dr. Silkworth had conveyed the attitude toward spirituality that seems to characterize some researchers? Why is it that some who choose to research Alcoholics Anonymous seem to bring to that task attitudes toward "the spiritual" that if held toward homosexuality would be termed homophobic? Why, to be more concrete, are pejorative terms such as *religiosity* and *authoritarianism* preferred to the as-descriptive-words *spirituality* and *commitment*? We carefully eschew ethnic epithets and gender slurs: Why can researchers not show a similar sensitivity to the sensibilities of the alcoholics we study? Is it fair to ask their respect if we are unwilling to offer them ours?[19]

Why do I raise so sensitive a point? Because research is that sensitive. An enduring issue in studying Alcoholics Anonymous has been "cooperation." Given the decentralized nature of the A.A. fellowship, the autonomy of its groups, the thrust of its Traditions, researchers are frequently frustrated in their attempts to get cooperation from members of Alcoholics Anonymous. I empathize: historical research, which relies on access to documents, also requires cooperation; and I have discovered that just as we generalize about "members of Alcoholics Anonymous," A.A.

members generalize about "researchers." And so if you gain respect, my research may be easier. And if I violate and lose respect, your research may suffer. As researchers into Alcoholics Anonymous, we are all in this together, whether we like that or not! A.A. members, after all, are human beings: one thing they do not like – any more than we do – is being scorned, having those realities that hold precious meaning for them demeaned and dis-respected.[20]

Let's review but one manifestation of this concern. Respect touches on *ethics*, and our research may require a special sensitivity in this area. Recall the questions raised by Fred Davis in his discussion of a research project of John F. Lofland and Robert A. Lejeune. Wishing to investigate "what features of the social structures of A.A. groups may facilitate or deter affiliation," Lofland and Lejeune undertook field observation of about 70 A.A. groups (all in Manhattan) to which they sent "agents" who "posed as" A.A. newcomers. Davis questioned whether there might not be an ethical problem in such "premeditated deception," objecting that in the name of scholarship, it "constitutes a travesty upon A.A.'s identity." Davis went on: "This is not to say . . . that the sociologist is compelled to accept as truth the ideology by which the organization represents itself to outsiders. But, it is a far cry from intellectually detaching oneself from an organization's values to engaging in acts which effectively make a mockery of them."[21]

Note that the point here – the *impartiality* that can be guaranteed only by *respect* – concerns not criticism of Alcoholics Anonymous, which has been available for over four decades, but the specific history of critical research on the fellowship and its program. That history reveals a consistently recurring motif: the problems inherent in attempts to research "the spiritual" in the broadest sense of that much abused term. The story of those research efforts suggests that, for our purposes, it may be helpful to approach that theme from a sensitivity to the distinction between quantitative and qualitative research – or, from another perspective, to the differences between the research approaches of distancing and of immersion.[22]

The earliest research into Alcoholics Anonymous was primarily qualitative, and that remained the norm until relatively recently when, paralleling alcoholism research's turn to the biologically concrete in preference to the psychologically and sociologically amorphous, research on A.A. also took a strong turn toward quantification. Unlike alcoholism research's yoking of this emphasis with the concretely physiological, however, researchers on A.A. set off on the quantitative trajectory at just the point where the most interesting research questions seemed to deal in some way with "the spiritual."

Why the turn to quantification took place, although an intriguing question, lies beyond our research concern here; but it does seem worthy of note that the explosion of quantitative studies and the burst of insistence on operationalizing directly correlate in time with the availability of funding disbursed by bureaucratically administered institutions.

At first glance, the turn to quantification would seem a real boon. How better guarantee accuracy and objectivity than by the quantitative approach? Numbers are so precise, so verifiable, so unemotional – apparently, at least, so objectively accurate. Yet quantitative research also has assumptions: not only do we look for what we expect to find, but we see what we look for, as was several times demonstrated at the Conference that gave rise to this book. Early in the proceedings, for one vivid example, Robin Room noted that "Nine per cent of the American population have at some time attended a meeting of Alcoholics Anonymous – that is a number greater than practically any other institution, save the public school and the Catholic Church." A bit later, Don Cahalan, citing the same research study, observed that "*Only* nine per cent of the U.S. population has even attended an A.A. meeting" (italics in his voice). Research practitioners, in other words, continue to rediscover the problems inherent in what Nietzsche termed "the doctrine of the immaculate perception." All data are theory-laden: "Perceivers without concepts, as Kant almost said, are blind."[23]

For the deeper difficulty arises from the assumption-turned-demand that "the spiritual" can and should be operationalized. The language is new, but the point at issue is ancient. And although the story of this effort does not necessarily reveal that it *cannot* be done, that history does suggest wariness of claims to achieve measurement of spiritual entities. Some campuses are still afflicted with the lecturer who each year convinces some freshmen that love can be equated with genital tumescence – a not inappropriate parallel, if we recall psychiatrist Leslie Farber's analysis of how the demand to prove love is but one example of the futility of demands to impose will on the spiritual, demands for which addiction affords such a fascinating metaphor.[24]

From our perspective, here, perhaps the best evidence that "the spiritual" cannot be directly measured may be found in our ready (and appropriate) acceptance that there exists no "scientific proof" of the efficacy of Alcoholics Anonymous – this despite descriptions by hundreds of thousands of members of Alcoholics Anonymous who attest that A.A. has saved their lives and made it possible for them to live lives worth living. If we have no such proof, despite all the efforts expended over the years by talented and sophisticated researchers, that very lack (1) supports A.A. members' claims that their program and the spiritual cannot be separated and (2) challenges us to think out research strategies that *respect* that reality.

A review of research suggests that past endeavors to operationalize the spiritual have produced the same results as attempts to trisect the angle or to prove that four colors suffice the map-maker. Yet recognizing that need not provoke despair. If we can lay aside demands that would require the spiritual to be somehow material, we discover that the spiritual can still be investigated. Historically, in fact, two lines of research into Alcoholics Anonymous have shown particular promise in this area: studies of the affiliation process, and the methodology of content-analysis.

Mindful of the danger of falling into thinly veiled re-pursuits of the alcoholic personality, researchers on affiliation have recently returned to exploring its *process*, in this recapturing a research suggestion implicit in a little-known aspect of A.A. history. A.A. co-founder Bill Wilson, together with medical researchers Abram Hoffer and Humphrey Osmond, discovered early on that some kind of *capacity for the spiritual* seemed to be required if an alcoholic was to get the A.A. program. They understood that capacity not as related to church-going or creedal affirmation or upbringing, but as some kind of process potentially present in every human being, a process that could be prodded. Their efforts to learn the nature of this process in fact underlay Wilson's experimentation with LSD. I do not recommend that readers continue that particular exploration, but awareness of it may help researchers deepen sensitivity to the complexity of the pursuit of spirituality, for which "sober intoxication" is a more than two-millennium old image.[25]

"Capacity for the spiritual" is not a new research category: John Clancy broached the topic three decades ago. Others have touched on it more recently, albeit less directly. To the best of my knowledge, only one person, a hobbyist rather than a scholar, is currently researching how early A.A.'s bibliotherapy worked – the practice of assigning certain books to be read, which was seen as an effective way of "opening to the spiritual." But studies of the A.A. practice of sponsorship do follow up on another early hunch about how to achieve that opening. If those who investigate the relationship that is A.A. sponsorship can approach that phenomenon not as a manifestation of "authoritarianism" or "infantilism" but as evidence of the capacity to learn by listening and of a potential for the classic virtue of *humility*, then perhaps we are on the road to researching "the spiritual."[26]

The second promising line of research, although so far more hinted at than carried out, is content-analysis – examining the words and concepts used by speakers or in discussions. Used sensitively, content-analysis can happily marry quantitative methodology with qualitative sensibility. I can point to no major formal study, but limited examples are sufficiently plentiful both to offer hope and to point out pitfalls. Murphy's study of the values expressed at A.A. meetings is one landmark here, and the method has been carried forward informally not only in the dissertations of Taylor and Johnson and Smith and O'Reilly, but in the studies of Denzin and Rudy and Rodin . . . not to mention the too often overlooked work of George Vaillant.[27]

Conclusion:

Accuracy . . . Objectivity . . . Respect: these must guide not only how we approach the topic of our research, but how we approach each other as fellow-researchers into a subject that transcends not only any one of us but, more importantly, any one discipline. The most recent history of research on Alcoholics Anonymous reveals a fault-line not between religion and science – whatever those terms may signify – but between the differing approaches of quantitative and qualitative methodologies . . . between those who believe that truth is best found by maintaining *distance from* the object of study, and those who think truth is best approached by *immersion in* the subject of interest.

On one side, quantifiers and those who fund research reasonably and responsibly request that the realities we claim to study be in some way operationalizable: let's be able to demonstrate that what we study is real, that we are giving, and getting, our money's worth. Those on the other side insist that to study only those aspects of some realities that *are* operationalizable is like undertaking to study non-human life-forms and then restricting the scope of investigation to four-footed fur-bearers: convenient as such a research-design may be, the sample will not be representative of the population.

How might we bridge this gap, so that we can – truly – learn from each other? Any solution must begin, I suspect, with acceptance that quantitative and qualitative research, the preferences for distancing and for immersion, are in a very real way two different *cultures.* As in most such cases, although real efforts may be made (as well as lip service given) to tolerance and mutual respect, there always seems to lurk the not-too-well-hidden conviction that one's own culture is best, that one's own methodology is "number one." The pattern, then, will almost certainly continue of operationalizing quantitative researchers decrying the fuzzy and unreplicable nature of qualitative studies, while qualitative researchers challenge whether what is being so precisely measured has any importance, as they gleefully point out the assumptions implicit in the supposedly objective quantitative studies.[28]

Two cultures, then; and on the assumption that this reality will resurface so long as differently-inclined researchers investigate Alcoholics Anonymous, I think the most apt conclusion to our examination of the historical context of research on A.A. is to frame this theme in historical experience made contemporary by recent film. Reviewing the motion picture *Black Robe*, one critic praised its avoidance of "easy romanticism" in portraying the clash of cultures. "Usually today," he noted, pointing implicitly at Costner's *Dances With Wolves*, "one culture does get romanticized and the other trashed." But in *Black Robe*:

> There is a massive, unvarnished dignity, flawed and vulnerable, in both the Native American leader and the French priest. The tragedy is that, for all their nobility and integrity, they inhabit utterly divergent worlds. What is home for one man is chaos for the other. What is beautiful for one is ugly for the other. What is heaven for one is devastation for the other.[29]

The story of past research on such topics does not conclusively demonstrate that such is also our fate, but that possibility remains real. Can we hope for more than that future historians will be as generous in viewing the equivalent of these two groups among us? I think we can, if the research inspired by, as well as the research reported in, this volume can become itself a contribution to healing . . . to the making whole of the very diverse efforts of very diverse researchers, by encouraging the commitment of all of us to accuracy, objectivity, and – especially – respect.

NOTES

1. Mark Keller, "The Oddities of Alcoholics," *Quarterly Journal of Studies on Alcohol* 33: 1147-1148 (1972); a strong echo may be found in Alan C. Ogborne and Frederick B. Glaser, "Characteristics of Affiliates of Alcoholics Anonymous: A Review of the Literature," *Journal of Studies on Alcohol* 42(7): 670-671 (1981). Charles Bishop, Jr. and Bill Pittman, *The Annotated Bibliography of Alcoholics Anonymous, 1939-1989* (Wheeling, WV: The Bishop of Books, 1989), list 218 scholarly journal articles, 267 chapters about AA in books, and 93 theses and dissertations on the subject.

2. Robert F. Bales, "Types of social structure as factors in 'cures' for alcohol addiction," *Applied Anthropology* 1:1 (1941); Walter L. Voegtlin and Frederick Lemere, "The Treatment of Alcohol Addiction: A Review of the Literature," *Quarterly Journal of Studies on Alcohol* 2: 717-803 (1941); Selden D. Bacon, "Sociology and the Problems of Alcohol: Foundations for a Sociologic Study of Drinking Behavior," *Quarterly Journal of Studies on Alcohol* 5: 402-445 (1944); Dwight Anderson, "The Process of Recovery from Alcoholism, *Federal Probation* 8(4): 14-19 (1944); Robert F. Bales, "The Therapeutic Role of Alcoholics Anonymous as Seen by a Sociologist," *Quarterly Journal of Studies on Alcohol* 5: 267-278 (1944).

3. J. M. Brandsma, Maultsby, M. C., Welsh, R. J. *Outpatient Treatment of Alcoholism. A Review and Comparative Study.* Baltimore, MD: University Park Press, 1990; K. S. Ditman, G. C. Crawford, E. W. Forgy, H. Moskowitz and C. MacAndrew, "A Controlled Experiment on the use of court probation for drunk arrests." *American Journal of Psychiatry* 124 (1967): 160-163;

4. Even Emrick, in a very uneven paragraph, says that the A.A. members' lives "remain alcohol-focused." Chad D. Emrick, "Overview," in Marc Galanter, ed. *Recent Developments in Alcoholism*, vol. 7: Treatment Research (New York: Plenum Press, 1989), p. 7; more balanced treatment may be found in Emrick, "Alcoholics Anonymous: Membership Characteristics and Effectiveness as Treatment," *in eodem*, pp. 37-53. The reference in the text is to Alan C. Ogborne, "Some Limitations of Alcoholics Anonymous," *in eodem*, p. 57; *cf. Alcoholics Anonymous* (New York: A.A.W.S., 1975 [1939]), p. 62.

For a recent clear and correct understanding, see Hazel Cameron Johnson, *Alcoholics Anonymous in the 1980s: Variations on a Theme*, Ph.D. dissertation in sociology, University of California at Los Angeles, 1987, p. 277: "In A.A. parlance, to be dry is to be not drinking; to be sober is to be not drinking and to be working on changing 'character defects' and 'making amends' to people who have been harmed. 'Sobriety' implies much more than not drinking; it involves a new way of life which would not include 13th stepping or using the A.A. meetings for dubious types of personal gain."

5. Johnson, as her title suggests, directly addresses the relevance of this point to recent research. At the beginning of her conclusion, she notes concerning her review of previous research: "These social scientists, by ascribing homogeneity to members and groups, were able to justify making generalizations about members, groups, and the social movement with small samples. Many of them then proceeded to examine the most vocal and visible groups in their local areas. I [say] that, although these groups may represent a valid statement about *some* members and groups, they did not speak adequately for the wide range of types found in Alcoholics Anonymous."

6. On the increasing numbers arriving at Alcoholics Anonymous by way of treatment programs, see "Comments on A.A.'s Triennial Surveys," which "is an analysis of the 1989 survey plus a review of comparable previous surveys from 1977 forward," available from Alcoholics Anonymous World Services. The most detailed treatment of A.A.'s variety, although limited to but one area of the United States (southern California), may be found in Johnson, *Alcoholics Anonymous in the 1980s: Variations on a Theme.* See also Annette R. Smith, *Alcoholics Anonymous: A Social World Perspective*, dissertation, University of California at San Diego, 1991, p. 129: "It is often assumed by outsiders that there is a single pathway to AA success, and that members follow that path in similar cookie-cutter fashion. But as revealed here, there are variations in members' patterns of integration into the social world of AA and in their conversion experiences."

7. Private correspondence to the author (San Diego, CA), 26 December 1991.

8. On the "kind of subjects" chosen for studies of Alcoholics Anonymous, note the importance of the point raised by Smith, *Alcoholics Anonymous: A Social World Perspective.* Noting that some (but too few) researchers insist on a full year of sobriety before using someone as an "A.A. subject," Smith observes (p. 72): "Based on some of the data in this research which suggests that many members do not experience full integration for two or more years, it may be questionable that one year is an adequate measure of successful affiliation. . . . It is estimated that as much as two years may be required for some alcoholics to fully recover neurologically."
    The observation that "*all* generalizations about Alcoholics Anonymous need careful qualification" of course includes that one -- although it is closer to tautology than to truth to say that "All members of Alcoholics Anonymous have a desire to stop drinking."

9. On "secularization," see Oliver Tschannen, "The Secularization Paradigm: A Systematization," *Journal for the Scientific Study of Religion* 30(4): 395-415 (1991); Wilson's letters offer many expressions of the point here . . . and the reasoning behind it:

> But as for the A.A. therapy itself, that could be practiced in
> any fashion that the group wished to practice it, and the same went
> for every individual. We took the position that A.A. was not the

final word on treatment; that it might be only the first word. For us, it became perfectly safe to tell people they could experiment with our therapy in any way they liked.

And on another occasion:

In the early days of A.A. I spent a lot of time trying to get people to agree with me, to practice A.A. principles as I did, and so forth. For so long as I did this . . . A.A. grew very slowly.

10. Harrison Trice and William J. Staudenmeier, "A Sociocultural History of Alcoholics Anonymous," in Galanter (ed.), *Recent Developments*, vol. 7, p. 32. The prevalence of the reaction noted here is verified by stories and interpretations offered by Frank M., current A.A. archivist.

It merits note that even today, although perhaps not on the level of scholarship represented here, there are individuals seriously studying A.A. according to the ancient split between its New York and Akron manifestations. One Texan, reports regularly how his investigations of the readings and the backgrounds of the earliest New York A.A.s proves (to his satisfaction, if not to mine) that Alcoholics Anonymous originated in the Theosophy of Madame Helena Blavatsky, shaped by aspects of Rosicrucianism. And sometimes the same mail brings me pages from a Californian who, immersed in the study of the books read by Dr. Bob Smith and other Oxford Group-adhering early A.A. members, demonstrates (again to his satisfaction more than to mine), that every idea in Alcoholics Anonymous derives directly from the King James version of the Bible.

11. Robert McFarlane, *A Stillness in the Pines: The Ecology of the Red-Cockaded Woodpecker*, as quoted and cited in *The New York Times Book Review*, "Noted With Pleasure," 5 January 1992.

12. Mary Catherine Taylor, *Alcoholics Anonymous: How It Works -- Recovery Processes in a Self-Help Group*, University of California at San Francisco, 1977 (University Microfilms #79-13241); Christine Helen Vourakis, *The Process of Recovery for Women in Alcoholics Anonymous: Seeking Groups "Like Me"*, University of California at San Francisco, 1989; Hazel Cameron Johnson, *Alcoholics Anonymous in the 1980s: Variations of a Theme*, and Annette R. Smith, *Alcoholics Anonymous: A Social World Perspective*, have already been fully cited.

13. Richard H. Seiden, "An Experimental Test of the Assumption that Members of Alcoholics Anonymous are Representative Alcoholics," master's thesis, Denver University, 1955; the research was reported more widely in R.H. Seiden, "The Use of Alcoholics Anonymous Members in Research on Alcoholism," *Quarterly Journal of Studies on Alcohol* 21: 506-509 (1960); one recent citation is Alan C. Ogborne and Frederick B. Glaser, "Characteristics of Affiliates of Alcoholics Anonymous," *Journal of Studies on Alcohol* 42(7): 661-675 (1984); the terms "infantilism," "authoritarianism" and "religiosity" appear in Ogborne, "Some Limitations of Alcoholics Anonymous," pp. 55, 58, and *passim*.

14. Robert Kenneth Jones, "Sectarian Characteristics of Alcoholics Anonymous," *Sociology* (Oxford), 4: 181-195 (1970). Jones informs, for example, that "One of the A.A. symbols . . . is an empty pint beer glass which is placed on the speaker's table." On the specific topic of "sect," although Jones mentions "Niebuhr" (with no indication of whether Reinhold or H. Richard), not Niebuhr nor Weber nor Troeltsch are cited; Jones's bibliographical citations on the topic of "sect" are to two books by Bryan R. Wilson, both of which are manifestly oriented to the British context. A more American-oriented treatment of the same question may be found in Robert C. Fuller, *Alternative Medicine and American Religious Life* (New York: Oxford University Press, 1989), see especially pp. 77ff. and 123 for the criticism, 132ff. for the perspective.

15. Charles Aharan, "A.A. and Other Treatment Programs: Problems in Cooperation," *Addictions* (Toronto), 17: 25-32 (1970). The direct quotation in the text here is from the CAAAL abstract: in the article itself, Aharan wrote that "in some [A.A.] groups, if a person wants to be recognized as a member in good standing, he does not speak about his fear of people, his inability to work . . . the program, the fact that he often behaves badly, or that he is unhappy and depressed -- even if all these things are true." This article is adapted from a talk Aharan presented at the 35th Anniversary International Convention of Alcoholics Anonymous. For a recent citation, Ogborne, "Some Limitations of Alcoholics Anonymous," p. 57. As to the questions raised in the text, all of these points, I am informed, were noted in the discussion after Aharhan's original presentation of his paper.

16. Joseph Boscarino, "Factors Related to 'Stable' and 'Unstable' Affiliation with Alcoholics Anonymous," *International Journal of Addictions* 15(6): 839-848 (1980), italics Boscarino's; Keith Humphreys *et al.*, "Factors Predicting Attendance at Self-Help Groups After Substance Abuse Treatment: Preliminary Findings," *Journal of Consulting and Clinical Psychology* 59(4) 591-593 (1991); B.E. Mavis and B.E. Stofflemayr, "Paraprofessionals, Staff Recovery Status, and Client Satisfaction in Alcohol Treatment," Paper presented at the 97th Annual Convention of the American Psychological Association (1989).

17. The reference here is to Ogborne and Glaser, "Characteristics of Affiliates of Alcoholics Anonymous," 663-664, reporting the research of Dorothee F. Mindlin, "Attitudes Toward Alcoholism and Toward Self; Differences Between Three Alcoholic Groups," *Quarterly Journal of Studies on Alcohol* 25: 136-141 (1964); Selden D. Bacon, "A Sociologist Looks at A.A.," *Minnesota Welfare* 10 (10), 35-44 (1957); Mel Tremper, "Dependency in Alcoholics; A Sociological View," *Quarterly Journal of Studies on Alcohol* 33, 186-190 (1972); Smith, *Alcoholics Anonymous: A Social World Perspective*, also offers sophisticated awareness of "which comes first" questions.

18. The dangers of bias, of course, run in two directions; and the fact that I have chosen to focus on one should not be taken to mean that I ignore the other -- see Note #10, above. Past research on Alcoholics Anonymous and "the spiritual" alerts to the

dangers of both opposed biases. On the one hand there is scorn of "the spiritual," evident disbelief in any such reality. Even if the scorn is muted, assumptions that "the spiritual" is something else, "nothing but" a psychological deficiency or mental aberration or whatever -- such assumptions clearly impede honest research. But as destructive, from the other direction, is the tendency of some committed to "the spiritual" to smuggle into the questions asked or the interpretations generated particular theological assumptions. Theology, thought on spirituality, has its own story: unawareness of or failure to advert to that whole story also undermines the value of research on "Alcoholics Anonymous and 'the spiritual.'"

Taylor, p. 6, offers an example of the kind of sensitivity to context, and the kind of valuable but still unresearched questions, that respect can generate. Commenting on criticisms of A.A.'s "ideological quality and rigidity," Taylor acknowledged the truth of the observation, but suggested that the criticism missed an important aspect of that phenomenon: "A.A. protects its members [from manipulation by pathological or irresponsible members] by providing a fairly rigid ideological structure which limits the goals of the program . . . and by specifying very precisely how recovery is to be achieved, thus limiting and focusing the influence members may have on vulnerable newcomers and one another." Thus, A.A.'s ideological quality and rigidity "serve a very vital function, and it is doubtful if A.A. could survive, or at any rate be as helpful and safe for its members, without these qualities." The very professionals who most criticize A.A.'s rigidity, she suggests, would be the most appalled were this protection lacking.

19. Trice and Staudenmeier, "A Sociocultural History of Alcoholics Anonymous," p. 17, opine that after calling Dr. Silkworth, "*Fortunately . . .* [Wilson] was assured that he was not mad . . ." (emphasis added).

20. Aharan treated this directly in his "AA and Other Treatment Programs: Problems in Cooperation." Among more recent studies, see Linda Farris Kurtz, "Ideological Differences Between Professionals and A.A. Members," *Alcoholism Treatment Quarterly* 1: 73-86 (1984), and "Cooperation and Rivalry Between Helping Professionals and Members of A.A.," *Health and Social Work*, 10: 104-112 (1985).

21. John F. Lofland and Robert A. Lejeune, "Initial Interaction of Newcomers in Alcoholics Anonymous: A Field Experiment in Class Symbols and Socialization," which appeared in *Qualitative Methodology: Firsthand Involvement with the Social World*, ed. William J. Filstead (Chicago: Markham, 1970), pp. 107-118, after originally appearing in *Social Problems*, 8: 102-111 (1960). Responding was Fred Davis, "Comment on 'Initial Interaction of Newcomers in Alcoholics Anonymous,'" in *Qualitative Methodology: Firsthand Involvement with the Social World*, pp. 271-274.

22. There is no time here to trace the history of criticism of A.A., which began with the *Journal of Nervous and Mental Diseases* review of the A.A. Big Book through Francis Chambers and Arthur Cain. The reviews of A.A.'s Big Book that appeared in the *Journal of the American Medical Association* and the *Journal of Nervous and Mental*

Diseases were far from laudatory; the latter in fact was downright snide. The JAMA and JNMD reviews are both reprinted in Kurtz, *Not-God*, p. 92; Francis T. Chambers, "Analysis and Comparison of Three Treatment Measures for Alcoholism: Antabuse, the Alcoholics Anonymous Approach, and Psychotherapy," *British Journal of Addiction* 50: 29-41 (1953); Arthur H. Cain, *The Cured Alcoholic: New Concepts in Alcoholism Treatment and Research* (New York: John Day, 1964), based somewhat on Arthur H. Cain, *Philosophical Psychology of the Socially Estranged Alcoholic*, Columbia University Dissertation, 1960. Bill Wilson's reaction when some members became irate at Cain's publishing his criticisms more widely in *Harper's Magazine* and *The Saturday Evening Post* may be of interest. In a letter to a member who complained about Cain, Bill wrote:

> Probably the Cain article kept some people away from A.A. Maybe some will stay sick longer, and maybe a few will die because of it.
>
> But so far as we who are in the fold are concerned, I think it is a rather good experience. . . . the practice of absorbing stuff like that in good humor should be of value.
>
> Despite its petulant and biased nature, the piece did contain some half-truths. It certainly applied to some A.A.'s at some places at some times! Therefore it should help us take heed of these natural tendencies.

[Wilson (New York) to Betty R., 11 February 1963.]

23. The final quotation is Alasdair MacIntyre's, *After Virtue* (Notre Dame, IN: University of Notre Dame Press, 1981), p. 76; a more extended discussion of this point may be found in Stanton L. Jones, "A Religious Critique of Behavior Therapy," in William R. Miller and John E. Martin (eds.), *Behavior Therapy and Religion: Integrating Spiritual and Behavioral Approaches to Change* (Newbury Park, CA: SAGE, 1988), pp.139-170, *via* whom the quotation of Nietzsche is borrowed.

24. On the futility – and frustration – of the demand to "prove" love, see several of the essays collected in Leslie H. Farber, *Lying, Despair, Jealousy, Envy, Sex, Suicide, Drugs, and the Good Life* (New York: Basic Books, 1976), especially "Will and Anxiety," "Our Kindly Family Physician, Chief Crazy Horse," and "My Wife, The Naked Movie Star," pp. 13-34, 106-119, 146-162.

25. The recent research of affiliation has been helped by rediscovery of Harrison Trice, "A Study of the Process of Affiliation with Alcoholics Anonymous," *Quarterly Journal of Studies on Alcohol*, 18: 39-54 (1957); among the more accessible recent studies are David R. Rudy, *Becoming Alcoholic: Alcoholics Anonymous and the Reality of Alcoholism* (Carbondale, IL: Southern Illinois University Press, 1986, and Norman K. Denzin, *The Recovering Alcoholic* (Newbury Park, CA: Sage Publications, 1987).

In earliest A.A., the reading of specified books and the practice of sponsorship were seen as especially useful in triggering this capacity.

The use of psychedelic chemicals has often resurfaced in the history of research into "capacity for the spiritual"; see, for example, Charles Savage, "LSD, Alcoholism, and

Transcendence," *Journal of Nervous and Mental Disease* 135: 429-435 (1962); Kenneth E. Godfrey, "LSD Therapy," in Ronald J. Catanzaro (ed.), *Alcoholism: The Total Treatment Approach* (Springfield, IL: C.C. Thomas, 1968), pp. 237-253; B.J. Albaugh and P.O. Anderson, "Peyote and the Treatment of Alcoholism Among American Indians," *American Journal of Psychiatry* 131: 1247-1250 (1974). Wilson's experiments are treated both in Ernest Kurtz, *Not-God: A History of Alcoholics Anonymous* (Center City, MN: Hazelden, 1979), pp. 136-137, and in even more detail in A.A.'s own *Pass It On: The Story of Bill Wilson and How the A.A. Message Reached the World* (New York: Alcoholics Anonymous World Services, Inc. 1984), pp. 369ff.

"Sober intoxication" is treated, *passim*, in both Bernard McGinn, *The Foundations of Mysticism* (New York: Crossroad, 1991), and E.R. Dodds, *The Greeks and the Irrational* (Berkeley: University of California Press, 1951).

26. John Clancy, "The Use of Intellectual Processes in Group Psychotherapy with Alcoholics," *Quarterly Journal of Studies on Alcohol* 23: 432-441 (1962); see some follow-up in David R. Rudy, *Becoming Alcoholic: Alcoholics Anonymous and the Reality of Alcoholism*, and Norman K. Denzin, *Treating Alcoholism: An Alcoholics Anonymous Approach* (Newbury Park, CA: Sage Publications, 1987); Several studies on A.A. sponsorship are reported by Emrick, "Alcoholics Anonymous: Membership Characteristics," p. 46; for more on the topic, see Joseph H. Fichter, "Survey on NCCA Membership," *NCCA Blue Book* 30: 11-16 (1978), and Fichter, *The Rehabilitation of Clergy Alcoholics* (New York: Human Sciences Press, 1982).

The in-process work on A.A.'s early bibliotherapy is by Dick B., *Dr. Bob's Library*, to be published in 1992 by The Bishop of Books, Wheeling, WV.

Two 1959 articles on sponsorship, one respectful and the other less so from its psychoanalytic perspective, still helpfully define this turf: Herbert S. Ripley and Joan K. Jackson, "Therapeutic Factors in Alcoholics Anonymous," *American Journal of Psychiatry* 116: 44-50 (1959), and Hendrik Lindt, "The 'Rescue Fantasy' in Group Treatment of Alcoholics, *International Journal of Group Psychotherapy* 9: 43-52 (1959).

On the wider but importantly related topic of what is classically termed "spiritual direction," see Kenneth Leech, *Soul Friend: The Practice of Christian Spirituality* (San Francisco: Harper & Row, 1977), and especially Edward C. Sellner, *Mentoring: The Ministry of Spiritual Kinship* (Notre Dame, IN: Ave Maria Press, 1990).

27. Mary Martha Murphy, "Values Stressed by Two Social Class Levels at Meetings of Alcoholics Anonymous," *Quarterly Journal of Studies on Alcohol* 14: 576-585 (1953); George E. Vaillant, *The Natural History of Alcoholism* (Cambridge, MA: Harvard University Press, 1983). Also informal, but useful for its cross-cultural perspective, is Joseph Kessel, *The Road Back: A Report on Alcoholics Anonymous* (New York: Knopf, 1962), translation of *Avec les Alcoholiques Anonymes* (Paris: Librarie Gallinard, 1960). Explicit but limited is Miriam B. Rodin, "Getting on the Program: A Biocultural Analysis of Alcoholics Anonymous," in Linda A. Bennett and Genevieve M. Ames (eds.) *The American Experience with Alcohol: Contrasting Cultural Perspectives* (New

York: Plenum Press, 1985), pp. 41-58; see also the dissertation by Edmund Bernard O'Reilly, *Toward Rhetorical Immunity: Narratives of Alcoholism and Recovery*, University of Pennsylvania, 1988.

28. My "two cultures," I hope needless to say, are closer to C.P. Snow's than to the more recent James Davison Hunter's.

29. Martin Marty, *Context* 24(3): 5, quoting John Kavanaugh, S.J., in the *St. Louis Review*, no further citation.

In mid-1985, I was invited to participate in a German - American Conference on "Religion and Philosophy in the United States of America" to be held in Paderborn, Germany, in the late Spring of 1986. The following paper was prepared for that conference. Unfortunately the paper was never given, though the organizers were kind enough to publish it in the Proceedings of the Conference: I suffered heart attacks in March and April of 1986 and in May underwent bypass surgery that also repaired a ventricular aneurism.

Some diligent friends, among them Jim Blair of Montreal, somehow came across the piece and have urged me to give it wider publication, so here it is.

For the record, this paper was first published as "Alcoholics Anonymous: A Phenomenon in American Religious History," in Peter Freese (ed.), Religion and Philosophy in the United States of America: Proceedings of the German American Conference, Paderborn, 1986 (Essen: Verlag Die Blaue Eule, 1987), vol. 2, pp. 447-462.

Alcoholics Anonymous:

A Phenomenon in American Religious History

Rarely must a scholar defend his choice of topic, and it is of course impolitic to begin with an *apologia*, but a decade's experience has taught that approaching Alcoholics Anonymous as an historically significant phenomenon requires such an introduction. In the context of this conference, if my topic needs defense, I would point less to the over one million now living human beings who attest that A.A.'s fellowship and program have enabled them to find and to live the meaning of their humanity – sheer numbers, after all, mean little – than to two other realities that it seems irresponsible to ignore.[1]

First, despite wide-ranging developments both philosophical and theological, we still live in the shadow of Bonhoeffer's call for a "religionless Christianity." Although the writhings of theologians over the last forty years have failed to concretize that reality, the same forty years have witnessed A.A.'s claim to be "spiritual rather than religious" find resonance both in the minds of a surprisingly large smattering of intellectuals and – even more surprisingly – in the experience of an ever more diverse spectrum of ordinary people.[2] Second, for whatever reasons of health-care economics or valid re-evaluation of the role of professional expertise in treating chronic illness, the burgeoning spread of "self-help mutual aid groups" that enable the healing and the recovery of human dignity is too obvious – and too obviously significant – to ignore. Such groups virtually all use Alcoholics Anonymous as model, and most of them adopt or adapt the "Twelve Steps" that are the core of A.A.'s program as their own modality of healing.[3]

What is Alcoholics Anonymous?

Alcoholics Anonymous is a fellowship of men and women who share their experience, strength and hope with each other that they may solve their common problem and help others to recover from alcoholism.

The only requirement for membership is a desire to stop drinking. There are no dues or fees for AA membership; we are self-supporting through our own contributions. AA is not allied with any sect, denomination, politics, organization or institution; does not wish to engage in any controversy, neither endorses nor opposes any causes. Our primary purpose is to stay sober and help other alcoholics achieve sobriety.[4]

That "Preamble," the reading of which begins most meetings of Alcoholics Anonymous, well summarizes the thrust of A.A.'s significance in American Religious History. Two points stand out. First, note the idea of a "fellowship," a *Gemeinschaft*, a *fraternité*, within which one seeks self-healing through sharing one's own "experience, strength and hope" – that is, telling one's story. Second, mark the wariness of the usual trappings of religion in the succinct detailing of the membership requirement, the attitude to money and to controversy, the explicit denial of belief-based or cause-based affiliation.

Although my approach to describing A.A.'s significance will be historical, it seems better to use the alloted time to analyze that significance rather than to detail its historical development. Thus, to frame understanding, let me merely list the conscious, explicit, and well-documented sources of the ideas embodied and enacted within Alcoholics Anonymous and then briefly sketch how those ideas got there.[5]

A.A.'s explicit sources are three: (1) the psychology of Dr. Carl Jung and most particularly his insistence on the importance of "religious experience"; (2) the Oxford Group (later Moral Re-Armament) vision of "First Century Christianity" as promulgated by the Pennsylvania-born Lutheran minister, Frank Buchman; and (3) William James's portrayal of *The Varieties of Religious Experience* and especially his description of the "conversion" experienced by the "twice-born" or the "sick-soul." T h e story of A.A.'s shaping by these sources can be told briefly. Over several months in 1931, Rowland Hazard, a Rhode Island businessman, sought treatment for his alcoholism from Dr. Jung, who suggested that his only hope was "a religious experience." Rowland joined the Oxford Group and carried that message of Jung to a friend, also alcoholic, who carried it to another alcoholic friend, Edwin Thatcher. Thatcher in turn, in November of 1934, conveyed it to the most hopeless drunk he knew, his old drinking-buddy William Griffith Wilson, a former Wall Street hustler. Scant weeks later, Wilson, while being detoxified in Towns Hospital in New York City, underwent a "spiritual experience" that his physician, Dr. William Duncan Silkworth, helped him to understand in Jamesian terms.

Upon his release from the hospital, Wilson for four months tried to carry the same message to others, both within the Oxford Group and at Towns Hospital, but without any success beyond the fact that he himself stayed sober. In May of 1935, Bill traveled to Akron, Ohio, in pursuit of a business opportunity that promptly failed. Fearing that he would again turn to alcohol, Wilson sought out another alcoholic not for the purpose of saving that alcoholic but to save himself. The alcoholic Bill found turned out to be a physician, a surgeon, Dr. Robert Holbrook Smith, and so rather than tell him about the malady, alcoholism, Wilson told Smith about himself, the alcoholic. Although familiar with Oxford Group ideas, Smith heard something different in Wilson. The date of Smith's last drink, June 10, 1935, is celebrated within Alcoholics Anonymous as its birthday, and "Bill W. and Dr. Bob" are revered as A.A.'s co-founders.

Mindful of those sources, some dismiss Alcoholics Anonymous as another example of the crutch that simplistic evangelical religion affords the intellectually deficient, seeing little difference between attending A.A. meetings and joining some revivalist congregation.[6] Others find in Alcoholics Anonymous more of a "mind-cure" or "positive thinking" approach, and of course Donald Meyer has taught us to see through all the heirs of William James.[7] Still others, perhaps more respectfully but no less reductively, concentrate on the "mysticism" of Jungian thought and present A.A. in terms of Aldous Huxley's "perennial philosophy" as updated by Milton Berman or, more fashionably, in the concepts of Gregory Bateson's "Cybernetics of Self."[8] Most recently, in response to A.A.'s continuing success, we find deeper psychological yet still religiously lacking analyses in the work of Harvard psychiatrists John Mack and Edward Khantzian in their explorations of "narcissism" and "The Governance of the Self."[9] Yet all these analyses of Alcoholics Anonymous, whether contemptuous or appreciative, overlook the same two things: A.A.'s context and A.A. practice.

My point in this paper is that in order to understand the religious and philosophical significance of Alcoholics Anonymous and its offspring in American history, two simple facts must be kept in mind. First, Alcoholics Anonymous came into being and attained final form in the decade between 1935 and 1945. Second, from its beginning and still today, the philosophy and the spirituality – the *healing* – of Alcoholics Anonymous is transmitted by the practice of storytelling, of telling a particular kind of story the very format of which inculcates a way of thinking that shapes a particular way of life.

First, the context. Ideas, perhaps especially if borrowed from varied sources, have implicit as well as self-conscious roots. There is both a climate and a soil of opinion. The years between 1929 and 1945 mark the dawn of a renewed awareness of human limitation. Less significant, for our purposes, than the Great Depression, the revelations of Auschwitz, and the use of atomic weapons, are the permeation of American thought by existentialist philosophy and neo-orthodox theology. However confusedly, Americans in this era found themselves confronting "the experience of nothingness" and distinguishing not only between doing and having but between doing and *being.*[10]

The earliest members of Alcoholics Anonymous, like most of their successors, were not readers of Heidegger and Sartre, nor even of Paul Tillich and the brothers Niebuhr. And although there is evidence of subtly shaping influence by the thought of Karen Horney and Harry Stack Sullivan, I prefer to rest my claim for affinity on the recognition of it by Reinhold Niebuhr in his 1960 "Letter to A.A.," in which he marked precisely the "acceptance of failure and limitation" as the key to A.A.'s success.[11]

The personal acceptance of human essential limitation permeates the whole A.A. program. It comes through most clearly in the Alcoholics Anonymous understanding of the "alcoholic" as someone who cannot safely drink any alcohol at all. The acceptance of that "cannot" does not take away freedom but bestows it. For if there is a *not* at the very core of one's being, then embrace of that *not* fulfills one's being.

Guided by an insight far older than the fifty or two hundred years usually accorded it by the historically naive, the A.A. member views his or her disease as an inherent attraction to the self-destructive – in psychological terms, as an obsession-compulsion. In a theological vocabulary, Alcoholics Anonymous understands alcoholism not as actually sinful but as a manifestation of "original sin." In the acknowledgment "I am an alcoholic," then, one professes less "I cannot drink" than "I can not-drink" – no small freedom for the obsessive-compulsive, for the addict.

A.A.'s focus on the "not-ness" of human essential limitation suggests a vision of human both-and-ness, of the human as a mixture or a meeting point of being and non-being. Because that concept is so abstract, let me break off from this exploration of what A.A. drew from the context of its formative decade and turn to *how* this abstract vision is conveyed within the very concrete format of an A.A. meeting – by the practice of storytelling.

The bridge between context and practice, between the abstract and the concrete, may be found in two understandings that undergird Alcoholics Anonymous as both program and fellowship. According to a key passage of the A.A. "Big Book": "Selfishness – self-centeredness! That, we think, is the root of our troubles."[12] That self-centeredness, which attempts to deny human both-and-ness, manifests itself in especially two ways in the drinking alcoholic. First, there is the claim and the demand to be in control, signaled by the way the alcoholic uses both alcohol and other people. Second, there is the denial of all dependence – again, both on alcohol and on others.

In reality, of course, as A.A. recognizes, the actively drinking alcoholic is both totally out of control, addicted, and utterly dependent on the chemical alcohol. A.A.'s prescription, the fundamental message of all the stories told at its meetings, is the middle course of limited control and limited dependence. "You can do something, but not everything." "You alone can do it, but you cannot do it alone." These acceptances, conveyed by the telling of stories, shape the nature of the A.A. fellowship. T h e telling of stories. Recall A.A.'s "Preamble": "share their experience, strength and hope." How is it that personal narrative – telling stories that "disclose in a general way what we used to be like, what happened, and what we are like now"[13] – can prove healing not only of chronic disabilities such as alcoholism but of one's humanity itself? For the answer, it seems most helpful to turn first not to the context of scholarly discussion in the fields of philosophy, theology, literary theory and historiography, but to the context of A.A.'s own history.[14]

When the fledgling fellowship left the Oxford Group – in 1937 in New York, in 1939 in Akron – its first one hundred members did so precisely because they objected to the Group's explicit religiosity. Philosophically, the Oxford Group's insistence on its "Four Absolutes" did not fit the emerging program's focus on essential limitation. Theologically, the Oxford Group practice of narrating tales of conversion offended the sensibilities of both the agnostics and the Roman Catholics who made up a significant part of early A.A. membership. But what, then, were they to do at their own meetings?

Newcomers attended those gatherings, and the neophytes had questions. They had failed at earlier efforts to avoid drunkenness, how was A.A. different? What did it mean when one suffered loss of memory? How complete need be the "inventory" and the "amends" spoken of in the Twelve Steps? Was wanting to get even the same thing as "harboring a resentment"? These and a hundred other questions were raised: no one is more skilled in denial, in finding a reason to drink again, than the newly dry alcoholic. But those sober for a year or two were not philosophers, theologians, psychologists, nor physicians – even Dr. Bob, after all, was a proctologist. And so they could answer only by telling of their own experiences with the same or similar concerns.

Thus developed the A.A. modality of story-telling: a modified "conversion narrative" that contained echoes of the classic story motifs of the hero and the pilgrimage. The themes explored by Joseph Campbell in his studies of heroic myth shed much light on A.A. stories.[15] Each teller, in the pursuit of "more," had entered the outer darkness and had explored the pit; now, having surmounted its dangers, he had returned, wiser and witnessing to hope. But the heroic plot of separation-initiation-return is leavened by another, deeper, theme – that of the pilgrimage.[16] A.A. storytellers are still "on the way," for they are ever mindful that A.A.'s promise is "spiritual progress rather than spiritual perfection,"[17] and the very fact that they are present testifies that they too need help.

"What we used to be like, what happened, and what we are like now" thus describes a dialectical process of both being changed and changing. Or, to put it another way, in the A.A. modality of storytelling, one is "saved," but not completely. Salvation – sobriety – remains operative only so long as one makes it available to others by telling the story of one's own.

Having limned A.A.'s context – the existentialist and neo-orthodox sense of limitation – and the implications of the A.A. practice of storytelling, it is now time to bring these together in a deeper unity. Through the program and within the fellowship of Alcoholics Anonymous, human beings are healed not by technique but by practice, not by science but by art. For A.A. has discovered – and tells and implements – a larger story.

One corollary of essential limitation, and therefore of the context of the sense that marks the post-modern sensibility, is the rediscovery of the ancient distinction between *techné* and *phronesis*, between knowledge and wisdom.[18] Perhaps the greatest significance of Alcoholics Anonymous in the history of ideas consists in its practical implementation of a mode of thinking that leads to a way of life that values the claims of *wisdom* without rejecting the validity of *knowledge*.

For those unfamiliar with or perhaps unsympathetic to the rediscovery of *phronesis*, let me suggest ten distinctions in an attempt not to explain but to describe the significance of the fundamental distinction and therefore of Alcoholics Anonymous.

1. Knowledge seeks to collect facts, data; concerned with technique, it hears the question "Why?" as asking "How?" Wisdom is concerned with meaning and thus with value; seeking reasons rather than causes, it hears the question "Why?" as inquiring "Wherefore?" Research demonstrates that A.A. stories offer better raw material for philosophy than for sociology.[19]

2. Knowledge is primarily a method; it seeks truth by experiments that aim at exactness. Knowledge focuses on quantity, and the mastery of knowledge produces experts. Wisdom is a vision; it seeks truth by understanding, which is concerned with adequacy. Wisdom focuses on quality: immersion in wisdom produces artists. There are no experts in Alcoholics Anonymous.

3. Knowledge can and must be added to, even replaced; it comes to us in textbooks and articles that we read once and then "refer to." Wisdom is less added to than deepened; it comes to us in "classics" –

works that we re-read and ponder because we change more than they do. As its nickname hints, A.A.'s "Big Book" falls in the latter category.

4. Knowledge gives answers: one possesses knowledge and therefore can sell it. Wisdom suggests new perspectives on ultimate questions; one does not possess wisdom but is rather possessed by it, and thus any claim to "sell" wisdom signals the charlatan. No one can "buy" Alcoholics Anonymous.

5. In the ancient classical understanding, the source of knowledge is leisure, either the possession of it or the desire for it. A.A. stories witness to what Edith Hamilton has suggested was a core Greek insight: "Wisdom's price is suffering, and it is always paid unwillingly although sent in truth as a gift from God."[20]

6. Knowledge attends to realities as things: biochemists and neurologists can offer us much knowledge about alcoholism. Wisdom attends to realities as personal: Alcoholics Anonymous is interested only in the alcoholic.

7. Knowledge locates human uniqueness in the capacity to think. Wisdom locates human uniqueness in the capacity to love. A.A. presents itself as both program and fellowship.

8. Knowledge, rejecting story for analysis, insists on the separation of "fact" and "value." Wisdom finds truth in stories because of its insistence that "What can I know?" and "How shall I live" are not two unrelated questions.

9. Knowledge is fascinated by the new; it is at least tempted to give the presumption of validity to novelty. Wisdom encourages mindfulness of the old, offering the presumption of value to that which has endured the test of time. The truest statement about Alcoholics Anonymous is that it is nothing new.

10. Knowledge accepts as reality only that which has been or at least can be proven. Wisdom acknowledges the possibility of the existence of

that which escapes strict proof, holding that there are some realities, such as love and sobriety, in the existence of which one must believe before one can see them.

Now let me blur those distinctions: according to the point of view represented by Alcoholics Anonymous, to be human is to be *both* scientist and artist, for to live humanly requires *both* knowledge and wisdom. If, as we have been warned and have even experienced in some modern cult and drug experiences, "Knowledge separates while mysticism unites," it is also true that wisdom distinguishes without either separating or uniting.

Wisdom's key distinction and the message of all storytelling concerns the complexity of human being. To be human is to be *both* a unique, individual self *and* somehow part of reality greater than the self. This insight underlies all religion, art, and love. To be human is thus also at the same time to be both more and less than *merely* human: it is to exist, essentially, in a mixed, middle, paradoxical condition. Over Emerson Hall, the philosophy building in Harvard Yard, there is inscribed the Judaeo-Christian version of one-half of that ancient wisdom: "You have made him a little less than the angels." The ancients knew that we are also a little more than the beasts, or, better, that to be human is to be neither beast nor angel yet somehow also to be *both*. Wisdom's vision is of human both-ness.

All comedy and all tragedy – all storytelling – witness to that vision. The core of comedy is the embrace of human both-and-ness. Tragedy details the effort to deny that same both-and-ness. And what of Alcoholics Anonymous, wherein the way in which tragic tales are met with laughter confuses so many observers? Long before A.A., some alcoholics – "compulsive drunkards," they were called in American colonial times – recovered. Until Alcoholics Anonymous, they thought of themselves as "ex-alcoholics," or perhaps as "reformed drunkards."[21] Now I am sure you know that the customary introduction of any storyteller within Alcoholics Anonymous runs: "My name is ____, and I am an alcoholic." Refer to an "ex-alcoholic," and most members of Alcoholics Anonymous will begin searching the obituary pages.

Wisdom's paradox of human both-and-ness, then, is contained in and taught by the very concept "sober alcoholic." That is why a recovering member need not even speak at all to tell his story at an A.A. meeting: simply *being there* as a sober alcoholic, tells the story . . . although it is of course useful and helpful to hear some of the details of each particular heroic pilgrimage quest. To accept the possibility of being a "sober alcoholic" is to accept the reality of human both-and-ness, and in the wake of that acceptance comes wisdom itself.

Does this embodiment of "wisdom" make Alcoholics Anonymous a philosophy or a religion? No, but A.A.'s claim to be a "way of life" does appear validated.[22] Remember Bonhoeffer's call for a "religionless Christianity." Both philosophy in the classical sense and theological religion have suffered eclipse in modern times, especially in the Anglo-American world that gave birth to Alcoholics Anonymous and first witnessed its widespread impact.[23]

My point in this paper concerns the significance for the story of wisdom of the story of Alcoholics Anonymous. For at least a millennium, until some time in the seventeenth or eighteenth century, human beings preferred wisdom to knowledge. Then, for some two or three centuries, they pursued knowledge at the expense of wisdom. In both contexts, some sought to reverse the trend, but almost always in an either-or, all-or-nothing fashion. The modern drug cult, and even some therapies, evidence that tendency. The significance of Alcoholics Anonymous, lies in its attempt to regain wisdom without sacrificing knowledge, in its witness to their complementarity, in the reality that the A.A. fellowship and program have transcended the religious "problems" of the past two or three centuries in a way that again makes Wisdom and its insights available to large numbers of very ordinary people without requiring them to reject knowledge.

But wisdom – *phronesis, sapientia* – is not the same as "religion" nor even as the reality for which Bonhoeffer called. Alcoholics Anonymous presents its fellowship as "spiritual rather than religious," and co-founder Bill Wilson was wont to parry challenges to its program by those who wanted it to be "more" by referring to A.A. as "a spiritual kindergarten."

Mindful that "only what does not have a history can be defined,"[24] I would suggest that no better description of wisdom can be found than A.A.'s portrayal of itself as "way of life."

My second contention in this paper, then, involves the claim that Alcoholics Anonymous is also significant because of what its way of life teaches, enables, and inculcates: an attitude – a posture before reality – that is at the same time both profoundly philosophical and deeply religious.

How describe such an attitude? Of what might it consist? Argument, although inevitable, proves fruitless. Rather than beginning with a definition and proceeding deductively, then, let me begin with A.A. practice, seeking to derive an at least possible model. To what does research indicate the practice of the A.A. program leads in the daily life of its members?

The literature on Alcoholics Anonymous recognizes four attitudes as characteristic of A.A.'s sober members.[25] Feeling a sense of *release* for which they are profoundly *grateful*, members of Alcoholics Anonymous in embracing their own both-and-ness as "sober alcoholics" reveal a *humility* from which flows profound *tolerance* – a joyous willingness to accept others' limitations. Would it be too much to claim that it is precisely these qualities – releasement and gratitude, tolerance and humility – that characterize any really "religious" attitude?

You will note that something is apparently missing. A philosopher has recently insised that the core of religion is to be found in *worship*.[26] But is "worship" so different from the "attitude of awe in the face of the universe" that the psychiatrist, John Mack, remarked in A.A. – especially if that attitude of awe be celebrated communally?[27] Alcoholics Anonymous not only has a program; it *is* a "fellowship." Releasement and gratitude, tolerance and humility, although A.A. members attempt to practice them "in all our affairs," are *celebrated* at A.A. meetings – celebrated *by* the telling of stories.

Often, religious professionals see in those meetings either too much or too little. In A.A.'s early years, Catholic clergy scented in its Oxford Group origins and in its usual use of "the Protestant Lord's Prayer" a forbidden *communicatio in sacris*. More recently, other clerics have more pragmatically resented the fact that at least some alcoholics seem to substitute going to A.A. meetings for attendance at church. Similarly, most non-religious professionals tend to view Alcoholics Anonymous as "just another form of religion," just another "church."

But these objections must be balanced by criticisms from the opposite direction. Others, beginning with the Jesuit theologian John Ford in the 1940s, have found A.A.'s claim to be "spiritual rather than religious" all too true, or even too much. They fault Alcoholics Anonymous less for its failure to worship than for its absence of theology. Some social scientists follow the same tack, viewing A.A. as primarily group socialization – but Durkheimian religion is not religion in any usual sense.[28]

Where does such disagreement leave the observer concerned primarily with A.A.'s continuing history? The revivification of religion, like the rebirth of philosophy, is of course beyond A.A.'s scope. Sober alcoholics are not that grandiose. But I would suggest that any interested in either question – and perhaps especially any scholars fascinated by the current revival of interest in story-telling among philosophers and theologians, critics and historians, might find suggestive hints in the ongoing story of Alcoholics Anonymous.

The significance of Alcoholics Anonymous as a phenomenon in American Religious or Philosophical History is quite simply that for the past half-century it has been in the center of a mainstream that most scholars have been led by ideological blinders to ignore. Two current revivals of interest render the continuation of that ignorance unconscionable. Within Alcoholics Anonymous and its Twelve-Step offspring, more and more people are asking more and more explicitly for guidance in spirituality. Indeed, "spirituality" bodes to become the next fad in an already over-fadded field. That outcome will be sad, for it will steal from all of us yet another important word. When a culture does not accept the existence of some reality, whatever term those who experience that reality use to name it quickly becomes debased, its original meaning perverted and lost.

Perhaps the second revival, then, can offer hope – if those engaged in it can prove more open-minded than their predecessors. The revival of interest in narrative, in storytelling, might learn much from the experience, strength and hope of Alcoholics Anonymous. I commend to you that task in the words of the only italicized sentences that appear in the book, *Alcoholics Anonymous*: "Willingness, honesty and open mindedness are the essentials of recovery. But these are indispensable."[29]

A.A.'s experience proves that that holds true for recovery from alcoholism. May I suggest that it might hold equally true for scholarship's recovery of humanity?

NOTES

1. Current membership figure by private communication with A.A.'s General Service Office, 10 January 1986; on the accuracy of such figues, *cf.* Barry Leach and John L. Norris, "Factors in the Development of Alcoholics Anonymous," pp. 441-543 in Benjamin Kissin and Henri Begleiter, *Treatment and Rehabilitation of the Chronic Alcoholic* (New York: Plenum, 1977), pp. 443-451.

2. "More of the Young and Cross-Addicted Now in A.A., Survey Reveals," *Box 459*, vol. 29 (1984), no.5, 1; similar articles on other diversity can be found in almost every issue.

3 Leonard D. Borman, ed., *Explorations in Self-Help and Mutual Aid*, (Evanston, IL: Northwestern Univ., 1975); Alan Gartner and Frank Riessman, eds., *The Self-Help Revolution* (New York: Human Sciences Press, 1984); Daniel J. Anderson, *Living With Chronic Illness*, (Center City, MN: Hazelden, 1985).

4, May be found on p. 3 of any issue of the *A.A. Grapevine*.

5. The history of Alcoholics Anonymous is recounted in two of its own publications: *Alcoholics Anonymous Comes of Age* (New York: A.A. World Services, 1957) and *"Pass It On"* (New York: A.A.W.S., 1984). Full sources for all the detailed points that follow may be found in my own study, *Not-God: A History of Alcoholics Anonymous* (Center City, MN: Hazelden, 1979).

6. *e.g.* R.K. Jones, "Sectarian Characteristics of Alcoholics Anonymous, *Sociology* (Oxford) 4: 181-195 (1970); Francesca Alexder and Michelle Rollins, "Alcoholics Anonymous: The Unseen Cult." *California Sociologist.* 1984; 7(1): 33-48.

7. Donald Meyer, *The Positive Thinkers* (Garden City, NY: Doubleday, 1965), pp. 315-324.

8. Morris Berman, *The Re-Enchantment of the World* (Ithaca, NY: Cornell Univ. Press, 1981); Gregory Bateson, "The Cybernetics of 'Self': A Theory of Alcoholism," in Bateson, *Steps to an Ecology of Mind* (New York: Ballantine, 1972), pp. 309-337.

9. John Mack, "Alcoholism, A.A., and the Governance of the Self," pp. 128-162; E.J. Khantzian, "Some Treatment Implications of the Ego and Self Disturbances in Alcoholism," pp. 163-188, both in Margaret H. Bean and Norman E. Zinberg (eds.), *Dynamic Approaches to the Understanding and Treatment of Alcoholism* (New York: Free Press, 1981); *cf.* also George E. Vaillant, *The Natural History of Alcoholism* (Cambridge, MA: Harvard Univ. Press, 1983).

9. William Barrett, *Irrational Man* (New York: Doubleday, 1958).

10. "Letter to A.A. from Reinhold Niebuhr," *Thirty-Five Years* (New York: A.A.W.S., 1960), p. 65; on the claim to influence by Horney and Sullivan, *cf.*, e.g. Dr. Esther Richards (Baltimore) to Wilson, 18 July 1938.

11. *Alcoholics Anonymous* (New York: The Alcoholic Foundation, 1939), p. 74; in the more readily available 2nd and 3rd editions (New York: A.A.W.S., 1955 and 1976), p. 62.

12. *Alcoholics Anonymous*, 1st ed., p. 70; 2nd & 3rd eds., p. 58.

13. The recent literature on story is vast; I rely especially on: Stanley Hauerwas, *Truthfulness and Tragedy* (Notre Dame: Univ. Press, 1977); Alasdair MacIntyre, *After Virtue* (Notre Dame, IN: Univ. Press, 1981); Terry Eagleton, *Literary Theory: An Introduction* (Minneapolis: Univ. of Minnesota Press, 1983); Paul Ricoeur, *Time and Narrative*, vol 1, trans. Kathleen McLaughlin and David Pellauer (Chicago: Univ. Press, 1984); Paul Veyne, *Writing History*, trans. Mina Moore-Rinvolucri (Middletown, CT: Wesleyan Univ. Press, 1984). Arthur C. Danto, *Narration and Knowledge* (New York: Columbia Univ. Press, 1985).

15. Joseph Campbell, *The Hero With A Thousand Faces*, (Princeton, NJ: Princeton Univ. Press, 1949).

16. Concerning pilgrimage, *cf.* MacIntyre, pp. 203-204.

17. *Alcoholics Anonymous*, 1st ed., p. 72; 2nd & 3rd eds., p. 60.

18. In addition to the sources cited in note #14, *cf.* Richard J. Bernstein, *Beyond Objectivism and Relativism* (Philadelphia: Univ. of Penn. Press, 1983); also Robert N. Bellah, Richard Madsen, William M. Sullivan, Ann Swidler, and Steven M. Tipton, *Habits of the Heart* (Berkeley: Univ. of Cal. Press, 1985).

19. *Why* this is true may perhaps best be grasped from a very insightful anthropology dissertation: Mary Catherine Taylor, *Alcoholics Anonymous: How It Works* (Univ. of California at San Francisco, 1977), Univ. Microfilms #79-13241.

20. Edith Hamilton, *The Greek Way* (New York: Norton, 1930), p. 59.

21. *Cf.* Mark Edward Lender and James Kirby Martin, *Drinking in America* (New York: Free Press, 1982), pp. 9-21.

22. [William G. Wilson], *Twelve Steps and Twelve Traditions* (New York: A.A.W.S., 1953), p. 15; [Wilson], *As Bill Sees It: The A.A. Way of Life* (New York: A.A.W.S., 1967).

23. *Cf.* Kurtz, *Not-God*, pp. 113, 185.

24. Attributed to Friedrich Nietzsche by Susan Sontag, "When Writers Talk Among Themselves," *The New York Times Book Review*, 5 January 1986, p. 22.

25. The pre-1979 literature is best perused in Kurtz, *Not-God*; more recently, *cf.* especially Vaillant, *Natural History*, pp. 197-208, and also "Dangers of Psychotherapy in the Treatment of Alcoholism," pp. 36-54 in Bean and Zinberg (eds.), as well as Mack, pp. 160 ff. and Khantzian, p. 172, as cited. A less technical and more comprehensive view is offered by Milton A. Maxwell, *The Alcoholics Anonymous Experience: A Close-Up for Professionals* (New York: McGraw-Hill, 1984), especially pp 70-128.

26. Leszek Kolakowski, *Religion* (New York: Oxford Univ. Press, 1982), pp. 175 ff.

27. Mack, "Governance," p. 144.

28. For an early example, *cf.*, e.g., R.F. Bales, "The Therapeutic Role of Alcoholics Anonymous as Seen by a Sociologist," *Quarterly Journal of Studies on Alcohol* 5:267-278 (1944); further references on this and the preceding points may be found in Kurtz, *Not-God*, pp. 306, 314.

29. *Alcoholics Anonymous*, 1st ed. (after the 1st printing), p. 400; 2nd & 3rd eds., p. 570.

In early 1989, an editor of Lear's Magazine asked if I would be interested in writing an article on Bill Wilson and LSD. This had been an interesting topic since the publication of Not-God. An A.A. Trustee had asked me to consider excluding that part of my dissertation from publication, but after consultation with my mentors, I decided to retain it as an essential part of the story. When the book was published, members and others who loved Alcoholics Anonymous did not object to the publication of this information but rather rejoiced that it revealed that Bill W. remained a flawed human being even in sobriety, just as did they.

Due to the demise of Lear's, the article was never published and so appears in print here for the first time. I am happy for this opportunity, because this piece offers the opportunity to clarify my understanding of this somewhat ambiguous episode in the life of the longer-lived co-founder of Alcoholics Anonymous.

Drugs and the Spiritual: Bill W. Takes LSD

A friend of mine, saved from alcoholism, during the last fatal phases of the disease, by a spontaneous theophany, which changed his life as completely as St. Paul's was changed on the road to Damascus, has taken lysergic acid two or three times and affirms that his experience under the drug is identical with the spontaneous experience which changed his life – the only difference being that the spontaneous experience did not last so long as the chemically induced one. There is, obviously, a field here for serious and reverent experimentation.

(Aldous Huxley to Father Thomas Merton, 10 January 1959)

California, August 29, 1956. Four men – a philosopher, a psychiatrist, and two recovered drunks – sit solemnly, waiting. One of the alcoholics, who after his death would become the most famed holder of that dubious title, has just taken a dose of the chemical d-lysergic acid diethylamide, soon to be popularly known as "LSD." The others are present to observe and to guide.

The expected, the desired, happens. Some twenty years earlier, in Towns Hospital in New York City, Bill W. had discovered the insight that became Alcoholics Anonymous in a "spiritual awakening": an experience of white light and the sound of rushing wind and a feeling of deep peace. And now, on this day, in this very different setting, he finally recaptured that experience. His "doors of perception" cleared, colors glowed more intensely, the voice of Dr. Cohen reverberated with new resonance, all motion flowed with languorous beauty, and, above all, he comprehended "the essential All-Rightness of the universe . . . the reconciliation of opposites."

A.A.'s own telling of this story in the book *Pass It On* describes Bill as "enthusiastic about his experience; he felt it helped him eliminate many barriers erected by the self, or ego, that stand in the way of one's direct experience of the cosmos and of God." Bill continued his experiments with LSD into the early 1960s.

HOW COULD HE!?

Addiction-obsessed as we tend to be in this era when drug use threatens our safety on the streets as well as the security of our homes, when we are bombarded by the feel-good theology of a thin new spirituality that claims all our malaises are rooted in "addiction," alarm and shock seem appropriate responses to the news that William Griffith Wilson, cofounder of Alcoholics Anonymous, experimented with LSD. We think of Alcoholics Anonymous and the Twelve-Step programs derived from it as the main hope for dealing with the demand-side of drug use. Why would Wilson, who so well knew the dangers of mind-altering chemicals, attempt such an experiment? How **could** he?! For in addition to confusion, we feel betrayal – is this not evidence that Bill W. let his followers down, that A.A. is flawed in its source?

Addressing such concerns requires perspective: the 1950s were not the 1990s. We find a hint of the difference, and of a similarity, in Bill's own activities at the time. Far from keeping secret his experience with LSD, A.A.'s co-founder judiciously but eagerly spread the word, inviting not only his wife and his secretary but also trusted friends to join his experiments. Some, like his favorite Jesuit, Father Edward Dowling, did so. Others such as Dr. Jack Norris, non-alcoholic chairman of A.A.'s trustees, declined. Clearly, Bill experienced no sense of shame or guilt over his activities. He in fact regarded them as in service to the A.A. fellowship.

But how could he think this? And the question remains, **why** did he get involved in such an endeavor? We have no complete answer, but what we do know suggests that in a strange but real way, Bill was still seeking a cure for alcoholism – not the kind of "cure" that would allow drinking alcohol safely, but a way of helping more alcoholics get sober in Alcoholics Anonymous. In fact, Wilson's experimentation with LSD reflects one more facet of his persistent pursuit of "the spiritual."

THE STORY OF LSD

The use of hallucinogens as a cure for alcoholism goes back at least as far as the Native American peyote cults and was reported by anthropologists as early as 1907. The story of LSD begins with the synthesizing of the chemical, d-lysergic acid diethylamide. Although he first produced the substance in 1938, Dr. Albert Hoffman, a Swiss research chemist employed by Sandoz, discovered its properties only in 1943. His findings attracted interest, for scientists saw in LSD-25, as it was then called, "a drug which would make a normal person psychotic." That implied a chemical basis for insanity, and further suggested that if such "aberrant enzymatic action" could be reversed, an antidote had been found that would "cure schizophrenia." A flurry of research began on "LSD-25 as an Aid in Psychotherapy."

In 1952, two Saskatchewan researchers, Doctors Abram Hoffer and Humphrey Osmond, began investigations along this line. Hoffer and Osmond worked in a mental hospital, treating alcoholics as well as schizophrenics, and their interest centered on patients suffering both disorders. These were their toughest cases, for the schizophrenia seemed to impede the kind of insightful experience thought to be required if an alcoholic was to stop drinking.

Gerald Heard, who had introduced Wilson to Aldous Huxley in the mid-1940s, also supplied the link between Hoffer and Osmond and A.A.'s co-founder. According to Osmond's later recollection, Bill had been "extremely unthrilled" about their research: "He was very much against giving drugs to alcoholics."

But the psychiatrists soon learned from their own experience as well as from observation that the main effect of the drug was to bring on an experience of illumination. They also discovered that that experience of illumination seemed to allow some of their patients who had previously resisted "the spiritual" to accept it and thus to "get" the A.A. program.

The results reported by Hoffer and Osmond fascinated Wilson. When LSD was given to alcoholics in mental hospitals, "of whom A.A. could touch and help only about five per cent, they had about 15 per cent recoveries." One of the Canadian studies reported a recovery rate of 70 percent.

BILL AND SPIRITUALITY

Here, then, is one clear reason why Bill Wilson experimented with LSD: he was seeking still further ways of helping alcoholics, of helping specifically those alcoholics who could not seem to attain sobriety in Alcoholics Anonymous because, apparently, they could not "get the spiritual."

But why this drive? The answer lies also in "the spiritual." Bill yearned not only to recapture his own spiritual experience: he sought to slake a new craving, for his thirst for alcohol had become a thirst for alcoholics. In 1940, when Father Edward Dowling walked into Wilson's life at the very nadir of the co-founder's personal depression, the priest had assured Bill that we all thirst: to be human is to thirst. The question is at what we direct our thirst. In a very real sense, the story of Bill's sobriety details his turning of his thirst for alcohol into a thirst for alcoholics. That is why and how Alcoholics Anonymous first came into being. And grew. But Bill also learned, in those first twenty years, that the main obstacle to drunks "getting" A.A. was "the spiritual."

Wilson understood. He knew of William James's observation that "The only cure for dipsomania is religiomania." Bill himself had been a skeptic, as reflected in the A.A. "Big Book" chapter, "We Agnostics," which details his own transition from conventional unbeliever to unconventional believer. Because that change had been precipitated by a "spiritual awakening," A.A.'s co-founder guessed that a similar experience could help others like himself "melt the icy intellectual mountain in whose shadow [they] lived and shivered."

AND TODAY?

Today, such ideas seem strange. Or do they? We may not be so removed from Wilson's world as we would like to think. Both an implicit medical materialism and the hope that spirituality will help us transcend ourselves continue to shape how we think of addictions. Few would absolutely deny the presence in our own baggage of those two impulses that also lay behind Bill Wilson's LSD experimentation.

William James minted the term *medical materialism* to denote the insistence that there must be a measurable, physical cause in order for any malady to be *real*. On this topic, we all tend to be materialists: it is the dominant faith. And so arguments are waged and dollars spent and effort expended to locate the evil, the trouble, the problems, the malady, in some physical form – in biochemistry, or "brain hormones," or in the alcoholism gene.

That belief, and those efforts, were as strong in the 1950s. Then as now, reaction against the extremes of pop psychologies and fad psychiatries led the scientifically inclined to emphasize the reality of the physical behind apparently mental and emotional disorders. This materialism penetrated far. Episcopal Church Bishop Pardue, consulted by Wilson's friend and sometime mentor, the Reverend Sam Shoemaker, about a parishioner's complaint over Bill's involvement with LSD, declared himself "in the utmost sympathy with what [Bill] is doing." The bishop, Shoemaker reported to Wilson, "is convinced that the biochemical factor is of the greatest importance. . . . half our problems are bio-chemical and do not go back to sin and cannot wholly be governed by prayer."

But as the history of LSD bears out, belief in a physically material disease engenders faith in its physically material antidote. For every target there must be a "magic bullet." And so if "brain hormones" were the problem, some other chemical would furnish the solution. "Medical materialism," that is to say, shares the core assumption of addictive thinking: the belief that whenever there is something wrong with me, something outside me can "fix" it. No less than addiction, medical materialism locates divinity in drugs.

AN AMERICAN SPIRITUALITY?

The second impulse shaping Bill Wilson's quest for spirituality was the American culture-religion, an Evangelical Protestantism watered-down by its subservience to the social science of its time. By the mid-1950's, sociology was replacing psychology as the lodestar of the American faith, but both apostasies gratified the demand for a spirituality that could be commanded.

Americans have never been good waiters. On the foundation laid by the Puritan "Half-Way Covenant," despite pristine Calvinist bemoaning of "Arminianism," the "calling down" of revivals early became standard practice. The mid-twentieth century version of this rationalization, for all its modern vocabulary, echoed the insights of Charles Grandison Finney a century earlier: "New measures" (such as taking LSD) were justified because they attempted not to manipulate reality, but to remove the barriers that impeded spiritual reality from asserting itself.

Wilson set forth his thoughts on how LSD might serve spirituality in a 1958 letter to Sam Shoemaker. "[LSD] seems to have the result of sharply reducing the forces of the ego," Bill noted, pointing out the "generally acknowledged fact in spiritual development that ego reduction makes the influx of God's grace possible. . . . [LSD] will never take the place of any of the existing means by which we can reduce the ego, and keep it reduced," Bill acknowledged. But he went on to roll out the classic justification for spiritual innovation by noting "the probability that prayer, fasting, meditation, despair, and other conditions that predispose one to classic mystical experiences do have their chemical components." If such exercises aided "in shutting out ego drives, opening the doors to a wider perception," why not evaluate the more honestly chemical LSD in the same way?

SPIRITUALITY AND CONVERSION

One feature of American Evangelical spirituality especially impelled Bill's fascination with LSD. The Evangelical vision insists on an experience of "conversion." It is this experience that validates the sense and hope of being somehow *changed*, somehow *different*, somehow **new**.

America began as a quest for a new beginning. The insistence on the possibility of a totally new beginning indeed defines America. In the religious arena, as Horace Bushnell pointed out in his Finney-contemporaneous treatise on "Christian Nurture," the discovery of that "new birth," *conversion*, could take place in two ways: suddenly and dramatically or more measuredly, through a kind of education.

Unlike inhabitants of more traditional cultures, citizens of the United States tend to suspect not the sudden, but the gradual. And so those who experience sudden conversion usually regard their change as somehow more **genuine**. Thus it was that in spite of the A.A. Big Book's measured words about "educational variety spiritual experiences," Bill W. was himself drawn to seek ways of making more available the "sudden and spectacular upheavals" that although not necessary, seemed very, very useful.

SPIRITUAL OR RELIGIOUS?

For a related consideration came into play, fashioning Wilson's fascination with the possibilities of LSD. From its beginnings, Alcoholics Anonymous had proclaimed its program to be "spiritual rather than religious." A dual strategy lay behind that insistence: it rendered A.A. acceptable to religious leaders; and it lured alcoholics, who often were idealists disillusioned with religion, into initial examination of the fellowship.

But in conveying the "spiritual" aspects of the program, Wilson faced the classic problem of religious mystics: how speak of that which cannot be captured by words? A.A. spirituality is founded in an experience of release, a free-ing – the sense that one has been *saved*. To those who do not experience such an event, spirituality ever remains total mystery. And they are comforted in their condition by the extremes to which some of those others who *have* experienced it have gone. For although anyone at all aware of spirituality knows the need to attempt to "eff the ineffable," those who actually think they achieve that are at best fanatics and at worst, bores.

Having so long refused the spiritual because of his disgust with those extremes, Wilson carefully eschewed the stock ways of describing spiritual experience. Even within Alcoholics Anonymous, he regretfully but readily admitted, both fanatics and bores flourished. Yet other members showed something else. The co-founder felt a responsibility to make that deeper, less glib experience available to a wider population of alcoholics.

But how? Bill realized that in spite of his identification with just about every alcoholic he ever met, his own background in matters of "the spiritual" was hardly typical. Unlike most drunks of his era, Bill did not in his drinking years throw over a religious background and upbringing. He had never had either, but was rather himself an early product of the secularization that in his lifetime became ever more the American culture-religion.

Bill's "spiritual awakening" had changed all that. His experience in Towns Hospital in December 1934 had perfectly replicated the ordeals detailed in William James's *Varieties of Religious Experience*: the lapsing into darkness, the seeing of "a great white light," the sense of "a wind blowing not of air but of spirit," and – especially – the final feeling of great peace and calm, the perception of "the essential All-Rightness of the universe." In his LSD experiments, Bill Wilson was seeking to recapture and to extend that spiritual experience. He of course sought that for his own benefit; but he also – and even especially – hoped thus to find a way of making that experience available to other alcoholics.

46

BILL WILSON, LSD, AND DR. CARL JUNG

In the midst of his experimentation, in 1961, Wilson finally got around to doing something he had long contemplated. Writing to Dr. Carl Jung, A.A.'s co-founder expressed gratitude for the famed psychiatrist's formative role in the pre-history of Alcoholics Anonymous. That correspondence has been often reprinted. And so it is well known that in his reply, Jung formulated an image that extended Dowling's metaphor of thirst, suggesting that alcoholism involved the struggle of *spiritus contra spiritum* – "spirits" destroying the **spiritual** in the lives of alcoholics.

It is less well known that Bill wrote a second, unreprinted, letter to the psychiatrist, one left unanswered because Jung's death intervened. In this response, Wilson apprized Jung of how much his "observation that drinking motivations often include . . . a quest for spiritual values caught our special interest." Building on that insight, Bill went on to tell Jung of his experiences with LSD, detailing his views on the "spiritual significance" of that substance. What is striking in Wilson's recital is less his rehearsing of the ideas earlier set forth to Shoemaker than how completely, albeit implicitly, Bill re-states concerning LSD what had always been known of the connections between **alcohol** and spirituality.

ALCOHOL AND SPIRITUALITY

The perception of connections between alcohol and spirituality, as the Jungian paralleling of "spirits" and *the spiritual* hints, is not peculiarly American, nor Protestant, nor even Christian: the intuition has a long and diverse history. The ancient Greeks embodied it in the figure of Dionysus. By the 1950s and 1960s, the vision, the vocabulary, and the chemical had all changed, but the era of Carlos Casteneda and Dr. Timothy Leary seemed about to bring to fulfillment Aldous Huxley's *Brave New World* prediction of "soma," the drug that would obviate the need for religion.

A relatively obscure Harvard professor at the time, Leary had in fact in 1958 sought Wilson out, asking to be included in the co-founder's experimental work with LSD. Whether this request sprang more from

47

scientific curiosity about Bill's specific line of inquiry or was motivated by Wilson's apparently more ready access to the substance remains unclear. We know only that Bill became wary and put Leary off, one of the few individuals so treated.

Huxley, meanwhile, in an October 1958 *Saturday Evening Post* article, "Drugs that Shape Men's Minds," declared baldly that alcoholism and other forms of drug addiction were "as much a consequence of self-transcendent yearnings as were mystical theology, spiritual exercises, and yoga." He summed up his thoughts neatly: "The pen is mightier than the sword. But mightier than either the pen or the sword is the pill."

A friend of Bill Wilson who was not "a friend of Bill Wilson," Huxley elsewhere quoted Housman, hinting the problem but suggesting a cure unavailable to most alcoholics:
Malt does more than Milton can
To justify God's ways to man.

CONCLUSIONS

Perhaps the best understanding of *addiction* presents it as an attempt to fill a spiritual void with a material reality. If there be any truth in that insight, Bill Wilson's experimentation with LSD occasions both caution and hope.

Caution, because even A.A.'s co-founder, despite his vast experiential knowledge of alcoholism in all its manifestations, despite all his very real albeit also very uneven personal spirituality, only most dimly recognized the extent to which his ongoing quests, even in sobriety, were expressions of what he liked to term his "malady." As Bill had written, what he was dealing with was "cunning, baffling, powerful!" More so, apparently, than even he knew.

But the story of Bill and LSD also occasions *hope*. At a moment when we seem about to be swamped by a self-centered age's guilt-mongering gurus who would label all compassion "co-dependence," it is refreshing to recall that even in his errors, A.A.'s co-founder was seeking ways to benefit other alcoholics. Bill never lost what recent self-styled spiritual mentors apparently never gain: the sense of humor that warned him that he could be wrong. Bill Wilson never forgot that if he, as an alcoholic in recovery, had **any** spirituality, it was a spirituality of imperfection.

The Twelve-Step program of Alcoholics Anonymous offers only "a spirituality of imperfection." To expect more is to reject that spirituality; to hope for more is only to be human; to demand more, even of that program's first expositor, is to forget what attracted us to it in the first place.

The "lesson" of Bill Wilson's experimentation with LSD? If perfection is your goal, don't go looking for models among the members – or even the founders – of Alcoholics Anonymous.

REFERENCES

Lears Magazine does not print notes, but in the hope of helping anyone interested in further investigation of this topic, I append the "Source Sheet" that their Research Department requested:

INTERVIEWEES QUOTED: NONE

PRIMARY BACKGROUND MATERIAL – Sources Interviewed but Not Quoted:

Lois Wilson (currently deceased)
Nell Wing, former secretary to Bill W.;
Frank Mauser, current A.A. archivist;
The ultimate primary background material is the research represented by my
    book, cited under Secondary Sources, and my continuing research on A.A.
    history.

SECONDARY SOURCES:

Ernest Kurtz, *Not-God: A History of Alcoholics Anonymous* (Hazelden 1979; rev. ed. 1991)

Bill Pittman, *AA: The Way It Began* (Glen Abbey 1988)

[Anonymous], *Pass It On*, (A.A. World Services 1984)

Nan Robertson, *Getting Better: Inside Alcoholics Anonymous* (Morrow 1988)

Charles Taylor Knippel, *Samuel M. Shoemaker's Theological Influence on William G. Wilson's Twelve Step Spiritual Program of Recovery* (unpublished dissertation, 1987, St. Louis University, available from University Microfilms International)

Joost A.M. Meerloo, "Artificial Ecstasy: A Study of the Psychosomatic Aspects of Drug Addiction," *Journal of Nervous and Mental Disorders* 115:246-266 (1952)

Charles Savage, "LSD, Alcoholism and Transcendence," *Journal of Nervous and Mental Disorders* 135: 429-435 (1962)

Kenneth E. Godfrey, "LSD Therapy," in Catanzaro (ed.), *Alcoholism: The Total Treatment Approach* (C.C. Thomas 1968)

Cole and Ryback, "Pharmacological Therapy" in Tarter and Sugerman (eds.), *Alcoholism: Interdisciplinary Approaches of an Enduring Problem*, pp. 721-733

E. Brooks Holifield, *A History of Pastoral Care in America*. Nashville: Abingdon, 1983.

Robert Thomsen, *Bill W.* (Harper & Row, 1975).

Alcoholics Anonymous (A.A.W.S., 1939, 1955, 1976)

Alcoholics Anonymous Comes of Age (A.A.W.S., 1957)

NOTES AND SUGGESTIONS TO RESEARCH DEPARTMENT:

Pass It On should ease any fears of libel charges, and the Savage article contains most of the LSD background data. Everything that appears in quotation marks is a checked quotation from the source indicated. Knippel offers different quotes from W's letter to Shoemaker than does *Pass It On*.

Invited to offer a paper at the 35th Conference of the International Congress of Alcohol and Drug Dependence, held July 31st to August 6th, 1988 in Oslo, Norway, I chose to address what seems the largest problem professionals have with Alcoholics Anonymous – its spirituality. This difficulty is, if anything, greater in Europe than in the United States, and especially so in the Scandinavian countries.

Yet my own investigations (as well as the testimony of many, many A.A. friends) have convinced me that spirituality is the essence of Alcoholics Anonymous, wherever it flourishes, and so I keep trying to make that point, in one way or another. This paper represents one of those efforts. It was published with the collected papers from the Conference in Prevention and Control/ Realities and Aspirations: Volume II, *ed. R. B. Waahlberg, pp. 678-86. Oslo, Norway: National Directorate for the Prevention of Alcohol and Drug Problems, 1989.*

"Spiritual Rather than Religious":

The Contribution of Alcoholics Anonymous

Many people remain confused about the place of Alcoholics Anonymous in the process of recovery from alcoholism. Some of the confusion results from a tendency to view the fellowship and its program as a kind of religion.[1] Few examine A.A.'s own claim to be "spiritual rather than religious." But that assertion, understood in the light of A.A.'s history, can help to clarify the qualities of a successful recovery from alcoholism.[2]

Alcoholics Anonymous came into existence in the late 1930s, an offshoot of what was then named the "Oxford Group," which was an attempt to recapture what its participants thought to be first-century Christianity. The founding members of Alcoholics Anonymous departed the Group primarily because they found its adherents too religious for their taste. Although unconnected with any particular church or sect, devotees of the Oxford Group tended to be aggressively evangelical Protestant Christians who sought to convince especially the wealthy and the prominent that they possessed "the truth" in some unique way.[3]

From the dawn of independent existence, A.A. members interpreted their program as offering a type of universal spirituality that can cohere with any religion or with none. First motivated by the desire to make Alcoholics Anonymous available to all, that effort was further shaped by the secularization from which in fact derives the modern usage of the term *spirituality*.[4] This emphasis has also been aided by A.A.'s self-consciousness of being influenced by the philosopher William James and the psychiatrist Carl Jung, two thinkers who reflected unconventional spirituality by their example of taking religious insight seriously without adhering to any specific theology.

But A.A.'s greatest self-awareness involves its members' sense that their program derives especially from their own experience. That experience issued in both a "way of life" and a way of conveying that way of life – the telling of stories that "disclose in a general way what we used to be like, what happened, and what we are like now."[5] What follows will examine the discoveries and the themes that emerge from that practice.

DISCOVERIES

Four assumptions, each discovered by the earliest members' experience, frame the A.A. understanding of spirituality and of its role in recovery from alcoholism.

The first discovery concerned the vital importance of "the spiritual," properly understood. Newcomers to Alcoholics Anonymous, it was recognized, required a new understanding of "the spiritual" as much as they needed an understanding of alcoholism as disease or malady or obsession-compulsion. Their earliest endeavors taught the first A.A. members that the alcoholic, in order to recover, had to abandon *two* misconceptions: his old notion of alcoholism/alcoholic, which thwarted recognition of his condition; and his old notion of "the spiritual," which impeded recovery from that condition. The stories told at meetings served to shatter *both* false stereotypes.[6]

Secondly, the earliest members of Alcoholics Anonymous soon came to realize that especially in the area of "the spiritual," there existed a deep difference between "magic" and *miracle*. "Magic" involved the claim and the demand to control, to manipulate, and seeking the magical was recognized to be the antithesis of recovery spirituality, for it replicated the experience of alcoholic drinking. The early A.A.s thus came to see the spirituality necessary to recovery as involving not the seeking of the magical, but being open to *miracle* – accepting life as *mystery* to be lived rather than "problem" to be solved.[7]

Related to "miracle rather than magic" was the third discovery – the earliest members' vivid experience of the *open-endedness* of "the spiritual." This awareness issued in the fellowship's emphasis on "progress rather than perfection" as well as in co-founder Bill W's favorite image of "Pilgrim's Progress."[8] Two manifestations of this third assumption have waxed and waned within A.A.'s story: the emphasis on being "teachable," wherein a classic virtue – docility – is given a new name; and an understanding of the essence of A.A. spirituality as its being a "spirituality of not having all the answers." Both preserve the original vision of Alcoholics Anonymous in establishing its own identity by leaving the Oxford Group.

Finally, those manifestations of open-endedness in turn bridge to the fourth experiential assumption concerning spirituality that the earliest members discovered despite their own many efforts to deny it: "the spiritual" necessarily *pervades*. It is not some kind of separate category, but is rather the glue that *makes* "the whole." As the stories in the "Into Action" and "Working With Others" chapters of the book *Alcoholics Anonymous* reveal, any attempt to segregate some aspect of one's life from "the spiritual," any failure of honest application of the whole of the A.A. program to the whole of one's life, inevitably led to relapse.[9]

Yet language limps, and so members of Alcoholics Anonymous commonly speak of "the physical, the mental, and the spiritual" as if distinct. This is one reason why "the spiritual" in A.A. is less talked about directly than transmitted by *story*. Such unity, the unity inherent in "the spiritual," is best conveyed by *story.* Only story can begin to reveal the connections between thinking and acting and willing and feeling, the unity that is at the core of the A.A. experience of sobriety.

A.A. storytelling, like all spirituality, involves not "talking about it" but the actual living of certain qualities. The practice of telling stories in the format of "what we used to be like, what happened, and what we are like now" actually elicits and reinforces those qualities – those thematic realities that we now turn to explore. Thus, storytelling is the primary way in which sobriety, spirituality, is not only transmitted but grown in. In the very telling of one's own story, one sees/feels/acts – one *experiences* – those qualities: Release, Gratitude, Humility, and Tolerance.

THEMES

RELEASE:

The first "theme" elicited even as it is described is that of freedom or, better, RELEASE. Its language may be of "weight lifted," or "chains fallen away," or perhaps of "a light turned on": what predominates is the sense, the experience, of being freed. Note that the experience is of *being freed* rather than of "gaining freedom" – which is why the term RELEASE seems more appropriate. The emphasis is on the sense of release rather than of any kind of control or triumph. RELEASE is not "gained"; rather, it *happens.*

Predominant in this first theme is the sense of *wonder.* The A.A. member does not tell his or her story in order to "attain" release; yet the experience of release does emerge from the practice of telling one's story. As one philosopher has observed, "When we let the truth about ourselves be revealed, we experience a kind of release"[10]: note "let", rather than some kind of exhibitionism. The sense of *wonder*, and therefore as we shall see of gratitude, arises in part because the experience is beyond one's purpose.

Also noteworthy is how this language of "Release" reflects the core insight of the mystical tradition: the paradox that one attains the sense of "release" only if one oneself releases, *lets go.* This mystery of "surrender" is urged by the Pietist "Let go and let God," which has become an A.A. axiom.

GRATITUDE:

GRATITUDE, the second theme, is the only one of the themes commonly mentioned by name within Alcoholics Anonymous. The significance of A.A.'s emphasis on *gratitude* may best be understood by borrowing words first spoken of a far more dire reality than alcoholism:

> No one is as capable of gratitude as one who has emerged from the kingdom of night. . . . We know that every moment is a moment of grace, every hour an offering; not to share them would mean to betray them. Our lives no longer belong to us alone; they belong to all those who need us desperately.[11]

Gratitude flows directly from the sense that "Release" is a *gift*: unearned, unmerited, not attained by being "deserved"; in fact, not "attained" at all. This sense of "gift" has been largely lost in our culture, with its ritual occasions of giving. We seem almost to need an excuse to give or to receive a gift!

For a true gift, a spontaneous boon such as "Release," the only possible response is *gratitude*. What is "gratitude?" It is the only possible response to *gift*. And what is that "response"? Especially within a "way of life" that necessarily involves a way of thinking, that response, that gratitude, is not a "feeling" but rather a kind of *vision* that enables recognizing how "gifted" we are, how much we have received. "Spirituality" has been defined as the ability to see the hand of God at work in the world.[12] In such an understanding, gratitude is the foundation and linchpin of spirituality.

Like the *release* experienced "when we let the truth about ourselves be revealed," gratitude connects in a special way with *story*. The concepts "think, thank, remember" are intimately related:

> "Think" and "thank" are kindred roots, and the German word *an-denken* – literally, "to think on" – means to *remember*; hence, think, thank, and remembrance are related notions. Real thinking, thinking that is rooted in Being, is at once an act of thanking and remembrance.[13]

Or again, from a different source:

Thinking is a kind of thanking. In thanking, we accept the gift of existence. In accepting ourselves, we become ourselves. As released, we gratefully enter into the play of which we are already a part. Releasement means "homecoming." Thinking as thanking means loving.[14]

Gratitude is that vision that enables recognizing – truly *seeing* – many such gifts. As the insight embodied in Japanese Naikan therapy attests, gratitude heals.[15] Most stories told in Alcoholics Anonymous further suggest that perhaps the greatest gift is that of the ability *to* give, without any expectation of return, precisely because one has discovered the nature of *gift*. Profound connections thus exist between gratitude and A.A.'s Eleventh Step, wherein the member seeks to improve "conscious contact with God."

HUMILITY:

The third theme, HUMILITY, refers to acceptance of the middleness, the *both-and-ness* of one's human condition. The spirituality of Alcoholics Anonymous here most clearly reveals its inspiration in that tradition of wisdom that has informed mainline Western understanding. To be human, the ancients suggested, was to be "less than the gods, more than the beasts, yet somehow also both." Later ages captured the same insight in the vision that to be human was to be *both* "beast and angel," as Pascal's "He who would be an angel becomes a beast" cautioned.

Humility, according to this insight, involves accepting that being thus in the middle, being human, is "good enough." As this acceptance has been urged in terms that did not originate in A.A. but are surely true to A.A. spirituality: "You can do something, but not everything"; "You alone can do it, but you cannot do it alone." Some find this significance reflected in the classic prayer-posture of kneeling, which is interpreted as an embrace of this "half-way" position.

Within A.A., humility is less addressed directly than as related to *humor*, for the source of all humor resides precisely in the *incongruity* that is the essence of the human condition. To laugh at oneself signals the humility that accepts one's own imperfect humanity. A sense of humor bespeaks recognition that, at least at certain of life's moments, the most profound choice available is between fighting self and laughing at self. As the "Big Book,"

Alcoholics Anonymous, observes in italics: "*. . . we have stopped fighting anybody or anything. We have to!*[16]

Humility issues also in the sense of belonging, of *fitting in*, the quest for which so many have suggested may be found at the root of alcoholism.[17] Thus arise the "peace," "harmony," and sense of "being at home" – with one's alcoholism, with one's humanity, with larger reality – that differentiate sobriety from dryness and that characterize what Alcoholics Anonymous presents as "serenity," which is but a synonym for spirituality and indeed for what an earlier generation termed "sanctity."

TOLERANCE:

A further note on the nature of "spirituality" affords an apt transition to the final theme of TOLERANCE. "The spiritual" is that which does not diminish as more participate in it. And it makes no difference whether they participate differently. Within A.A., the term *tolerance* sometimes passes under the aliases of "serenity" or "acceptance."[18]

The root of tolerance within Alcoholics Anonymous is obvious. If one accepts one's own both-and-ness -- and, perhaps even more importantly, the both-and-ness or imperfection of those whom one loves and respects -- one may become able to move toward accepting the imperfections of others of whom one is not so fond. This lesson did not come easily to early A.A., as many of co-founder Bill W's letters reveal.

> Nobody can cause more grief than a power-driven guy who thinks he has got it straight from God. These people cause more trouble than the harlots and drunkards. . . . I have had spells of that very thing, and so I ought to know.[19]

> In the early days of A.A. I spent a lot of time trying to get people to agree with me, to practice A.A. principles as I did, and so forth. For so long as I did this, . . . A.A. grew very slowly.[20]

As early as 1945, confronting a tendency in which he foresaw danger to Alcoholics Anonymous, Bill had observed in the newborn *A.A. Grapevine*:

The way our "worthy" alcoholics have sometimes tried to judge the "less worthy" is, as we look back on it, rather comical. Imagine, if you can, one alcoholic judging another![21]

A bare month before, in a presentation to the Yale Summer School of Alcohol Studies, Bill responded to a somewhat truculent request for "a brief summary of how A.A. works" by quoting his fellow co-founder, Dr. Bob Smith: "Honesty gets us sober, but tolerance keeps us sober."[22]

The popular A.A. slogan, "Live and Let Live," of course inculcates tolerance, but that quality is more effectively fostered within Alcoholics Anonymous by the *variety* of stories offered at each meeting. Members are encouraged, "Identify, don't compare"; but they then hear many different examples of how different sober alcoholics implement A.A.'s simple Twelve-Step program. The stories told reveal both sameness and difference. But the sameness that is rooted in shared weakness allows the differences that arise from diverse strengths to be appreciated rather than resented, to be seen as enriching rather than threatening. This is not *mere* "tolerance" but active appreciation.

The world has known religious wars, but spirituality has historically been spread precisely by "heresy." Perhaps the greatest proof that Alcoholics Anonymous is "spiritual rather than religious" may be found in the reality that A.A. grows by heresy. Probably half the A.A. groups in existence originated when some small number of sober alcoholics, dissatisfied with how their group conducted a meeting or whatever, split off and began holding their own meeting and eventually formed their own new group. The welcoming of that outcome is as common within Alcoholics Anonymous as it is rare outside its fellowship.

A Note on Conversion

Most spiritualities recognize as crucial some point at which an individual experiences a sense of fundamental change. This crisis is classically termed *conversion*. In the A.A. story format detailing "what we used to be like, what happened, and what we are like now," *what happened* generally describes some kind of "turn around" or "about face." This is "conversion" in the ancient sense of *metanoia*: a sense of movement in a different direction. One way of understanding "the spiritual" is as that by which people believe they have been and are profoundly changed.

A classic formulation of the process of this conversion views its change as involving four stages. According to this insight, conversion begins with a "first awareness" of some defect or lack in oneself, and this awareness includes also the discovery of one's own impotence, one's inability to do anything about that flaw.

There follows the "first response," which involves *acceptance* of self as flawed, which in its turn entails a "letting go," a "turning over to," an "asking for help." This final dimension is the first "religious" act, the cry for help that is prayer.

Next, usually after some time, there follows the "second awareness": one begins to notice the flaws and lacks of others, *and* that those others are as unable to rid themselves of those defects as one had oneself been.

This second awareness is thus succeeded by the "second response", a sense of likeness to and of oneness with other humans *precisely as flawed*. So it is that one comes to experience pity and compassion, rather than blame and separation, when confronted by reality's imperfection.

In the thought of Julian of Norwich, a recently rediscovered fourteenth-century mystic who reflected this understanding, a corollary followed – one profoundly appropriate to the experience of Alcoholics Anonymous: "What hinders our spiritual growth more than anything is our failure to believe that God will bring and is now bringing to completion in us the work he has begun."

This classic understanding parallels the conversion actually experienced within Alcoholics Anonymous in three ways. For A.A. members, the difference between active alcoholism and sober recovery is (1) experiential rather than dogmatic, (2) involves essentially a movement from falseness to truth, and (3) comprises new understandings arrived at through a re-thinking and re-telling of one's story.

CONCLUSION

This paper has examined, in historical context, nine topics that illuminate the claim of the fellowship of Alcoholics Anonymous that its program is "spiritual rather than religious." From A.A.'s origins, most members have found in that claim an encouragement that has fostered a way of life and of thinking that has contributed to their recovery and sobriety. In some ways, for at least some individuals, A.A.'s revelation that and how one might be "spiritual" without being "religious" may be its greatest contribution. And I suspect that, given the opportunity, this may prove to be even more significant in nations other than the United States and Canada.

NOTES

1. *Cf.*, e.g. Robert Freed Bales, "Social Therapy for a Social Disorder," *Journal of Social Issues* vol. 1, no. 3 (1945), 14-22; Margaret Bean, "A.A. and Religion," *Psychiatric Annals*, vol. 5, no. 5 (1975), 52-55; more recently, James Christopher, *How to Stay Sober: Recovery Without Religion* (Buffalo, NY: Prometheus Books, 1988).

2. The analysis that follows derives from the research represented by my book, *Not-God: A History of Alcoholics Anonymous* (Center City, MN: Hazelden, 1979), but also from continuing research in the monthly journal of Alcoholics Anonymous, *The A.A. Grapevine*, which has been published continuously since June 1944.

3. *Cf.* Walter Houston Clark, *The Oxford Group: Its History and Significance* (New York: Bookman Associates, 1951); Reinhold Niebuhr, "Hitler and Buchman," *The Christian Century* (October 7, 1936), 1315-1316; Kurtz, *A.A.: The Story*, pp. 48-51.

4. *Cf.* Simon Tugwell, *Ways of Imperfection: An Exploration of Christian Spirituality* (Springfield, IL: Templegate, 1985) pp. vii-ix; Richard Wightman Fox, "Putting Religion in Its (Pivotal) Place," *Reviews in American History*, vol. 16, no. 1 (March 1988), 59-64.

5. *Alcoholics Anonymous*, 3rd ed., (New York: Alcoholics Anonymous World Services, 1975), p. 58.

6. *Cf.*, for two very early and very clear statements of this discovery, Bill W. [A.A. co-founder] (New York) to Dorothy S., 8 January 1940; and to Ted P., 25 March 1940.

7. This emphasis first appears in *A.A. Grapevine* articles by two non-members important in A.A.'s earliest history, Rev. Samuel Shoemaker and Rev. Edward Dowling, S.J.; for an early use of these terms by members, *cf. AAGV*, February, 1948, page 5, reporting a discussion on the topic "What makes A.A. work?"

8. *Cf.* Kurtz, *Not-God*, pp. 244-247.

9. *Alcoholics Anonymous*, pp. 72-103.

10. Michael E. Zimmerman, *Eclipse of the Self* (Athens, OH: Ohio University Press, 1981). p. 58.

11.   Elie Wiesel, 1986 Nobel Peace Prize Acceptance Speech, as reported in *The New York Times*, 11 December 1986.

12.   Paul V. Robb, "Conversion as a Human Experience," *Studies in the Spirituality of Jesuits*, vol. 14, no. 3 (May 1982), *passim*.

13.   William Barrett, *Irrational Man* (New York: Doubleday-Anchor, 1962), p. 235.

14.   Zimmerman, *Eclipse of the Self*, p. 247.

15.   David K. Reynolds, *Naikan Psychotherapy* (Chicago: University of Chicago, 1983).

16.   *Alcoholics Anonymous*, p. 103.

17.   *Cf.*, e.g., John E. Mack, "Alcoholism, A.A., and the Governance of the Self," and E. J. Khantzian, "Some Treatment Implications of the Ego and Self Disturbances in Alcoholism," in Margaret H. Bean and Norman E. Zinberg (eds.), *Dynamic Approaches to the Understanding and Treatment of Alcoholism* (New York: Free Press, 1981), pp. 128-162 and 163-188.

18.   Bill W., "What Is Acceptance?" *A.A. Grapevine*, v.28, n. 10, (March 1962), 3-5.

19.   Bill W. (New York) to Ollie J., 15 December 1950.

20.   Bill W. (New York) to May M., 24 August 1964.

21.   Bill W., "'Rules' Dangerous", *A.A. Grapevine*, vol. 2, no. 4, (September 1945), 2-3.

22.   Bill W., "The Fellowship of Alcoholics Anonymous," talk given at the Yale Summer School of Alcohol Studies, August, 1944, reprinted in *Alcohol, Science, and Society* (New Haven: Quarterly Journal of Studies on Alcohol, 1945), pp. 461-473

Although I am not a psychologist and thus not a member of the American Psychological Association, that August group invited me to present a paper at its 98th Annual Convention, held in Boston in August of 1990, the occasion on which its membership cele-brated the centenary of William James's The Principles of Psychol-ogy. *The topic assigned was "The Spirituality of William James."*

THE SPIRITUALITY OF WILLIAM JAMES:

A LESSON FROM ALCOHOLICS ANONYMOUS

INTRODUCTION:

In this paper, I propose to illuminate the place of William James in the ongoing history of American understandings of spirituality. The paper will argue that rather than being a precursor of "New Age" spirituality, James was a vehicle of the more ancient tradition that finds modern expression in the fellowship of Alcoholics Anonymous. Examining especially James's vision of human nature and his treatment of **will**, what follows will touch also on the philosopher/psychologist's roles as a popularizer and an opponent of all reductionisms.[1]

1. The Older Challenge and the Newer Data

The proximate context for my treatment of William James and spirituality is a generation-old scholarly opinion that has deteriorated into a kind of semi-popular lore, begetting a misunderstanding that calumniates James.

In this not-very-new age of the so-called "New Age," many ascribe to William James – blame seems a not inaccurate word – many *blame* William James for New Age ideas on "spirituality." Intriguing as this suggestion of James's continuing impact may be, recent developments demonstrate the need for caution. Popular spirituality has more than one face, and the attribution to William James of responsibility for its more bizarre manifestations is less than accurate.

Yet this is an understandable error: James's tolerance reveled in a breadth that included ample room for the bizarre, and our hero would no doubt have been more fascinated by New Age phenomena than am I. But there is a difference between tolerance of and *responsibility for*. My point is to deny the latter, and so it seems well to begin by looking at the indictment – as first leveled in 1965 by Donald Meyer, then repeated by William Clebsch in 1973, whose version was adopted by Gerald Myers in his 1986 biography of James.[2]

The stage was set twenty-five years ago, with the treatment accorded James by Donald Meyer in his useful study of *The Positive Thinkers*.[3] A detailed "Postscript" argues that William James was "the authority" for later generations of "positive thinkers." To the best of my knowledge, that interpretation was not disputed at the time; there seemed neither reason nor basis to do so. Nor did the observation by William Clebsch that "Nobody exerted a wider influence [than James] on the palliative-peddlers of twentieth-century American popular religion," an attribution accepted uncritically by Gerald E. Myers, awaken much comment, although with each repetition of the charge, the cultural context may be seen in hindsight more and more to have invited some sort of challenge.

Today's late-twentieth-century "palliative-peddlers," the instant gurus whose promotions dot the pages of such journals as *New Age* and *Gnosis*, continue, on occasion, to appeal to James. But claimed influence is not necessarily real impact, and just as "patriotism is the last refuge of the scoundrel," mention of William James has become the ultimate appeal of the religious nut (if I may be pardoned the use of that technical psychological term). With all due respect to two great students of the human condition, it seems somewhat sadly accurate to observe that most modern references to the religious insights of William James and Carl Jung signal fuzzy thought and a use of language that can be most charitably described as "singular."

*　　　*　　　*

64

This paper begs to differ with Professors Meyer and Clebsch and Myers, because more recent history suggests that the significance of William James in the area of spirituality lies in a very different direction. Like any "story," history is not over with until all the data – all the outcomes – are in. They never are "*all* in," of course, but later developments do help us better to understand earlier events. And the "spirituality" of the so-called "New Age," although accurately categorized as our era's manifestation of the hoary tradition of "mind-cure" by "positive thinking," differs broadly and distinctly from another modern expression of a far more ancient tradition of spirituality, the one first articulated in modern form over fifty years ago by the Twelve-Step program of Alcoholics Anonymous.

If we would understand not only William James's ideas on spirituality but also his own spirituality, we need look not to the "New Age," nor to the proliferation of claimed offshoots of A.A., claims generally based solely on a sloppy concept of addiction: we must look to Alcoholics Anonymous itself. A.A.'s claim to have been influenced by William James, and specifically by its early members' reading of *The Varieties of Religious Experience*, rests on more solid ground. Alcoholics Anonymous came into being out of the Oxford Group, and James's *Varieties* appeared on that organization's list of "required reading" and was in fact read carefully by members who had difficulty accepting "the spiritual," a common difficulty with most alcoholics then as indeed also now.

2. James on the Topic of Alcohol

But that somewhat tenuous claim on William James is not the main reason behind A.A. co-founder Bill W.'s reference to him as "one of our founders." The reference is manifestly hyperbolic. What is striking, in fact, in A.A.'s advertence to James, is the almost studious ignoring, at least by Bill Wilson himself, of James's many mentions of alcohol, and **especially** in *Varieties*. Midway through that work, in describing the work of Jerry M'Auley's Water Street mission, James tosses off a footnote observation the absence of advertence to which in the literature of Alcoholics Anonymous is striking: "The only radical remedy I know for dipsomania is religiomania."[4]

Most of the early members of Alcoholics Anonymous (like most of the later members) would have found that reference unwelcome: most alcoholics would rather be drunk than "religious." Nor is this the only "obvious" Jamesian passage ignored by A.A. members. James's direct treatment of alcohol and its use is rightly celebrated:

> The sway of alcohol over mankind is unquestionably due to its power to stimulate the mystical faculties of human nature, usually crushed to earth by the cold facts and dry criticisms of the sober hour. Sobriety diminishes, discriminates, and says no; drunkenness expands, unites, and says yes. It is in fact the great exciter of the Yes function in man. It brings its votary from the chill periphery of things to the radiant core. It makes him for the moment one with truth. Not through mere perversity do men run after it. To the poor and the unlettered it stands in the place of symphony concerts and of literature; and it is part of the deeper mystery and tragedy of life that whiffs and gleams of something that we immediately recognize as excellent should be vouchsafed to so many of us only in the fleeting earlier phases of what in its totality is so degrading a poisoning.[5]

Surprising as this may be to some, such an understanding of the power of alcohol would not have been foreign to members such as A.A. co-founder Bill Wilson. In his brief correspondence with Dr. Carl Jung shortly before the psychiatrist's death, and in a far more lengthy exchange with a prominent Philadelphian who had been treated by Jung, Bill revealed a very Jamesian understanding of the affirming, even mystical place of alcohol in the lives of many drinkers who become alcoholics. There is, in fact, a profound similarity between James's description of his experimentation with nitrous oxide and Wilson's thoughts on his own explorations with the chemical popularly known as LSD, which enjoyed in the late 1950s a brief vogue among some scientists as a potential cure for alcoholism.[6]

Let me be clear on the point here: there is no evidence that Wilson's understanding of the possible connections between mind-altering drugs and religious experience was drawn from James. Indeed, the bulk of evidence points in the direction of Bill being one of the few early members who did *not* read *Varieties* very thoroughly. Wilson may, of course, have picked up an awareness of William James's ideas on the topic in conversation (which is how Bill gained most of his knowledge: like James, he was an extraordinary listener). The point here is that although the affinities between Jamesian thought and A.A. understanding run far deeper, even some more superficial apparent discrepancies are only apparently discrepancies.[7]

3. Main Direct Impact:
"Spiritual" Taken Seriously and Unconventionally

For facile references such as the James quotation on alcohol, although interesting, serve mainly to distract. Both James's main direct contribution to Alcoholics Anonymous, and the very different chief way in which A.A. practice illuminates James's own spirituality, are more substantial – and more subtle.

The main direct contribution of William James to Alcoholics Anonymous can be simply stated. William James, like Carl Jung, was a world-class intellectual who took religion seriously, declaring it in fact to be "the great interest of my life."[8] More accurately, in the more modern vocabulary that their example encouraged, both Jung and James took *the spiritual* seriously, for neither was in any way a "conventional believer" in any traditional religion. They witnessed, if that term may be used here, to the possibility of being "spiritual rather than religious," which became a keynote claim and real conviction among Alcoholics Anonymous. That, quite simply – the openness to unconventional spirituality, the lived example that such was possible – was James's greatest direct contribution to Alcoholics Anonymous [9]

Openness to the unconventional may also seem to characterize "New Age" spiritualities, but the deep conventionality of their all-too-traditional "positive thinking" approach is set in relief by another Jamesian animus that is itself clarified by the very different example of Alcoholics Anonymous. As Herbert Schneider has pointed out, James's revolt against "absolute" philosophical idealisms involved a refusal of all *gnosticisms* – a rejection of those approaches, ever re-current, that seek to find religious satisfactions in philosophy instead of exploring how metaphysics might need to be reconstructed in view of the facts of religious experience.[10] Albeit in very different language, the same animus informs Alcoholics Anonymous, to the constant chagrin of many and diverse professionals as well as New Agers.

4. Main Deep Point: Open to Dark Side of Being Human

For here as in this next main point of my presentation this afternoon, my concern is less with the impact of William James on A.A. than how Alcoholics Anonymous illuminates James's spirituality. A.A. spirituality differs from "New Age" approaches precisely in its acceptance of the reality of "the dark side" of human experience. A.A. members, that is to say, in their embrace of the identity "sober alcoholic," accept in that vocabulary the reality that they are – in Jamesian terms – "sick souls." The thin spirituality of the New Age, on the other hand, is emphatically the religion of "healthy-mindedness."

Two key passages in co-founder Bill W.'s telling of A.A.'s story detail his debt to William James. Describing how he came to understand his own "spiritual experience," Wilson tells of reading in *Varieties* of "the great common denominators of pain, suffering, calamity. Complete hopelessness and deflation at depth," Bill read, "were almost always required." *Then* it was that "The significance of all this burst upon me. *Deflation at depth* – yes, that was *it*. Exactly that had happened to me."[11] Six months later, Wilson went on to record, after the total failure of all his efforts to sober up even one other drunk, his physician, Dr. William Duncan Silkworth, "again reminded" Bill "of Professor William James' observation that truly transforming spiritual experiences are nearly always founded on calamity and collapse."[12] That insight, Wilson always felt, undergirded his first successful approach, a month later, in Akron, Ohio, to the person who would become A.A.'s other co-founder, Dr. Robert Holbrook Smith. Alcoholics Anonymous thus learned, from the very beginning, the importance of acknowledging "the dark side." The often echoed axiom "Remember When" combines with the repeated profession of the identification, "I am an alcoholic," to ensure embrace of identity as, in Jamesian terms, a "sick soul."

James, of course, identified *himself* as one of the "sick souls." "The constitutional disease from which I suffer," he once casually confided, "is what the Germans call *Zerrissenheit* or torn-to-pieces-hood."[13] William James knew the paradox, the two-sidedness of human nature and of human beings; knew the truth of the Islamic insight: "All sunshine makes a desert."[14]

What James termed "the religion of healthy-mindedness" is a vigorous, full-bodied, optimistic type of spiritual sensibility that sees nature as beneficent and God as intimately, affirmatively, related to all His creatures. Characterized by the "inability to feel evil," this spirituality "looks on all things and sees that they are good." This *is* the "simpler" view, and it is aptly captured by the spiritualities of the New Age. The problem with this uncomplicated affirmation of the goodness of creation, as James points out with an uncharacteristic restraint that perhaps reflects his own continuing tussles with "melancholy," is that it is bought at the cost of a certain amount of blindness to the reality of evil in life.

James's description of twice-born religion, the spirituality of the sick soul, runs far differently. These individuals remain ever aware of the sense of risk, danger, and pervasive moral evil running through the world. They are people possessed by a divided self – knowing an inner instability, tension, and conflict between the various elements of their lives.[15] James's "sick-souled" express in vivid relief the traditional insight that the self of every human being is an unstable, even conflictual phenomenon. This is not a self about which to be glum, but it is a self that will find vacuous those philosophies that can be formulated on bumper-stickers and those theologies that can be encapsulated by smiley buttons. James may not be explicit about preferring such a self, but he is frank about the reason for his preference for such religions: they work better. "The completest religions would therefore seem to be those in which the pessimistic elements are best developed."[16]

And this is precisely the insight of Alcoholics Anonymous, the intuition that sets A.A. off from the New Age healthy-mindedness that sometimes claims to imitate it. Members of Alcoholics Anonymous identify themselves as alcoholics, even though they are sober. The acceptance, the insistence, on the identity, "sober alcoholic," both signals and teaches acceptance of the reality of human duality. What was new in the A.A. vision at its birth in 1935, the element of the A.A. vision that still confuses so many of the modern "once-born," is that one can be sober and yet still "alcoholic."

Alcoholics got well before Alcoholics Anonymous: they called themselves "ex-alcoholics," a wording that through borrowing crept into the first printings of A.A.'s own "Big Book." But that wording was excised – the *only* change of wording in what quickly became a kind of sacred text. It is the centrality of this vision, this very Jamesian vision, that more recent and very different spiritualities fail to grasp. The point, for "the spirituality of William James," is that James understood the highest levels of spirituality to emerge only from an honest confrontation with the evil in oneself and the world.[17]

5. Tolerance and Open-mindedness as Flowing from This:
From this central vision flow the related Jamesian points of tolerance, popularization, and opposition to reductionism, the last of which will also afford transition to a few final animadversions on the connections between Jamesian spirituality and his thought on will.

James's vaunted tolerance and open-mindedness were rooted in and sprang from precisely his awareness of human duality. And A.A.'s flows similarly: "Who can imagine one alcoholic judging another?!" Bill Wilson once queried, tongue only partly in cheek. For from the recognition of human duality flows the understanding that the line between good and evil, between brilliance and stupidity, runs not between nations or peoples or classes or individuals, but **through** each individual human being. James's key insight of *homo duplex* affords the only sure undergirding of true tolerance, of the capacity for that forgiveness that heals the *resentiment* named within Alcoholics Anonymous as "the number one offender" that "destroys more alcoholics than anything else."[18]

6. James as "Popularizer" and on "Reductionism"
In William James's own life, as in the experience of most members of Alcoholics Anonymous, recognition and acceptance of the *mixed* human

condition flowed into readiness to assume that everyone is teachable. To the scandal of some later philosophers and psychologists, James reveled in his role as popularizer.[19] Already as early as 1868, as Gerald Myers points out, James had "adopted the posture that would become his philosophical trademark – the middle term in a Hegelian triad, in this instance between academia and the populace." The Varieties of Religious Experience affords perhaps the best example; in it most explicitly, James "took religious experience to academics and philosophical interpretations of that experience to the people."[20]

Not unrelated to James the popularizer was James the staunch adversary of all forms of reductionism. In decrying what he saw as a tendency to "medical materialism," William James was taking the larger stance of opposing all reducing of **any** reality to "nothing but." More than his explicitly labeled "Progressive" contemporaries, James recognized the anti-democratic implications of the nascent modernist tendency to identify the "hidden" with the real. This was, indeed, one reason for his wariness of the thought of Sigmund Freud.

For James, like the Progressives who gave us Prohibition, was a moralist; but unlike the Progressives and the Prohibitionists, he was a moralist who looked first to himself and those like him. As Gordon Allport observed, William James "wanted psychologists to confront the fundamental moral fact that by their own theories of human nature they have the power of elevating or degrading this same human nature. Debasing assumptions debase the mind; generous assumptions exalt the mind."[21]

For James, "health" was a term that took on full meaning only when placed in the context of broader concepts about the meaning of the good in ethical terms.[22] The key to William James as both "pluralist" and "pragmatist" is to be found in his insistence on looking **always** to the whole – a realization that should undergird especially any re-reading of "The Sentiment of Rationality." James's chief argument with W.K. Clifford concerned not the scientific approach as the criterion of "belief," but whether in its necessary activity of analysis and dividing up, science did not lose that contact with **the whole** that is necessary for ultimate credibility. And for James, "religious experience" was an undeniable part of "the whole life" actually lived by most people.

7. Divergence from "New Age" in "The Strenuous Mood"

The Jamesian war on all forms of reductionism and "medical material-ism" is important not least because it once again helps to distinguish between Jamesian insight and New Age distortions of that insight. There is a world of difference between tolerant open-mindedness and the insipidness that flows from the absence of principles – and this is one of those Jamesian "differences that make all the difference." James's own vocabulary sometimes obscures this point. Coinages such as "The Gospel of Relaxation" may seem to suggest affinity with the New Age world-view, but those word usages came out of a context so different that it is in fact the opposite that is true. The most obvious divergence between Jamesian thought and the therapeutic narcissism of the New Age may be found in the philosopher-psychologist's lauding of the strenuous mood.

James's "strenuous mood" was not the hardiness of Theodore Roose-velt, although our philosopher borrowed that contemporary vocabulary, which was truer to his purpose than would have been a less sanguine phrase. For as his treatment makes clear, James emphasized the "strenuous mood" as the opposite of the "easygoing mood" – the "laid back" attitude of "I don't care." James's "strenuous mood," then, involves not the blasé labeling of every inclination to responsibility a manifestation of "co-dependence," but urges precisely the opposite: a positive and active attitude of care – care for oneself, for one's family, for the wider commu-nity, for possible future communities that may extend beyond the limits of one's own individual life.[23]

8. Will

For the final point on William James and spirituality, and how Alcoholics Anonymous throws light on that spirituality, concerns a contribution as central as James's model of unconventional spirituality and his vision of *homo duplex* – his thought on **will**. As unwelcome a topic as may be "the spiritual" in academic psychological settings, the subject of will seems even less seemly. Yet William James knew the reality of human will, its possibilities and its limitations, and he expressed and lived that reality as well as any twentieth-century thinker, at least up to the time of the psychiatrist, Leslie Farber, the title of whose book of collected essays would surely have delighted James: *Lying, Despair, Jealousy, Envy, Sex, Suicide, Drugs, and the Good Life.*[24]

Central to James's treatment of will was his understanding of *attention*: although some of our behaviors may appear "determined," we shape that very "determination," for we can *choose* that to which we will attend, at least to the extent of naming it. William James knew the nature of obsession.[25] But even more powerful is his description of the "drunkard's" games of naming, in a passage that shows sufficient insight to qualify James posthumously as an alcoholism counselor, if not a member of Alcoholics Anonymous!

> *How many excuses does the drunkard find when each new temptation comes! It is a new brand of liquor which the interests of intellectual culture in such matters oblige him to test; moreover it is poured out and it is sin to waste it; or others are drinking and it would be churlishness to refuse; or it is but to enable him to sleep, or just to get through this job of work; or it isn't drinking, it is because he feels so cold; or it is Christmas-day; or it is a means of stimulating him to make a more powerful resolution in favor of abstinence than any he has hitherto made; or it is just this once, and once doesn't count, etc., etc., ad libitum – it is, in fact, anything you like except being a drunkard. That is the conception that will not stay before the poor soul's attention. But if he once gets able to pick out that way of conceiving, from all the other possible ways of conceiving the various opportunities which occur, if through thick and thin he holds to it that this is being a drunkard and is nothing else, he is not likely to remain one long. The effort by which he succeeds in keeping the right name unwaveringly present to his mind proves to be his saving moral act.*[26]

As strikingly as reads that passage, this is not the moment to belabor *will*, nor indeed even to attempt to say anything further about James's spirituality itself. Rather, following the example of the many illustrative stories James used in *Varieties*, an example echoed in the A.A. practice of storytelling, let me conclude by summarizing will, spirituality, and I trust more in a well-known story about James, as told by Sigmund Freud.

The two men, Freud and James, met only once, at G. Stanley Hall's Clark University Conference in September of 1909, a conference attended also by Freud's student, Carl Gustav Jung, as well as by such American luminaries as James Jackson Putnam, Morton Prince, and Adolf Meyer. Later, in 1925, two years after his own first operation for the cancer that would ultimately kill him, Freud recalled the meeting and his most vivid memory of James:

> *I shall never forget one little scene that occurred. [As we were walking, James] stopped suddenly, handed me a bag he was carrying and asked me to walk on, saying that he would catch me up as soon as he had got through an attack of angina pectoris which was just coming on. He died of that disease a year later; and I have always wished that I might be as fearless as he was in the face of approaching death.*[27]

Conclusion:

James's life and career attest that all explanation need not be reductive. James's point, in *Varieties* and "The Sentiment of Rationality" as well as *The Principles of Psychology*, was that *explanation* becomes flawed as a vehicle of understanding if we insist on making it the *only* vehicle of understanding. On the topic of "spirituality," William James was less scientist than artist. Art describes rather than explains, as both William James and the storytelling members of Alcoholics Anonymous knew. I hope that on the topic of James's own spirituality, I have succeeded in following that example in a way helpful to your understanding.

NOTES

1. Although I recognize that this presentation is occasioned by the centenary of William James's *The Principles of Psychology*, I will draw the majority of my argument from his *The Varieties of Religious Experience*, for I agree with Jacques Barzun that this later work is "Volume Three of the *Principles*": *A Stroll With William James* (New York: Harper & Row, 1983), p. 242.

2. Gerald E. Myers, *William James: His Life and Thought* (New Haven, CT: Yale University Press, 1986), p. 607, cites William A. Clebsch, *American Religious Thought* (Chicago: University of Chicago Press, 1973), p. 153.

3. Donald Meyer, *The Positive Thinkers* (Garden City, NY: Doubleday, 1965).

4. VRE, p. 213, quoting, with apparent approbation, Samuel Hadley.

5. VRE, p. 297.

6. For James, *VRE*, p. 298; the best description of Wilson's taking of LSD, although it does not mention him by name, may be found in Aldous Huxley, *Moksha* (Los Angeles: J.P. Tarcher, Inc., 1977), ed. Michael Horowitz and Cynthia Palmer; on the scientific practice of the time, *cf.* the "Foreword" by Humphrey Osmond.

7. In a formulation offered by Jung in 1961, alcoholism and the use of other such chemicals represent an example of *"spiritus contra spiritum"* – a warring of "spirits against the Spirit" evident in the lives of many such chemical-users. William James shared the same insight, as the quoted and cited passages on alcohol and nitrous oxide make clear.

8. To the scandal of Morton White, who offers this information in a very different context in his *Science and Sentiment in America* (New York: Oxford University Press, 1972), p. 171, quoting Perry, TCWJ, vol. 1, p. 165.

9. On this aspect of James as not conventional in belief, *cf.* William Barrett, *The Illusion of Technique*, pp. 272 ff: "Among all the things that James says about religion he never speaks from within faith" – and Barrett goes on the explore the significance in a chapter titled, "The Faith to Will."

10. Schneider is treating especially of the James of *A Pluralistic Universe, cf.* Herbert W. Schneider, "Varieties of Religious Experience Since William James," in Herbert W. Schneider (ed.), *Religion in Twentieth-Century America* (1952), pp. 173 ff.

11. *AACA*, p. 64.

12. *AACA*, p. 13.

13. Perry, *The Complete William James*, vol. 2, p. 679.

14. Harriott, John F.X., "The Aspirin Society," *The Tablet*, 244:2809, 334.

15. *Cf.* VRE, pp. 141, 126, 135.

16. VRE, p. 139.

17. Meyer, p. 321, does seem to grasp this, noting that "James made no less an assertion of human values than did liberalism, but he registered the decisive point . . . : if human values were to count for anything, they had to endure fear with strength for experiencing the non-human and inhuman, subconscious depths and unmeasured transcendencies. . . . James's orientation was similar to . . . Dostoevski's portrait of the saint as one with the most profound awareness of evil."

18. VRE, p. 141: "The psychological basis of the twice-born character seems to be a certain discordancy or heterogeneity in the native temperament of the subject, an incompletely unified moral and intellectual constitution." In the recent literature, this aspect has been most helpfully treated by Don S. Browning, *Pluralism and Personality: William James and Some Contemporary Cultures of Psychology* (Cranbury, NJ: Associated University Presses, 1980); the quotation on "resentment" is from *Alcoholics Anonymous*, p. 64.

19. Among those scandalized, Morton White, who relates this specifically to James's interest in religion.

20. Myers, p. 464.

21. Quoted by Browning, *Pluralism and Personality*, pp. 33-34.

22. Browning, p. 27.

23. *Cf.* Browning, pp. 41 ff., for a fuller treatment of this point, although it also pervades Browning's book.

24. Leslie H. Farber, *Lying, Despair, Jealousy, Envy, Sex, Suicide, Drugs, and the Good Life* (New York: Basic Books, 1976), is probably the most Jamesian book to appear in the last quarter of the twentieth century.

25. The discussion of craving – under the heading of "monomania" – appears in *Principles*, vol. II, p. 543.

26. *Principles*, vol. II, p. 565.

27. Freud, "An Autobiographical Study," Standard Edition, vol. 20, p. 52, as quoted and cited by Nathan G. Hale, Jr., *Freud and the Americans* (New York: Oxford University Press, 1971), p. 19.

An earlier version of this brief piece was published in The Alcoholism Treatment Quarterly *vol. 4, no.2 (1987), 1-6, as "Shame in the Eighties," where it served as an "Introduction" to a special issue on "Shame." This revision dates from 1991, when I was invited to address a plenary session at the "First National Conference on Shame," sponsored by John Bradshaw and held in Las Vegas, Nevada, from May 8th to 11th of that year, on which occasion this talk was presented to an increasingly restless audience.*

SHAME IN THE NINETIES

A decade ago, in 1979, when I first suggested that distinguishing between shame and guilt and focusing attention upon shame seemed one of the contributions of Alcoholics Anonymous insight, most to whom I mentioned that idea expressed horror. "You can't talk about shame, Ernie," they cautioned. "That word will turn everybody off, especially alcoholics."

Well, we have come a long way. For the last decade, the surest way to make a buck has been to convict people of their shame and then to find a way of blaming someone else for it. As useful as extensions and applications of the core ideas concerning shame may be, a use of those ideas that denies or remains ignorant of their origins in the story of religious thought can become only twisted and dangerous. And so I wish to use my time today, in this plenary session, to explore that origin and those roots.

Let me state boldly what is both my initial insight and my main point. Alcoholics Anonymous works not because it is new but because it makes available an ancient wisdom. For other peoples, in earlier times, that healing wisdom was made available by other vehicles. The religion of the churches, immersion in classic literature, a sense of belonging to a community that was greater than and had claims on the individual: each of these experiences, in general no longer available to most of us, afforded a healing that facilitated living with the imperfection of the human condition.

1. The Personal and the Professional

In an era when those involved in the healing of chronic disabilities recognize that technical competence in the modalities of therapy must be complemented by sensitivity to the specifically human dimension of hurt, distinguishing between shame and guilt and attending to shame's specific pain both serve that recognition and enhance healing abilities. For if there be one over-riding albeit implicit theme in all the literature on shame, it is that one's personal experience of one's self cannot be separated from one's professional approach to the phenomenon of shame in the experience of others.

Guilt concerns doing, and what we do professionally and personally can be held separate. But shame has to do with *being*, and what we **are** personally and professionally necessarily touch. Here as rarely elsewhere in professional endeavor, only one who has experienced shame is capable of touching and healing shame. It seems, indeed, that only by understanding shame in one's own life does one become able accurately to identify its impact in another's. How to reconcile this awareness with the valid requirements of professionalism remains an ongoing challenge.

2. Sense of Failure, Lack, Flaw

The core of shame consists in the experience of failure – the sense that one is somehow flawed, defective, lacking. Ultimately, shame is an experience of nothingness – the experiencing, however veiled, of one's own non-being. One becomes more fully human by and in the processing of that experience. But that process does not necessarily occur. Shame is so painful, our defect of being can feel so hollow, that one may become mired in its misery. There is no disablement more profound than the inability to be human – to *be* humanly – that afflicts a person locked in shame.

Because the demand for all-or-nothing signals the attempt to be other than human, the sufferer becomes locked in shame not by the acknowledgment of flaw but by its denial. An age addicted to "pride," a context in which only "number one" matters, sets up its participants for disablement by shame.

3. Denial – Self-deception

For as commentators so regularly note, *denial* is the characteristic defense against shame.[1] Denial signifies not the dishonesty of lying but rather the self-deception that Sartre termed *mauvaise foi* – "the attempt to flee what one cannot flee, to flee what one is."[2]

Individuals disabled by shame tell lies, but they are not liars. To be disabled by shame means to be unable to be honest *with oneself.* Shame blinds to shame itself – one reason why the terms and the concept, shame's naming and its experiencing, tend to fall apart, to be sundered by the very namelessness that springs from shame as an experience of nothingness. It is the abandonment of "simple truths" that entails the need for "vital lies."[3]

4.The Interpersonal: Needing Others and Mutuality

Such an indescribable experience of nothingness, so well concealed even from self, of course cuts one off from others. The characteristic judgment associated with disablement by shame runs: "No one can possibly know how I feel, for no one has ever felt this way." Uniqueness sets off. The resulting isolation is rarely splendid, but it may prove terminal. Those mired in shame suffer terminal uniqueness.

Paradoxically, however, the sense of isolated separateness can lay the foundation for the bridge across which shame may be healed. For such uniqueness becomes too painful to bear, and that very pain can open the sufferer's eyes not only to the reality of the human need for others but also to its specification in the mode of mutuality. One reason why shame is good, one reason why "shameless" is an epithet, lies in that understanding. We attain full humanity only through those realities that we get only by giving, that we bestow only by being open to receive. The experience of shame thus teaches that and how human beings need each other in order to become whole.

5. Enough-ness

Both shame and its healing connect with sufficiency – with the sense of *enough*. Appropriately, then, shame seems specified most sharply in all forms of addiction. Addiction signals the failure of enough-ness.

Although the refusal of "enough" hallmarks modern identity, a fascination with *boundaries* has emerged as characteristic of our post-modern age. Parallel experience in the healing of shame seems to suggest that "only when however we are becomes good enough do we become free to be our very best."[4] The deeper meanings of that truth apply to more than the experience of addiction, but it seems likely that those who work in the field of addiction treatment may be the first to discover them. And they may thus discover the responsibility of making what they learn available to others, to the larger culture.

6. Relationship to "The Spiritual" and Virtue –
Light on Co-dependence

For "being responsible" is not an evil concept, nor is needing others some kind of illness. Shame has to do with *being*, and therefore with those qualities the ancients termed *virtue*.[5] Although this is but one source of shame's claim to a profound relationship with "the spiritual," it affords the title that merits direct attention here. The rediscovery of shame serves to offset the recent intrusion into even therapeutic understandings of the narcissistic, me-first fixations of the larger contemporary cultural context.

Those who love or live with someone afflicted by a malady such as alcoholism suffer very real pain and shame, and those who awaken sensitivity to that specific shame merit praise. But blithe inattention to the spirit of the age that has spawned the concept of "co-dependency," combined with an inadequate understanding of shame, have together issued in far too many treatments that serve mainly to view as "sick" such qualities as loyalty and commitment. If the first spiritual insight involves acceptance of one's own flawed reality, then the first spiritual response involves meeting another's defect not with the labeling blame that distances but with the compassionate pity that unites.[6]

Proper attention to shame may lead to a rediscovery of virtue. Meanwhile, sensitivity to the sources of disabling shame can free, if itself freed from the blinding trammels of the narcissistic vocabulary of this passing moment. "Feeling responsible" need not signify sickness. By reminding of both-and-ness and recalling to its acceptance, shame's pointing to *enough* may help restore to sanity, sobriety, and even sanctity.

NOTES

1. Helen Block Lewis, *Shame and Guilt in Neurosis*, New York, 1971.

2. The classic work on shame remains Jean-Paul Sartre, *Being and Nothingness*; for useful insight, *cf.* the also-classic William Barrett, *Irrational Man*, New York, 1958.

3. *Cf.* Daniel Goleman, *Vital Lies, Simple Truths*, New York, 1985.

4. Gershen Kaufman, *Shame: The Power of Caring*, Cambridge, 1980, p. 129; on the modern/post-modern point, *cf*, Arthur C. Danto, *The Philosophical Disenfranchisement of Art*, New York, 1987.

5. *Cf.* Alasdair MacIntyre, *After Virtue*, Notre Dame, 1981; and, for a usefully critical perspective on MacIntyre, Don S. Browning, *Religious Thought and the Modern Psychologies*, Philadelphia, 1987.

6. *Cf.* James Joyce, *Portrait of the Artist as a Young Man*, p. 239; also Donald P. McNeill, Douglas A. Morrison, Henri J. M. Nouwen, *Compassion*, New York, 1982; Browning, as cited; Miguel d'Unamuno, *Tragic Sense of Life*, New York, 1954; and Paul V. Robb, S.J., "Conversion as a Human Experience," in *Studies in the Spirituality of Jesuits*, vol. 14, no. 3 (May 1982).

Pergamon Press each year puts out an Annual Review of Addictions Research and Treatment. Each volume consists of many topical areas on each of which several scholarly essays offer comment or report research. In order to help readers better understand the significance of the individual articles, each topical area is introduced by a Commentary that attempts to set the context for understanding the significance of the pieces that follow.

For the 1992 edition, the Rutgers-based editors incautiously – or perhaps mischievously – prevailed on me to offer the Commentary on the section on "Lay Treatment," which to most of the contributors meant Alcoholics Anonymous. Although the articles on which I comment are here referenced rather than reproduced, I trust that there is enough context for this essay to stand on its own.

COMMENTARY ON "LAY TREATMENT."

Examining Alcoholics Anonymous under the heading of "treatment" is like studying the formation patterns of bears flying South for the winter. Reality constrained into the wrong category is reality distorted. Both bears and Canadian geese change their usual activities with the onset of winter. Both Alcoholics Anonymous and alcoholism treatment can benefit people whose lives are disrupted by the drinking of alcohol. But to leap from either observation of shared likeness to a larger equation that implies identity is as false in one case as in the other.

More than any phenomenon in recent history, Alcoholics Anonymous resembles the fabled elephant described by the legendary blind men. Each commentator reports what is seen through the lens of his or her particular discipline. Psychologists discover a behavioral or a cognitive program (Miller & Hester, 1980); those psychoanalytically-inclined uncover a psycho-dynamic program (Mack, 1981); those enamored of the medical model detect a living out of the disease-concept of alcoholism (Vaillant, 1983); sociologists find "interpersonal factors" dominant (Maxwell, 1951), or discern a manifestation of a "social movement" (Room, 1992), or a "self-help" enterprise (Mäkelä, 1992); those spooked by religion find "cult" or other manifestation of sectarianism (Jones, 1970; Galanter, 1989, 1990); those enthralled with "New Age" insight discover expressions of a "postmodern spirituality" (Corrington, 1989); and it goes on. As an historian, I too bring the lens of my discipline: and so rather than claiming to describe what Alcoholics Anonymous is, I will content myself with detailing how well the accompanying articles remain true to what A.A. has been.

Let's begin by admitting that the term, *lay treatment*, is oxymoronic. Such mixing of the religious and the medical metaphors does not work. The term *lay* means simply "of the ordinary people," and therefore lacking the set-apart-ness of special qualification (Onions, 1969; Shipley, 1984). The term *treatment*, on the other hand, necessarily denotes some degree of expertise and professionalism – as concern over licensing laws, certification procedures and credentialing of various kinds consistently confirms.

Efforts to overcome the confusion are not new. In 1970, the General Service Conference of Alcoholics Anonymous rejected as inappropriate the term "A.A. counselor." Reporting a "consensus reached on terminology," the 1975 Conference extended its disapproval to the term, "two-hatter" (Kurtz, 1991, p. 291). Both actions attest to the dissonance in all such concepts, of which "lay treatment" is a particularly mischievous example.

The first A.A.-connected usage of the term *treatment* was by Akron's Sister Ignatia, who began using the word as early as 1939 on the alcoholic ward of St. Thomas Hospital as a way of emphasizing that that hospital and ward had no "cure" for alcoholism (Darrah, 1992). Members of Alcoholics Anonymous visited the ward and were indeed its sole source of admissions: the St. Thomas program was in fact for a time called "the A.A. ward," in that era before the Twelve Traditions were even conceived. But despite that confusion, those earliest members of Alcoholics Anonymous knew as well as did Sister Ignatia and the medical staff of St. Thomas that A.A. was neither "cure," for there was none, nor "treatment," for that was why they needed the medical setting of a hospital. Consistently, then, Alcoholics Anonymous has been most usually described by those who know it most intimately as a "program of recovery," or, more recently, as "relapse prevention" (Nowinski, 1992).

How do A.A. and treatment differ? "The Twelve Steps are philosophy, not technology," a psychologist recently observed (Beutler, 1992). At least since 1979, when analyses by Kurtz and by Antze from two very different directions drew attention to the philosophical underpinnings of what A.A. prefers to term its "way of life" ([Anonymous], 1953, p. 15), evidence has been available that Alcoholics Anonymous is more than treatment. But could it *also* be "treatment"? And if Alcoholics Anonymous is not treatment, what are some of the relationships between A.A. and treatment?

Mäkelä brings to these questions not only sociological skills, but an anthropological perspective. Both Alcoholics Anonymous and alcoholism treatment, as specifically American innovations, can be observed most accurately by someone who stands outside the assumptions of American culture. Mäkelä's Finnish background and cross-cultural research permit him to avoid with equal adeptness the biases of behavioral researchers, of treatment marketers, and of mystical enthusiasts. His phenomenological approach, as in seeing A.A. meetings as "speech events," discovers several differences between A.A. and treatment. True to the religious practice of its Oxford Group origins, for example, traditional A.A. discourse involves a form of "disclosing secrets" in a setting that guarantees the absence of cross-talk.

The treatment approach may seem similar, but its confrontational style and aim of "searching for the authentic self" impose quests far more daunting than A.A.'s simple emphasis on "honesty." Anderson and Gilbert take up the same point with their observation that "mere self-disclosure is not enough." No, it is not . . . for the treatment setting, which is what they investigate. Their "communication training" is technique, not philosophy.

As Mäkelä points out, "treatment A.A." is not *real* A.A. – Alcoholics Anonymous as handed down by the alcoholics who produced the book, *Alcoholics Anonymous.* This issue is important, for it is a confusion unfortunately common among researchers . . . almost as common as mistaking court-mandated A.A. for A.A. as it is usually lived in most groups.

In reality, of course, treatment and A.A. are often mixed together, and so each does influence the other. The articles presented here thus address a valid question: *How **well** do treatment and Alcoholics Anonymous mix?* Many early "treatment" programs employed individuals whose sole credential was that they themselves were sober alcoholics – almost invariably through their participation in Alcoholics Anonymous (Anderson, 1981). Even in those earliest days, as expressed wariness over "appearing to sell the Twelfth Step" and the quick rejection of the term "A.A. counselor" for the name "two-hatter" (also eventually rejected) suggest, the distinction between Alcoholics Anonymous and even those primitive treatment programs was perceived to be very real. In time, however, as pressures toward validation for the acceptance of third-party payments became paramount, concern over credentialing and certification led to the explicit professionalization of alcoholism counselors – and some practitioners of this "new profession" (Royce, 1989) began less to bring their A.A. understandings into their treatment practice and more to import their treatment ideology into their Alcoholics Anonymous participation.

The effects of confusing Alcoholics Anonymous and treatment have become ever more clear in the codependency crusade. In a process not yet detailed in the literature, when economic imperatives became more important than philosophy in moving treatment providers to broaden the concept of addiction, that process led inevitably to an ever-increasing proliferation of therapy-oriented progeny such as the "adult children" movement.

Some of the tensions between the two insights have been pointed out by Robin Room (1992). The ideology of codependence emphasizes self-regard and self-sufficiency, teaching a "quintessentially individualistic" ideology that undermines altruistic behavior, thus subverting such important features of traditional Alcoholics Anonymous as 12th-stepping, sponsorship, and the service ethic. But the ideology of treatment (and of the "co-" movements that derive from the therapeutic world-view) conflicts even more directly with traditional A.A. practice. A.A. members learn to be wary of rationalizations of their behavior; the "co-" movements start from a rationalization that interprets one's own behavior in terms of external factors – the behavior of others. And while most A.A. members cherish co-founder Dr. Bob Smith's final injunction – "Let's not louse it all up with psychiatry" (Darrah, 1992) – the thinking of the "co-" movements has always been dominated by professional, even if at times dubiously credentialed, therapists.

Mäkelä adduces data showing how treatment has changed the pattern of A.A.'s international diffusion. His Swedish example – the openness to expressed affect and the language of "sharing" – adds useful perspective. More significantly for the future of "self-help" groups, Mäkelä's highlighting of the difference between *necessity* and *choice* as the source of affiliation provides a helpful way to distinguish between groups genuinely Twelve-Step and feel-good manifestations of "the triumph of the therapeutic" (Rieff 1966).

A benefit of examining other groups is that they may suggest measurable realities to assess in observing the changes that take place within Alcoholics Anonymous as that fellowship is ever more overwhelmed by treatment ideology. But the benefit carries with it a danger: to impose on A.A. any Procrustean pattern such as "cult" is as unhelpful as forcing it into the category of "treatment." Perhaps the most telling point of Galanter *et al.* (1990) for our purpose is that their emphasis on the importance of Alcoholics Anonymous *for* therapy may be seen as a recognition that A.A. is not *itself* therapy.

Mäkelä's strictures about Corrington's implicit assumption of "the new American spirituality" are perceptive and well taken, but there is a deeper problem here than the use of research scales modeled on "New Age" notions. Corrington tells us that he obtained volunteers for his study at meetings of Alcoholics Anonymous. Although such recruitment is not a clear violation of A.A.'s "Guidelines," some members would find in that practice less than full respect for the A.A. traditions, and so they would not participate. Thus, any sample derived in this way is already sorted and so necessarily weighted, biased. And it is biased toward those who would not recognize that violation, and so most likely toward those who came to A.A. by way of treatment and who have not yet internalized something as basic to Alcoholics Anonymous as its Twelve Traditions. Given the centrality of A.A.'s Traditions to *its* spirituality, such members are not the best representatives of A.A. spirituality.

Where does all this leave us – or, more importantly, where does the research reported here leave our understanding of Alcoholics Anonymous as "lay treatment"? Hopefully, the diverse points of view so well represented in the articles presented here, in Mäkelä's review, and in this "Commentary," will finally lay that confusion to rest – to the benefit of both Alcoholics Anonymous and the very real treatments that are available. Perhaps we may then better see *why* we best serve *both* by refusing the temptation to measure either against the other.

REFERENCES

Anderson, D. J. (1981). *Perspectives on Treatment: The Minnesota Experience.* Center City, MN: Hazelden.

Anderson, J., & Gilbert, F. S. (1989). Communication Skills Training with Alcoholics for Improving the Performance of Two of the Alcoholics Anonymous Recovery Steps. *Journal of Studies on Alcohol,* 30(4), 361-367.

[Anonymous] (1953). *Twelve Steps and Twelve Traditions.* New York: A.A. World Services.

Antze, P. (1979). Role of Ideologies in Peer Psychotherapy Groups. in *Self-Help Groups for Coping with Crisis.* (pp. 272-304). San Francisco: Jossey-Bass.

Beutler, J. (1992). Process Research Perspectives. In B. S. McCrady & W. R. Miller (eds.), *Research on Alcoholics Anonymous: Opportunities and Alternatives.* (pp. in process). New Brunswick, NJ: Alcohol Research Documentation.

Corrington Jr., J. E. (1989). Spirituality and Recovery: Relationships Between Levels of Spirituality, Contentment and Stress During Recovery from Alcoholism in AA. *Alcoholism Treatment Quarterly,* 6(3/4), 151-165.

Darrah, M. C. (1992). *Sister Ignatia: Angel of Alcoholics Anonymous.* Chicago: Loyola University Press.

Galanter, M. (1990). Cults and Zealous Self-Help Movements: A Psychiatric Perspective. *American Journal of Psychiatry,* 147(5), 543-551.

Galanter, M. (1989). *Cults: Faith, Healing, and Coercion.* New York: Oxford University Press.

Galanter, M., Talbott, D., Gallegos, K., & Rubenstone, E. (1990). Combined Alcoholics Anonymous and Professional Care for Addicted Physicians. *American Journal of Psychiatry,* 147(1), 64-68.

Jones, R. K. (1970). Sectarian Characteristics of Alcoholics Anonymous. *Sociology (Oxford),* 4, 181-195.

Kurtz, E. (1991). *Not-God: A History of Alcoholics Anonymous* (orig. ed. 1979). Center City: Hazelden.

Mack, J. E. (1981). Alcoholism, A.A., and the Governance of the Self. In N. E. Zinberg, & M. H. Bean (eds.), *Dynamic Approaches to the Understanding and Treatment of Alcoholism.* (pp. 128-162). New York: Free Press.

Mäkelä, K. (1992). Alcoholics Anonymous and the New Self-Help Movement. *Annual Review of Addictions Research and Treatment,* 2, Working paper, in process.

Maxwell, M. A. (1951). Interpersonal Factors in the Genesis and Treatment of Alcoholism. *Social Forces,* 29(4), 443-448.

Miller, W. R., & Hester, R. K. (1980). Treating the Problem Drinker: Modern Approaches. in W. R. Miller (ed.), *The Addictive Behaviors: Treatment of Alcoholism, Drug Abuse, Smoking and Obesity.* New York: Pergamon Press.

Nowinski, J. (1992). Research and the A.A. Traditions. In W. R. Miller, & B. S. McCrady (eds.), *Proceedings of Conference: Research on Alcoholics Anonymous.*

(pp. in process). New Brunswick, NJ: Center of Alcohol Studies/Rutgers University Press.

Onions, C. T. (ed.) (1969). *The Oxford Dictionary of English Etymology*. New York: Oxford University Press.

Rieff, P. (1966). *The Triumph of the Therapeutic*. New York: Harper & Row.

Room, R. (1992). Alcoholics Anonymous as a Social Movement. In B. S. McCrady & W. R. Miller (eds.), *Research on Alcoholics Anonymous: Opportunities and Alternatives*. (pp. in process). New Brunswick, NJ: Alcohol Research Documentation.

Royce, J. E. (1989). *Alcohol Problems and Alcoholism: A Comprehensive Survey* (rev. ed.). New York, New York: The Free Press: A Division of Macmillan Publishing Company, Inc.

Shipley, J. T. (1984). *The Origins of English Words: A Discursive Dictionary of Indo-European Roots*. Baltimore: Johns Hopkins University Press.

Vaillant, G. E. (1983). *The Natural History of Alcoholism*. Cambridge: Harvard University Press.

After the Albuquerque conference in 1992 (see the opening article in this book) and the publication of its papers the following year, Bill Miller suggested to me that perhaps the best way to get some important points across would be to write an article jointly. Since most viewed Miller as a critic of A.A. and me as a friend of the fellowship, we hoped that the mere conjunction of our names would draw attention to the piece. It did, as this became one of the most requested reprints in our experience. The article appeared in the Journal of Studies on Alcohol *55(2): 159-166 (1994), as William R. Miller and Ernest Kurtz. "Models of Alcoholism Used in Treatment: Contrasting A.A. and Other Perspectives with Which It Is Often Confused."*

Models of Alcoholism Used in Treatment:

Contrasting A.A. and Other Models with Which it is Often Confused

In January of 1992, we participated in the first national conference on "Research on Alcoholics Anonymous: Opportunities and Alternatives," jointly sponsored by the University of New Mexico and Rutgers University (McCrady & Miller, 1993). Among the insights that emerged during that meeting was the realization that the essential nature of an A.A. model of alcoholism and recovery is often misunderstood. In particular, key elements of three other models are often confused with, mistakenly attributed to, or blamed on A.A. (e.g., Heather & Robertson, 1983; Miller & Hester, 1989; Peele, 1985).

Drawing on a survey of alcoholism treatment professionals in New Mexico and California, Moyers (1991) examined the factor structure of beliefs about alcoholism. A strong first factor blended endorsement of items drawn from A.A. publications with non-A.A. items reflecting *genetic* ("A person's genes determine whether he or she will become an alcoholic"), *personality* ("The denial of alcoholics is so strong that it is often necessary to use very strong confrontation to get them to accept reality"), and *moralistic* beliefs ("Drinking alcoholics are liars and cannot be trusted"). Two other relatively unrelated factors embodied social learning theory and a view of alcoholics as a heterogeneous group with different needs and problems. Simultaneous endorsement of disease and moralistic beliefs seems to be the norm (Moyers & Miller, 1992). Milam and Ketcham (1983) have decried this dominant confusion of moral, spiritual, personality, and biological models.

As the treatment of alcoholism becomes increasingly professionalized, and as interest in research on A.A. grows, it will be important for treatment and research professionals to have a clear, accurate understanding of the essential nature and tenets of A.A.. At an experiential level, there is no substitute for attending A.A. meetings, and we believe that professionals in this field should do so. In thinking through the relationship of A.A. with treatment (Brown, 1985) or the design of new research in this area (McCrady & Miller, 1993), it is also helpful to have a sound conceptual grasp of how A.A. historically has understood alcoholism and the process of recovery. We seek, in this article, to offer a step in that direction by distinguishing among core A.A. precepts and other beliefs peripheral or even antithetical to A.A., with which it is often confused.

Four Models of Alcoholism

Many different descriptive and etiologic models of alcoholism have been proposed (Chaudron & Wilkinson, 1988; Miller & Hester, 1989; Paredes, 1976; Tarter & Schneider, 1976). We will focus here only on four which have been blended in current U.S. beliefs about alcoholism.

Volitional-Moral Model

The oldest model of drunkenness, which long predates Huss's (1849) coining of the term "alcoholism," saw it as volitional, the result of personal choice (Keller, 1979; Sournia, 1990). The ancients at times honored this choice, but the understanding that drunkenness was chosen, that people become intoxicated by their own willful actions, moved most in later times to pass negative moral judgment on such drinkers (Trotter 1778, as quoted by McCarthy 1958). In this view, social sanctions (punishment, loss of status or freedom) are appropriate responses to drunkenness. If adherents to this model adverted to any "loss of control" on the part of chronic drinkers, it may be interpreted as further evidence that drunkards are generally of weak and depraved character – an understanding furthered by temperance movements (Lender & Martin, 1987; McCarthy, 1958; an entertaining treatment may be found in Lender & Karnchanapee, 1977).

This perspective – that alcoholism is a matter of choice – is very much alive. Civil and criminal courts in the U.S. continue to show a reluctance to hold defendants blameless for actions committed under the influence (e.g., toughening laws on impaired driving). The U.S. Supreme Court has ruled that alcoholism can be regarded and treated as "willful misconduct" (Connors & Rychtarik, 1989). An assumption of freedom of moral choice lies behind all "Just say no" campaigns.

Personality Models

A second view emerged with the rise of psychoanalysis around the turn of the century. Alcoholism here is assumed to be a symptom of an underlying personality disorder, a disturbance of normal development. Though varying in specific content, writings in this area generally cast alcoholics as immature, fixated at an early childish level of development (Strecker, 1937). Thus arose the notion of the alcoholic personality – the idea that alcoholics share a common set of (undesirable, immature) traits which precede and continue or worsen with the development of drinking problems. Despite the elusiveness of such a personality in hundreds of studies of alcoholics (e.g., Miller, 1976; Vaillant, 1983), the belief strongly persists that alcoholics have a consistent and abnormal personality. Current popular manifestations include: (1) the notion that alcoholics characteristically overuse primitive ego defense mechanisms such as denial; (2) the belief that alcoholism in particular and addictive behaviors in general are results of growing up in dysfunctional families, and (3) the idea that there is a pervasive personality disturbance (e.g., co-dependence) which characterizes all people with addictions as well as those who live with them. The treatment, it follows, is psychotherapy, or some other process of working through, reparenting, etc.

American Disease Model

Within U.S. society, a third view emerged in the 1930s and 1940s, growing rapidly in popularity after World War II (B. Johnson, 1973; Wilkerson, 1966). Inspired by the observations of Dr. Benjamin Rush at the end of the 18th century, some 19th-century scientists had investigated the senses in which "inebriety," as chronic drunkenness was then generally termed, might be a disease. By century's end, however, the pressures of Prohibitionist political correctness had forced the abandonment of such research. With the repeal of Prohibition in 1933, a new "alcoholism movement" appeared in the United States, soon revealing itself to be dedicated less to research than to propagating the view not only that alcoholism is a disease, but that it is a particular *kind* of disease (B. Johnson, 1973). This model is succinctly set forth in one of the most popular and representative books of this movement (Milam and Ketcham, 1983).

Four core assumptions underlie the American disease model:

1. Alcoholism is a unitary disease entity that is qualitatively distinct and discontinuous from normality. As with pregnancy, there are no grey areas; one either is or is not alcoholic.

2. The causes of alcoholism are solely biological, rooted in heredity and physiology. Behavioral, family, and personality disturbances are merely symptoms of the underlying physical abnormality in how the body reacts to alcohol.

3. The definitive symptom of developed alcoholism is an inability to control consumption after the first drink. This is an inexorable reaction to the chemical ethanol, resulting from the physical abnormality.

4. This condition is irreversible and cannot be cured, only palliated.

In this view, alcoholics bear no responsibility for the development of their problems. They are, in fact, viewed as incapable of making rational decisions, warranting social intervention to coerce them into treatment. The therapy of choice consists of detoxification, education about the disease, admonition to abstain from all psychoactive substances, and medical procedures to alleviate related physical problems such as nutritional deficits (Milam & Ketcham, 1983). Psychotherapy is contraindicated, but referral to A.A. is seen as helpful for follow-up support. Nonalcoholics, on the other hand, are seen as able to handle alcohol normally, and thus in need of no treatment: "Alcohol is an addictive drug only for the minority of its users who are physically susceptible" (Milam & Ketcham, 1983, p. 24).

Alcoholics Anonymous

Alcoholics Anonymous is fundamentally a spiritual program. It is not a treatment, but a way of living and being. Though its sole purpose is to help alcoholics become and stay sober, the program attends to much more than the mere imbibing of alcohol. Only the first of A.A.'s Twelve Steps even names alcohol. The rest are concerned with spiritual processes: knowledge of and relationship with God or a Higher Power, self-searching, confession, openness to being changed, amends, prayer, seeking God's will, carrying the message to others (Kurtz, 1979; Kurtz & Ketcham, 1992). Alcoholic drinking is seen as a reflection of the human need – gone wrong – for spiritual life and growth. Abstinence, then, signals only embarkation on the A.A. way of life, which is seen as a continuing journey toward wholeness and serenity (Alcoholics Anonymous 1953, Wilson 1967). Spiritual experience is not a byproduct, but the means by which an alcoholic recovers. Many A.A. writings in fact question whether it is even possible to recover by nonspiritual means.

In the A.A. understanding, the core of alcoholism, the deep root of alcoholic behavior, lies in *character* (which is not to be confused with personality). "Selfishness – self-centeredness! That, we think, is the root of our troubles" reads a key passage of A.A.'s delineation of "How it works" (A.A. 1976, p. 62); and A.A.'s members habitually use the vocabulary of faults ("defects of character") such as grandiosity, resentment, defiance, dishonesty, and obsession with control. Practice of the twelve steps brings a recovery characterized by growth in such character traits as acceptance, honesty, humility, and patience.

Points of Departure

Physiologic Factors

Because of its spiritual focus, A.A. is by nature inclusive rather than exclusive. It is therefore easier to say what A.A. *is* than what it is not. For example, although the primary focus of A.A. is on spiritual factors in etiology and recovery, A.A. writings explicitly leave room for physiological, psychological, and social factors, and for whatever new knowledge may emerge through scientific inquiry. Thus A.A. cannot be represented as saying that alcoholism is *not* caused or influenced by a particular factor. A.A. specifically refuses, by its traditions, to take any stand on such issues.

It is entirely out of character with A.A., however, to assert that alcoholism is caused only by a physical abnormality (or, for that matter, by any single factor). To do so is to deny the spiritual, psychological, and social aspects of alcoholism and of humanity, and A.A. consistently names, includes, and examines such influences. Its encompassing implicit model might be called spiritu-bio-psycho-social.

This is one way, then, in which A.A. differs from the American disease model. Milam and Ketcham (1983) specifically deny any except physiological causal factors, and criticize A.A. for being "a powerful obstacle to accepting the otherwise overwhelming evidence that biological factors, not psychological or emotional factors, usher in the disease" (p. 141). A.A., in contrast, does not "take any particular medical point of view" (A.A., 1976, p. xx), asserts that "the main problem of the alcoholic centers in his mind, rather than in his body" (p. 23), and consistently describes alcoholism as an illness with many dimensions. "Of necessity," the book *Alcoholics Anonymous* notes early in its "There is a solution" chapter, "there will have to be discussion of matters medical, psychiatric, social, and religious" (A.A., p. 19).

The absolute, black-or-white tone in which the American disease model is often expressed is likewise at variance with the character of A.A.. Bill Wilson's writings consistently allow for exceptions, referring to "most alcoholics" and "many of us." Even on the disease model's anathematic issue of controlled drinking, a term introduced in the original 1939 A.A. "Big Book," Wilson wrote: "If anyone who is showing inability to control his drinking can do the right-about-face and drink like a gentleman, our hats are off to him." Even in the midst of observations that "demonstrated again and again: 'Once an alcoholic, always an alcoholic,'" the tone of A.A. remains one of openness, inquiry, and allowance for differences. For though "Physicians who are familiar with alcoholism agree there is no such thing as making a normal drinker out of an alcoholic," Wilson recognized in the next sentence that "Science may one day accomplish this, but it hasn't done so yet" (all quotations from Alcoholics Anonymous 1976, p. 31).

Alcoholic Personality

On the question of whether alcoholics have a consistent personality, Wilson expressed some support for the idea:

When A.A. was quite young, a number of eminent psychologists and doctors made an exhaustive study of a good-sized group of so-called problem drinkers. The doctors weren't trying to find how different we were from one another; they sought to find whatever personality traits, if any, this group of alcoholics had in common. They finally came up with a conclusion that shocked the A.A. members of that time. These distinguished men had the nerve to say that most of the alcoholics under investigation were still childish, emotionally sensitive, and grandiose. . . . In the years since, however, most of us have come to agree with those doctors. . . We have seen that we were prodded by unreasonable fears or anxieties into making a life business of winning fame, money, and what we thought was leadership. So false pride became the reverse side of that ruinous coin marked "Fear." We simply had to be number one people to cover up our deep-lying inferiorities (A.A., 1953 p. 127).

97

Wilson did offer other generalizations about alcoholics' *character*. As always, he carefully allowed for exceptions, but after 17 years of sober experience with A.A. members, Bill depicted alcoholics as "largely a band of ego-driven individualists (p. 150), "bankrupt idealists" and perfectionists (p. 160), and "certainly all-or-nothing people" (p. 165).

Yet it is doubtful that Wilson thought any of these to be *uniquely* the characteristics of alcoholics, distinguishing them from other people. Both his published writings and his many letters (to individuals both alcoholic and non-alcoholic) exude the sense that A.A.'s co-founder is writing about general traits of humankind. It is not surprising, then, that recent years have seen A.A.'s twelve-step program applied to many different problems by a wide variety of people. Immersion in A.A. literature indeed suggests a parallel with John Milton's comment on the word "presbyter": the "alcoholic" is simply a *human being* "writ large" (quoted by Haller, 1963 p. 180). There is no sense that alcoholics are peculiarly weak or fallen, wicked or malicious – and this is one very large way in which A.A. departs from a moral model.

On the now popular notion that alcoholics have universal defense mechanisms, Wilson had little to say. The language of defense mechanisms is from psychoanalysis, not from A.A., and the word "denial" does not even appear in Wilson's major writings. He characterized alcoholics as resistant to pressure, and reluctant to admit alcoholism while drinking, but no implication is made that alcoholics as a group – before, during, or after drinking – are characterized by generally primitive defensive styles. This idea, and the notion of "breaking down" defenses, are concepts of psychotherapy, and characteristic of confrontational programs such as Synanon, rather than of A.A. Although Synanon was pioneered by an A.A. member, Charles Dederich started Synanon precisely because there seemed no room in A.A. for the confrontation he deemed essential (Yablonsky 1965).

Coercion

With the rise of a treatment industry, it became increasingly accept-able for alcohol-impaired people to be coerced into treatment by the courts, employers, and planned family interventions – an uncommon practice in most of medicine and psychology. Vernon Johnson (1973) opined: "The primary factor within [the alcoholic] is the delusion, or impaired judgment, which keeps the harmfully dependent person locked into his self-destructive pattern. . . . The alcoholic evades or denies outright any need for help whenever he is approached. It must be remembered that he is not in touch with reality" (p. 44). Milam and Ketcham (1983) similarly argued that alcoholics "are sick, unable to think rationally, and incapable of giving up alcohol by themselves. Most recovered alcoholics were forced into treatment against their will" (p. 14).

Members of A.A. might well disagree with such a view. As their stories make clear, no one really comes to A.A. "freely," but the coercion described is more internal than external. "I finally got sick and tired of being sick and tired," runs one common explanation of why a member first came to A.A. The idea of externally coercing an alcoholic to do *anything* is utterly foreign to A.A.'s way. The guidelines set down by Wilson in 1939 for "working with others" have never been revised:

> If he does not want to stop drinking, don't waste time trying to persuade him. You may spoil a later opportunity. . . If he does not want to see you, never force yourself upon him (p. 90). . . Be careful not to brand him an alcoholic. Let him draw his own conclusion (p. 92). . . He should not be pushed or prodded by you, his wife, or his friends. If he is to find God, the desire must come from within (p. 95).

Contrast this with the following excerpt from an "intervention" with an executive, presented as exemplary on page one of the *Wall Street Journal* (Greenberger, 1983):

> They called a surprise meeting, surrounded him with colleagues critical of his work and threatened to fire him if he didn't seek help

quickly. When the executive tried to deny that he had a drinking problem, the medical director . . . came down hard. "Shut up and listen," he said. "Alcoholics are liars, so we don't want to hear what you have to say."

As the stories that continue to appear in *The A.A. Grapevine* attest, for over 50 years members of A.A. have generally continued to intervene in the supportive, listening, and patient manner suggested by their Big Book – a style that differs radically from the aggressive, confrontational methods sometimes advocated to "break down defenses" (Miller & Rollnick, 1991).

Willful Misconduct

While A.A. writings clearly support alcoholics' right and ability to choose their own way, Wilson was clear in his understanding that drinking was not a willful choice for true alcoholics. Here A.A. differs from a volitional-moral model, which regards drinking a matter of will and decision:

> But what about the real alcoholic? . . . At some stage of his drinking career he begins to lose all control of his liquor consumption, once he starts to drink (A.A., 1976, p. 21). We know that while the alcoholic keeps away from drink as he may do for months or years, he reacts much like other men. We are equally positive that once he takes any alcohol whatever into his system, something happens, both in the bodily and mental sense, which makes it virtually impossible for him to stop (p. 22).

The A.A. understanding is evident in Wilson's description of his first meeting with co-founder Dr. Bob Smith. Speaking to Bob, Bill "bore down heavily," using the words of Dr. William Duncan Silkworth, "describing the alcoholic's dilemma, the 'obsession plus allergy' theme" (A.A. 1957, p. 69). "Obsession" clearly implies that the alcoholic's lack of control extends to *taking the first drink*. In a 1966 letter reprinted in *As Bill Sees It: The A.A. Way of Life*, Wilson delineated his understanding of the alcoholic's power of choice: "As active alcoholics, we lost our ability to choose whether we would drink. . . Yet we finally did make choices that brought about our recovery. . . . we chose to 'become willing,' and no better choice did we ever make" (Wilson, 1967, p. 4).

In Jellinek's (1960) terminology, members of A.A. were thus understood by Wilson to be both "gamma" (unable to stop) and "delta" (unable to abstain) alcoholics. The hopelessness and powerlessness of this picture – unable to abstain, and unable to stop once started – provides a context to understand the need for help from a higher power. A.A. was meant, from its inception, as a last resort, when all else had failed. The lack of control is not limited to the second drink, or even to the first drink, but is described as a condition of the alcoholic's prior life in general. *Life* had become unmanageable.

Responsibility

Even a cursory examination of the twelve steps reveals A.A.'s sense of the alcoholic's responsibility to act: to admit, ask, accept, confess, pray, etc. The power to transform is not the alcoholic's, but God's – as members delight in reminding careless observers: "A.A." is not a self-help program: we tried that, and it didn't work. A.A. is a God-help program." Yet it is the alcoholic who must take the initiative for recovery, who must, by choice, "become willing."

The A.A. way differs from the American disease model in its sense of responsibility for actions prior to sobriety. Milam and Ketcham (1983) argued that A.A. "fixed the blame for contracting the disease squarely on the victim" and "has mistaken the psychological consequences of alcoholism for its causes" (p. 140). They warned that "The alcoholic should be assured throughout treatment that his personality did not cause his disease and that he is in no way responsible for it" (p. 156). They further advised that the fourth step of A.A. – making a searching and fearless moral inventory – should be based only on actions *after* treatment, not on what the alcoholic did before sobering up.

A.A., in contrast, advocates acceptance of responsibility for one's own actions, period. It is difficult to imagine an A.A. meeting at which someone claims, "I am not responsible for anything I did before I quit drinking." In the fourth through seventh steps, members specifically take responsibility for examining their past lives, recognizing and acknowledging their shortcomings. In the eighth and ninth steps, this responsibility is extended to making amends for past wrongs. Only then does the "from here on" advocated by Milam and Ketcham enter. A.A.'s final three steps are often referred to as "the maintenance steps." They assume a clearing away of "the rubbish of the past," not ignoring or denying it. Thus, the sense of avoiding moral responsibility for one's condition – a criticism sometimes leveled at A.A. – is characteristic of the American disease model, but clearly not of A.A.

Unitary Condition and Unitary Treatment

The American disease model is notably binary: either one is an alcoholic (and needs treatment) or a nonalcoholic (and needs no treatment). It was this very unitary disease model against which Jellinek (1960) cautioned.

There is much in A.A. writings to indicate an early, pre-Jellinek recognition of different types of alcohol problems. Phrases such as "seriously alcoholic," "not too alcoholic," "true alcoholic," and "real alcoholic" imply variations, as does Wilson's evident caution in using qualifications such as "most alcoholics" and "many alcoholics." Although the term *alcoholic* is manifestly used in different meanings in Wilson's prolific writings, it is clear that he consistently distinguished A.A. alcoholics from other types of drinkers, including "hard drinkers." Neither A.A. literature nor A.A. members speak as if there were one and only one type of alcohol problem. A.A. simply takes no position on anything except the experience of alcoholism described in its Big Book, by its members, for it is with this experience that potential new members must identify.

In describing a "model treatment program" (Milam's own), Milam and Ketcham (1983) prescribed a set of essential ingredients for success including an unnegotiable abstinence goal, education about the exclusively physical cause of alcoholism, and nutritional counseling. Other approaches to treatment (e.g., medications, psychological therapies) were specifically denigrated as ineffective or detrimental, and inferior to their American disease model treatment.

Bill Wilson's writings, in contrast, describe A.A. not as the one only way, but as only one way: the way its members had found to be effective for alcoholics "like us." As the foreword to the second edition (reprinted in the third edition) of *Alcoholics Anonymous* states: "Upon therapy for the alcoholic himself, we surely have no monopoly" (A.A., 1976, p. xx). Even in the essential area of "the spiritual," the Big Book's instructions for "working with others" cautioned from the very beginning: "If he thinks he can do the job in some other way, or prefers some other spiritual approach, encourage him to follow his own conscience. We have no monopoly on God; we merely have an approach that worked with us" (A.A., 1976, p. 95).

According to A.A.'s Tenth Tradition, "Alcoholics Anonymous has no opinion on outside issues; hence the A.A. name ought never be drawn into public controversy" (A.A., 1953, p. 180). As both Bill Wilson's writings and a variety of articles in the *A.A. Grapevine* have consistently made clear over the years since the Yale Clinic confusion in 1944, modalities of treatment and other approaches to recovery are "outside issues" (Kurtz, 1979, p. 118). For diverse reasons, over the same years, some in both the treatment and the research fields have forgotten or ignored that fact. Yet like any entity that claims to be "spiritual," A.A. eludes capture. The exploration undertaken here, we hope, will aid understanding not only of that reality, but of why it is so.

Conclusion

In sum, A.A., as reflected in its own literature, differs in several important respects from the volitional-moral, personality, and American disease models with which it is commonly confused in current public and professional conceptions of alcoholism. These differences are summarized in Table 1, which schematizes the foregoing discussion. Assumptions derived from these other models have been grafted onto A.A. concepts to form the opinions that dominate both treatment and research in the U.S.

alcoholism field. Yet key constructs from these models are incompatible and contradictory, as reflected in current confusion about the nature, causes, and treatment of alcoholism. Is it a binary condition, a continuum, or a group of subtypes? Is it a moral problem? To what extent are alcoholics responsible for their actions? Is there only one way to recover?

Table 1
Summary of Points of Agreement and Divergence

	A.A.	Disease	Moral	Personalty	Behavioral
What Causes Alcoholism?					
Moral/Spiritual Factors	Yes	No	Yes	No	No
Biological Factors	Yes	Yes	No	No	No
Psychological Factors	Yes	No	No	Yes	Yes
Social/EnvironmentalFactors	Yes	No	No	Yes	Yes
Prime Causal Emphasis	Spir	Physiol	Voliti	Dvlpmntl	Psych+
What Is Alcoholism?					
Disease/Illness	Yes	Yes	No	Yes	No
Unitary Entity	No pos.	Yes	No	Yes	No
Personalty	Char flaws	Irrelevant	Wkwill	Immatur	Irrelvant
Moral Issues					
Choice About Drinking	Earlier, not Later	No	Yes	Yes	Yes
Responsblty for Past	Yes	No	Yes	Yes	Yes
Responsblty to Recvr	Dn't Drink; Work Steps	Accept Tx	Behave	Accept Tx	Change Behave
Coercion acceptable	No	Yes	Yes	Yes	Yes
Recovery					
Source of Healing	God	Medical	Morality	Psychthrpy	Psych.
Helping Style	Empathic	Expert	Exhort'n	Confrntatn	Educ
Attitude To Moderatn	Skeptical	Prohbitve	Permissv	Variable	Variable

"The only requirement for A.A. membership is a desire to stop drinking" (A.A., 1953, p. 143). One aspect of A.A.'s claim to be "spiritual rather than religious" is that it imposes no creed, no dogma. It is important to remember this, at a time when pressures imposed by political and economic interests, some of which at least give the impression of reflecting A.A. thinking, promulagate views that go far beyond the "experience, strength and hope" described in A.A.'s own literature.

Several of the most contentious political-economic issues within the U.S. alcoholism field do not arise from A.A., but from an amalgamation of the viewpoints outlined above. A.A. writings do not assert: (a) that there is only one form of alcoholism or alcohol problem, (b) that moderate drinking is impossible for everyone with alcohol problems, (c) that alcoholics should be labeled, confronted aggressively, or coerced into treatment, (d) that alcoholics are riddled with denial and other defense mechanisms, (e) that alcoholism is purely a physical disorder, (f) that alcoholism is hereditary, (g) that there is only one way to recover, or (h) that alcoholics are not responsible for their condition or actions. These assertions involve outside economic, political, social, moral, legal, and disciplinary issues on which A.A. takes no stand (although A.A. members, as individuals, and political organizations such as the National Council on Alcoholism, do so).

It would be helpful for treatment and research professionals to separate these issues from A.A. itself, and to understand the essential nature of A.A. as a spiritual program of living. Therapists can, for example, better choose and prepare their clients for A.A. referral if they have a clear understanding of how A.A. differs from other models and approaches. Well-informed designers of needed research could, for example, better choose process and outcome measures appropriate to reflect progress through the program, as A.A. understands itself.

Perhaps more than any other reality born in modern times, Alcoholics Anonymous has become the proverbial elephant described by unsighted examiners. Immersion in the literature on A.A. indeed suggests that as with the classic Rorschach inkblots, those who tell about A.A. may reveal more about themselves than about the fellowship and its program. That *caveat*, of course, also applies to us. We have sought to respond to its warning by staying as close as possible to A.A.'s own literature. We hope this will encourage those who continue this discussion to be as cautious in claims that are made using the name of Alcoholics Anonymous.

REFERENCES

Alcoholics Anonymous (1953). *Twelve Steps and Twelve Traditions*. New York: A.A. World Services.

Alcoholics Anonymous (1957). *Alcoholics Anonymous Comes of Age*. New York: A.A. World Services.

Alcoholics Anonymous (1976 [orig. 1939, 1955]). *Alcoholics Anonymous*. New York: A.A. World Services.

Brown, S. (1985). *Treating the alcoholic: A developmental model of recovery*. New York: John Wylie and Sons.

Chaudron, C. D., & Wilkinson, D. A. (Eds.) (1988). *Theories on alcoholism*. Toronto: Addiction Research Foundation.

Connors, G. J. & Rychtarik, R. G. (1989). The Supreme Court VA/disease model case: Background and implications. *Psychology of Addictive Behaviors*, 2, 101-107.

Greenberger, R. S. (1983, January 13). Sobering method: Firms are confronting alcoholic executives with threat of firing. *The Wall Street Journal*. 1, 26.

Haller, W. (1963 [orig. 1955]). *Liberty and reformation in the puritan revolution*. New York: Columbia University Press.

Heather, N. & Robertson, I. (1983). *Controlled drinking* (Rev. ed.). London: Methuen.

Huss, M. (1849). *Alcoholismus chronicus. Chronisk alkoloisjukdom: Ett bidrag till dyskrasiarnas känndom*. Stockholm: Bonner/Norstedt.

Jellinek, E. M. (1960). *The disease concept of alcoholism*. New Brunswick, NJ: Hillhouse Press.

Johnson, B. H. (1973). *The alcohol movement in America: A study in cultural innovation*. Unpublished doctoral dissertation, University of Illinois at Urbana-Champaign. (University Microfilms No. 74-5603).

Johnson, V. J. (1973). *I'll Quit Tomorrow*. New York: Harper & Row.

Keller, M. (1979). A historical overview of alcohol and alcoholism. *Cancer Research, 39*, 2822-2829.

Kurtz, E. (1991 [orig. 1979]). *Not-God: A History of Alcoholics Anonymous.* Center City, MN: Hazelden.

Kurtz, E., & Ketcham, K. (1992). *The spirituality of imperfection.* New York: Bantam.

Lender, M. E., & Karnchanapee, K. R. (1977). "Temperance tales": Antiliquor fiction and American attitudes toward alcoholics in the late 19th and early 20th centuries. *Journal of Studies on Alcohol, 38*, 1347-1370.

Lender, M. E., & Martin, J. K. (1987 [orig. 1982]). *Drinking in America: A history.* New York: Free Press.

McCarthy, R. G. (1958). Alcoholism: Attitudes and Attacks, 1775-1935. *The Annals of the American Academy of Political and Social Science, 315*, 12-21.

McCrady, B. S. & Miller, W. R. (1993). *Research on Alcoholics Anonymous: Opportunities and Alternatives.* New Brunswick, NJ: Rutgers Center of Alcohol Studies.

Milam, J. R., & Ketcham, K. (1983). *Under the Influence: A Guide to the Myths and Realities of Alcoholism.* New York: Bantam.

Miller, W. R. (1976). Alcoholism scales and objective assessment methods: A review. *Psychological Bulletin, 83*, 649-674.

Miller, W. R. & Hester, R. K. (1989). Treating alcohol problems: Toward an informed eclecticism. In R. K. Hester & W. R. Miller (Eds.), *Handbook of alcoholism treatment approaches: Effective alternatives* (pp. 3-13). Elmsford, NY: Pergamon Press.

Miller, W. R. & Rollnick, S. (1991). *Motivational interviewing: Preparing people to change addictive behavior.* New York: Guilford Press.

Moyers, T. B. (1991). Therapists' conceptualizations of alcoholism: Implications for treatment decisions. Doctoral dissertation, University of New Mexico.

Moyers, T. B. & Miller, W. R. (1992). Therapists' conceptualizations of alcoholism: Measurement and implications for treatment decisions. Manuscript submitted for publication, University of New Mexico.

Paredes, A. (1976). The history of the concept of alcoholism. In R. E. Tarter and A. A. Sugerman (Eds.), *Alcoholism: Interdisciplinary approaches to an enduring problem* (pp. 9-52). Reading, MA: Addison-Wesley.

Peele, S. (1985). *The meaning of addiction: Compulsive experience and its interpretation.* Lexington, MA: Lexington Books.

Sournia, J. C. (1990). *A history of alcoholism.* Oxford: Basil Blackwell. (First published 1986 in French as *Histoire de l'alcoholisme.* Paris: Editions Flammarion. Translated by Nick Hindley and Gareth Stanton)

Strecker, E. A. (1937). Some thoughts concerning the psychology and therapy of alcoholism. *Journal of Nervous and Mental Disease, 86:* 191-205.

Tarter, R. E., & Schneider, D. U. (1976). Models and theories of alcoholism. In R. E. Tarter & A. A. Sugerman (Eds.), *Alcoholism: Interdisciplinary approaches to an enduring problem* (pp. 75-106). Reading, MA: Addison-Wesley.

Vaillant, G. E. (1983). *The natural history of alcoholism.* Cambridge, MA: Harvard University Press.

Wilkerson, A. E. (1966). *A history of the concept of alcoholism as a disease.* Unpublished doctoral dissertation, University of Pennsylvania. (University Microfilms No. 67:188)

Wilson, W. G. (1967). *As Bill Sees It: The A.A. Way of Life.* New York: A.A. World Services.

Yablonsky, L. (1965). *Synanon: The tunnel back.* New York: Macmillan.

On several occasions, in the late 1980s and early 1990s, I had the privilege of addressing the National Clergy Conference on Alcoholism. These presentations, although not "scholarly" in the sense of offering a critical apparatus, were presented to a highly educated audience very knowledgeable about alcoholism and Alcoholics Anonymous. Perhaps because I had some seminary training myself, I feared these occasions more than any others in my presentations around the world. Even official government physicians in Moscow and the faculty of Hebrew University in Jerusalem did not present such a challenge to the serenity of my gut.

But I also loved the men and women of N.C.C.A. because I knew first-hand of the good they did. And so my fear became a motive to give my very best. I hope that comes through in this final presentation that I offered them in January of 1996 in Scottsdale, Arizona.

Each of my N.C.C.A. talks was transcribed and eventually published in The N.C.C.A. Blue Book. This one appeared in the 1996 issue, volume 47, pp. 5-29, and includes the question-periods in the middle of and after the talk itself.

Spirituality and Recovery: the Historical Journey

Let's organize these immense topics under two large headings: (1) the journey that is A.A.'s story, its history, and (2) where that journey intersects with our own, in imperfection. The more astute among you may recognize in that arrangement a reflection of the two books mentioned in my introduction: *Not-God: A History of Alcoholics Anonymous* and *The Spirituality of Imperfection*. As someone remarked at the meeting last night, "We talk about what we know about." History and imperfection are my specialities – not necessarily in that order.

The History of Alcoholics Anonymous: Its Importance

History is important less because, in Santayana's often quoted but rarely grasped caution, "Those who do not remember the past are doomed to repeat it" than because, in words variously attributed to Dickens and Goethe: "Those who have no memory, have no hope." There is a link between memory and hope: both are fragile, and so each sustains the other, and each needs all the help it can get from the other. And this is why the *real* story of Alcoholics Anonymous is important. We need hope, and our hope is founded in memory.

Recent Publications and Scholarship

There are a couple of things going on right now on the topic of A.A.'s story. First, and most exciting, we have new works offering insight into A.A. history and more. Some of you may be familiar with Father Bob Fitzgerald's book, *The Soul of Sponsorship*, which draws on the letters between Bill Wilson and Father Edward Dowling, the Jesuit priest to whom Bill referred as his sponsor, although Dowling was not an alcoholic. Himself a Jesuit, Bob drew on the Society's archives as well as A.A.'s, and he not only has gathered some of the letters into that book, but he offers connective material that puts the letters in a context that help readers appreciate their significance in the lives of both men.

There is also Mary Darrah's work on Sister Ignatia. We need still more on Ignatia and St. Thomas Hospital in Akron and the program at St. Vincent's in Cleveland. Also, in the area of recently published histories, you may be familiar with Nell Wing's reminiscences, *Grateful to Have Been There*, and Arizona's A.A. archivist Wally P.'s new book on the History of A.A. Intergroups, *But For the Grace of God*. Wally offers interesting glimpses into local early Alcoholics Anonymous. For example, in Los Angeles, they used to have a screening committee. You could get kicked out of A.A. in Los Angeles in the early days: if you slipped twice, word was passed around and no group would admit you.

Beyond the directly historical, we are being blessed with some excellent dissertation studies of aspects of Alcoholics Anonymous. An Episcopal priest, Michael Wyatt, last December defended a dissertation at Emory University on the relationship between A.A. spirituality and American pragmatism. Wyatt's dissertation is unlikely to be published as a book, but be alert for the articles Michael may spin off: he offers some challenging interpretations of A.A. spirituality and how aspects of an American spirituality filters into the churches.

There is a recent dissertation out of Northwestern University by Kathleen Flynn. Its direct subject is the story-style of A.A. talks – Kathi's field is performance studies – but along the way she offers a telling analysis of A.A. convention gatherings and the developing A.A. shrines such as Dr. Bob's house in Akron. And at the University of Rochester, an anthropology candidate, Maria Swora, is completing a dissertation on what happens in A.A. meetings and how that has changed over time. Rochester, New York, had one of the early "Wilson Clubs" and for a long time was a bastion of the old-time A.A. that had definite membership requirements, so Maria is working a rich lode.

On the level of scholarship beyond the dissertation level, of most interest to you may be a book coming out in the Fall of 1996 by a theologian, Linda Mercadante, who measures A.A. and theology and the Church against each other. The proliferation of the Twelve-Step insight, genuinely or not, complicates this study, but it is the most competent scholarly study of which I know that brings to bear on Alcoholics Anonymous the insights of the theological tradition. Some points are sure to enlighten you; and some points you will as surely wish to argue. Mercadante is especially critical of the expansion of addiction as a metaphor, and she takes on various theologians as well as non-theologian popularizers such as Gerald May.

So not only A.A. but serious study of A.A. is vibrantly alive, and no matter what the explicit field of study, each of these works sheds further light on A.A.'s continuing story. I maintain a bibliography of serious literature on Alcoholics Anonymous, and it currently comprises some 2,000 items, with about five or six new additions each month.

The Dangers in Distortions of A.A.'s Story

That was the good news. Less happily, there have also recently appeared people who in pursuit of particular agendas tell A.A.'s story in ways that distort its history. Of particular concern are the Oxford Group enthusiasts who try to provide historical underpinning for what has become a movement to Christianize Alcoholics Anonymous by reinterpreting A.A.'s early history. Some of these zealots at times directly denigrate the contributions of Sister Ignatia and Father Dowling in their single-minded, indeed narrow-minded, attempts to prove that A.A. came out of "Bible Christianity." It is unlikely that you will confront many of these people directly, because usually they do not have much contact with Catholic clergy. But they tell their versions, and some of the distortions and half-truths get spread around.

There is nothing wrong with reinterpretation, so long as it is based on evidence. One reason we tell stories is to upgrade memory, and we revise our stories and our memory as more information comes in. But there are three guidelines that should undergird that process in any genuinely historical study.

First, there has to be evidence for any claim. Just because you think "it would be nice" if something happened in a certain way does not mean that it did. Some people think that Bill Wilson must have known Dr. Bob before Bill ever went to Akron back there in April of 1935. Maybe he did. I do not know, for certain, but all the evidence that we have says that he did not and, therefore, if someone says that he did, please show me your evidence. This may not seem like such a big deal, except that it would call into question Bill's fundamental honesty on a key issue. And so it is not merely trivial, like whether Dr. Bob had his last drink on June 10th or June 17th. Thanks to the research and evidence turned up by a New Jersey attorney, it seems probable that June 17th is the correct date, and the same evidence suggests how naturally such a memory error might have occurred. So we have been celebrating A.A.'s birthday a week early each year: I doubt that discovery impacts anyone's sobriety much, one way or the other.

The second requirement is that you have to look at *all* the available evidence. Yes, certain things did happen in Akron. But other things were also happening in New York and elsewhere. The historical storyteller has to take into account *everything* that we know, not just the facts that he or she happens to like. Actively drinking alcoholics are pretty good at the latter – just looking at those truths that they like. You can make a marvelous story out of the things that you like. "Well, I always got up and got to work in the morning; I never missed a day's work." But you do not bother mentioning that you had to be poured into bed every night and how often you went home from work at midday, or whatever the rest of the story was. Truth and honesty require examining and incorporating *all* the available evidence.

Third, you also look at what else is going on at the time, the context, the wider "climate of opinion." Yes, the book *Alcoholics Anonymous* shows signs of being influenced by Oxford Group literature. But also being read at the time were Karen Horney's 1937 book, *The Neurotic Personality in Our Time*, glimmers of which can also be found in the Big Book. And in Dale Carnegie's 1935 best-seller, *How to Win Friends and Influence People*, you will find a chapter titled, "When You Are Wrong, Promptly Admit It." Some early A.A. members had been in therapy with Horney or her disciples. Bill Wilson, for one, revered Carnegie. In discussing influences on early A.A. thinking, then, these names merit mention along with those of William James and Henry Drummond and Emmet Fox.

Sister Ignatia, Father Dowling, and the Oxford Group

Too often, at least for my taste, the distortion that overplays the role of the Oxford Group in the origins of Alcoholics Anonymous also underplays the roles of Sister Ignatia and Father Dowling.

In this area, too, there are trivia. For example, did the practice of passing out chips originate in Sister Ignatia's practice of giving Sacred Heart badges to the hospital program's graduates? It would seem so. But far more important are questions such as what shaped Bill Wilson's ideas on discernment. Did those understandings derive from his conversations with Father Dowling, which might suggest thinking about those ideas within the larger Ignatian tradition? Or did his ideas on discernment come from the Oxford Group tendency to label everything in either-or, good-bad, categories?

If we look at the rest of Bill's writings, especially his description of humility as an avoidance of either-or and an acceptance of both/and, you can sense the Dowling influence. This is not a trivial matter, because how Bill understood discernment comes through in the way he presents spirituality in the *Twelve Steps and Twelve Traditions* book. Bill was not God. Bill Wilson not only probably made mistakes: he surely made mistakes. Some people write Bill off totally because of one or another of his mistakes, for example, his mistress. Others concentrate on the fact of Bill's faithfulness and loyalty to that woman. Similarly, some seem determined to be scandalized by Bill's experiments with LSD, while others see in them evidence of his determination to find ways of helping even those alcoholics who seemed tone-deaf to the spiritual. A lot depends on the eyes that you bring. In general, in fact, as in so many other matters, what people tell us about Bill Wilson tells us even more about themselves. Not exactly a new insight to those schooled in psychology or Patristics, eh?

The Oxford Group began in the first decade of this century as the "First Century Christian Fellowship." It was one of the many periodic attempts to recapture first-century Christianity. Later, it would be known as Moral Re-armament, the name-change coming after Frank Buchman, its founder, made some rather incautious statements praising Adolph Hitler. By that time, 1938, New York A.A. had departed Oxford Group auspices, though that connection with what has been called the womb out of which Alcoholics Anonymous was born continued longer in Akron.

But perhaps less "maternal womb" than "surrogate parent," for to concentrate only on the relationship of A.A. to the Oxford Group misses the always present shadow and awareness of Carl Jung, among others. Even though Wilson did not write to Jung until 1961, there was abroad in the fellowship awareness of the story of Rowland Hazard and what Jung had said to Rowland. As much as that may have been twisted and partially forgotten, the essence of it was still there – so much so that when Bill got around to writing to Jung in 1961, the psychiatrist recognized in Bill's letter what he had said to Rowland. That is a good check on whether it had been distorted: Jung did not answer, "No that is not what I said. What I really said was. . . ." I find it fascinating, in this era of suspicion about memory, that A.A.'s oral tradition maintained that story that accurately for close to thirty years.

There is also the continuing impact of Dr. William Duncan Silkworth. In 1937, two years before the publication of the Alcoholics Anonymous Big Book, Silkworth published, in the journal of the Medical Society of New York, an article dealing with the distinction between two terms, two words: decision and resolution. If you read that article, I suspect you will never hear the words of the Third Step in exactly the same way again. Under the title, "Reclamation of the Alcoholic," Silkworth observed to his fellow physicians:

> Without quibbling over words, I wish to differentiate between a decision and a resolution or declaration of which the alcoholic has probably made many already. A resolution is an expression of a momentary emotional desire to reform. Its influence lasts only until he has an impulse to take a drink. A decision on the other hand is the expression of a mental conviction based on an intelligent conception of his condition. Often when a resolution is made, individual must fight constantly with himself. The old environment forces are still a raid against him and he finally succumbs to his old means of escape. However, if he has made a decision through understand of facts appealing to his intelligence, he has changed his entire attitude. No will power is needed because now he is not tempted.

That article is of course not the whole story of Silkworth's impact. "Silky" was always there, always available, in those days when Bill was hanging around Towns Hospital seeking out new prospects. It was Silkworth, remember, who gave Bill the advice that shaped how Bill told his story when he first met Dr. Bob Smith. And evidence suggests that Silkworth's brief advice did more to shape how A.A. storytelling developed than did all the Oxford Group's ranting about "sharing for witness."

Then too, many of the early A.A.s had been in treatment, some with followers of Richard Peabody or others influenced by the Emmanuel Movement, some with students of Karen Horney. The emphasis on the Oxford Group derives from a blinkered view of early A.A. Yes, there were three times as many members in Akron as in New York City well into 1940. And most of the Big Book stories in the first edition come out of Akron. Even that early, however, the New Yorkers had a disproportionate influence on the development of A.A. nationally. Because many worked in sales and traveled, when inquiries came in, they were the ones who were more likely to go to those places and meet those people. And when other Americans traveled, they were more likely to visit New York than Akron or even Cleveland. Especially after the publication of the Big Book and the Jack Alexander article, when people inquired about A.A., they wrote to New York: that's the address that was given. So despite their initial small numbers, the New York A.A.s had an impact out of proportion to those numbers. You don't just count members to tell where the center of gravity is: you look also at relative weight.

Even in the midwest heartland, the 1939 split of the Clevelanders from Akron was over the Oxford Group connection. And immediately there were splits in Cleveland itself, and this fact and process tells us something else that was not only important in early Alcoholics Anonymous but that may have increasing significance today, not least because so many forget this early history.

A Bridge Between History and Spirituality: Varieties

A theme that bridges A.A. history and A.A. spirituality – and probably history and spirituality in general – is openness to *difference* and therefore the cherishing of *varieties*. Because we are finite, there is no "once and for all"; or, in the words of Chapter Five: "First of all, we had to quit playing God. It didn't work."

If I were to write another book on A.A., its title would be *Varieties of the Alcoholics Anonymous Experience*. The vast diversity of meetings and groups is surely the outstanding characteristic of A.A. today. But this is not some new, postmodern thing. From the very beginning there were these varieties of A.A. understanding and experience. They have always been with us. The main problem of those who exaggerate the Oxford Group influence is that they are looking at only one small part of the story – small even in 1937 and surely by 1939.

Secrets

A final note on the Oxford Group, and A.A.'s departure from its auspices and rejection of many of its thrusts – an important final note, because the recent trend toward the therapizing of Twelve-Step spirituality intriguingly brings in its wake an Oxford Group understanding originally and vigorously rejected by the early members of Alcoholics Anonymous.

One Oxford Group saying that the early A.A.s definitely rejected has come into strange re-use in some of the ersatz Twelve-Step groups that have proliferated in more recent times – the sick saying that "You are only as sick as your secrets." That is not Alcoholics Anonymous; that is Oxford Group. In fact, one of the reasons why A.A. left the Oxford Group was that the idea of group guidance meant public confession. The A.A. insight is captured in the formulation of its Ninth Step, with its sensitivity about ". . . except when to do so would injure them or others." The Oxford Group distinguished "sharing for confession" and "sharing for witness" but encouraged both. Early Alcoholics Anonymous adopted, slowly, the telling of stories that "disclose in a general way," but the members adamantly rejected the intrusive lack of respect inherent in what a later generation would term "letting it all hang out" – lack of respect for both others and self.

Bill Wilson and Dr. Bob Smith and Anne Smith had all died by the time I began my research, but I had many long and fruitful sessions with Lois Wilson. Vivid in memory is that gentle lady's continuing deep disdain for what the Oxford Group termed "soul surgery." In pursuing with Lois her thoughts and feelings on the subject, I learned that that type of display was viewed not as honesty but as exhibitionism, and that those who reveled in it not only rarely stayed sober but were as obnoxious sober as they were when drinking. I find it sadly ironic, then, that this destructive aberration has crawled back into Alcoholics Anonymous under different auspices. Even if it be valid, which most sane philosophies would deny, it is not A.A.; it comes from a different source and it was in fact one reason why A.A. departed that different source.

Alcoholics Anonymous and "Treatment"

Quite a bit has been made recently about the difference between Alcoholics Anonymous and "treatment," which is a professional prerogative. That should be clear in the very origin of the application of the word *treatment* to recovery from alcoholism, for that usage was originated by Sister Ignatia, God help her. What happened in Akron, at St. Thomas Hospital, was that the alcoholics who were patients were visited by the sober alcoholics. And some of the visitors, using the familiar vocabulary of the time, sometimes mentioned that so-and-so was there "to take the cure." (The common claim a bit later in Cleveland, by the way, a take-off on a billboard advertisement, was "We fix drunks.")

Now Ignatia did not know much about alcoholism in those early days, but one thing she knew from what Dr. Bob taught her was that there was no "cure" for alcoholism in the medical sense of a condition totally repaired and restored to the *status quo ante*. And so Ignatia would say to the visitors, "No, he is not here to be cured. You *can't* cure it. He is here for treatment." And that is where the word "treatment," applied to alcoholism, comes from – as a way of emphasizing the permanence of the condition.

After St. Thomas Hospital in Akron, Ignatia went up to Cleveland and began the ward at St. Vincent's Hospital, Rosary Hall. Some have over-enthusiastically claimed that "A.A. ran that ward." No way: Ignatia ran her ward. What she did implement was a requirement that admissions be sponsored by an A.A. member. Rosary Hall did not accept admissions from physicians, except some few physicians whom Ignatia knew. Only those physicians whom Dr. Bob approved received admission privileges.

So although most physicians could not admit to this ward, if an A.A. member vouched for someone, that person would most likely be admitted.

So Alcoholics Anonymous members could sponsor an admission. And A.A. members were welcomed as visitors, but Ignatia set the conditions, such as no reading material except the A.A. Big Book. Neither St. Thomas nor St. Vincent's was the anarchic democracy that is Alcoholics Anonymous: you cannot run an institution like that. In those early days, they emphasized the importance of identification. A.A.s visited, and what they insisted on in early A.A. was that *different* people visit. The idea was to offer a variety of opportunities for identification. In fact, there is an article in the May 1946 *A.A. Grapevine* describing how, in Memphis, Tennessee, when A.A.s gained admittance to Bolivar State Hospital, they made a rule that no A.A. member could visit any particular patient more than once. Ignatia thought along the same lines. She did not approve of anyone spending all their free time hanging around the ward. The idea was to bring others, especially those that had been out more recently. Ignatia had control over visitors and she excluded some people whose language she did not like or who she felt did not have good sobriety. In fact, she quickly instituted in Cleveland that you have to be sober a full year before you could sponsor an admission.

In the midst of so much current confusion about treatment for alcoholism and its necessity, you might find it enlightening as well as refreshing to look up an article that Sister Ignatia published in the hospital management journal, *Medical Progress*, in October 1951: "Care and Treatment of Alcoholics." In the article, Ignatia describes her five-day program: reception, realization, moral inventory, resolution, plans for the future. Notice, by the way, the word "resolution" here: intriguing evidence how Akron's more Oxford Group vocabulary got carried over into Ignatia's thinking as opposed to the point Dr. Silkworth had made and its impression on the New Yorkers.

It is difficult to find that journal, of course, but Mary Darrah's biography of Sister Ignatia virtually reproduces the article. If you would like to see what an effective five-day treatment plan might look like – and in these days of "mis-managed care" even five days may soon be a luxury – you might find it worthy of examination and especially of thought.

Another aspect of Alcoholics Anonymous illuminated by what we know of Sister Ignatia: Ignatia was the admissions clerk at St. Thomas, which is why Dr. Bob approached her. She was not a nurse. Her field had been music, but she had suffered a kind of "breakdown" and so was sort of shunted off to the hospital work that was her order's main mission. Sometimes, ignorant people – and especially ignorant professionals – say that "Alcoholics Anonymous teaches that only an alcoholic can help an alcoholic." Sister Ignatia is only one of many whose story overturns that canard. Look at all the non-alcoholics who were so significant in early A.A. history: Sister Ignatia, Father Dowling, Willard Richardson, Frank Amos, Dr. Silkworth, and many others. They were not alcoholic, but they did all have something in common: each, in his or her own way, had experienced tragedy in their lives. They all had known *kenosis*; they had been emptied out; they had hit bottom . . . whatever vocabulary you want. They had stared into the abyss. They had lived through a dark night of the soul. Each had encountered and survived tragedy. This is why I am so interested in the biographies of those early people: I want to understand what is it that allows non-alcoholics to understand alkies. For you do not have to be an alcoholic to understand one. But it seems that you do have to have had this confrontation with tragedy in your own life. You have to have stared into that abyss. You have to have known utter hopelessness or utter helplessness. You have to have screamed the first prayer, "*God: help me.*" And Ignatia had.

Ignatia did not know much about medicine. She had no medical training. She was an admissions officer, which of course gave her the chance to smuggle people into the hospital. Dr. Bob was not stupid: He knew whose help he needed to sneak alcoholic patients into the hospital. The reason why hospitals did not admit alcoholics, by the way, was not because they did not like alcoholics, nor even because they did not seem able to help them very much. It was because alcoholics never paid their bills. There was no health insurance back in those days. You were responsible for paying your own bill, and experience taught hospitals that alcoholics never paid theirs. Therefore, they tried very hard, for simple economic reasons, not to admit alcoholics. Alcoholics Anonymous was instrumental in changing that, not so much by propagandizing its understanding of alcoholism but by seeing that the bills got paid. That was the first meaning of "sponsorship" in A.A. as the practice started in Cleveland: when you sponsored someone to be admitted to a hospital, it meant that if that person did not pay the bill, you would. At that time the cost was between $90 and $100, and that was a lot of money back then, in the aftermath of the Great Depression. Well, as you can imagine, you did not agree to sponsor someone unless you were pretty sure that they were serious about getting sober. And you did a good job being a sponsor in what has become the later meaning of that term, fostering full sobriety.

Earlier, in Akron, Ignatia would smuggle patients into St. Thomas Hospital on Dr. Bob's assurance that there was some hope for them and that someone would take care of their bills. Bob would usually admit them under a diagnosis of acute gastritis. Sometimes, when there were no empty rooms in the hospital and there was concern that the new admission might become disruptive in withdrawal, Ignatia would put them in the flower room. Some of you may recall the old hospitals, where they used to have a room where they put overnight the flowers from the patients' rooms. The theory was that flowers give off oxygen during the day but at night they absorb oxygen so it was unhealthy to leave flowers in a room with a sick patient. Anyway, that was also the room they put the corpses in, if someone died during the night, until the undertaker came in the morning to pick up the body.

So . . . I'm sure you can guess what would happen on occasion. Some poor drunk would be stuck in the flower room, and a stiff would be wheeled in on a table, and the gregarious, loquacious, probably hallucinating alkie-in-withdrawal would strike up a conversation. Then, the next day . . . . There are lots of ways of hitting bottom. I do not think any of those flower room people are still living, but I interviewed some, and others taped their stories so you may come across one. There are some experiences that our modern treatment centers just cannot replicate!

I mentioned the origin of the chip system. Its history is a bit muddled, but supposedly it was the Irish temperance movement that Father

Matthew brought to this country in the nineteenth century that started using a lapel pin to signify membership. The "Pioneers" picked that up, but they also encouraged distribution of the Sacred Heart badge at the time of First Communion or sacramental Confirmation as a symbol of the same pledge. Anybody here remember that? I do sort of vaguely. Anyway, Ignatia, as any patient of whatever religious background or preference was about to be discharged from the hospital, Ignatia, this little tiny nun, would go to the big lug and say, "Now, George, I want you to take this as a reminder of what you have learned here, that you are an alcoholic. And I want you to promise me that before you ever take a drink you will come and you will give this back to me." And, blubbering likely in inverse correlation with religious practice, the newly sober drunk would take that piece of cloth and store it in wallet or pocket, and . . . well you know.

The use of actual poker chips began, so far as I have been able to discover, in Elmira, New York, in 1947. Still, though it probably will bother members of this group less than it does some of our separated brethren in the rural South, how does it feel to realize that that poker chip or medallion some of you have in your pocket is really a Roman Catholic sacramental?

Question: I have always been curious since I was an unwilling patient in Hazelden: they had this small statue sitting up there kind of quietly. And I asked, "Well, who is that?" And they said it was a statue of Sister Ignatia. But it was a more of a caricature . . . this ugly statue . . . and I always kind of wondered is there a story behind that?

[EK]: I do not know. My guess is that it was something that was done by a patient out of love and the patient was not too talented. But since the love was what counted . . . it's like a child who brings home a drawing and mother puts it on the refrigerator. It is not great art, but that is not what it's there for. From what I know of Hazelden people, at least back then, that would fit. I do not know of any statues of Ignatia. I think Ignatia would wince at the idea, and probably a lot of church officials would wince even more at the idea of statues of Ignatia. My hunch though, knowing how some things at Hazelden used to operate, is that it is love-art, and no one throws that away until everyone forgets the story behind it.

Question: I am seeing in my clients many with dual problems. Some of them have trouble fitting into A.A. They have trouble especially because they have to be on medication, and many A.A. members tell them they should not be, and that confuses them.

[EK]: That question goes beyond the history of A.A. in part, but my study of the history of research on A.A. may offer some light. First, let's be clear that by "dual problems" you do not mean alcohol-and-other-drugs but a separate psychiatric diagnosis?

[Assent from the questioner: "Yes, another psychiatric problem."]

[EK]: Though it's not my area, you're in some luck, because that is an area that my wife has researched. She did a study of "double-trouble" groups, A.A. groups intended precisely for such people as you mention. And it seems that for such people to succeed in sobriety, it really helps to have such groups. Research indicates that most of them cannot make it in just straight A.A. However, the research also suggests that those who are capable of going to both "double-trouble" and regular meetings do better if they do go to both, go to straight A.A. as well as their dual meetings.

But of more concern is the idea that early A.A.s did not tolerate psychiatric medication: that is simply and totally false. If you look at the first mentions of psychiatric medications in the *A.A. Grapevine* in 1945 and 1946, "The Pill Problem: Chewing Your Booze," there is a distinction made even back then between psychiatric medication and what we would call today minor tranquilizers. They did not have the name then, but they had the pills – even before Miltown. They were talking about barbiturates, and their concern was self-medication. But from the time lithium came on the scene (1949, I believe), most people in A.A., and surely Bill Wilson, recognized that psychiatric medication should not be interfered with by A.A. members.

On the other hand, never forget A.A.'s prime axiom: "Some are sicker than others." You are going to find some A.A.s who are going to insist that *anything* is a violation of the program. But that is one reason why alcoholics with dual problems need special groups, and a large reason why we should speak up and teach what we know. For it is also true, on the physician side, that some are more knowledgeable than others: not all physicians are knowledgeable about alcoholism. In such cases, the usual A.A. practice has been to suggest not a medication change but consultation with a physician known to be aware of the realities of alcoholism. Some physicians still treat alcoholism as a Valium deficiency, as Dr. Russ Smith used to put it. But most A.A. groups keep track of physicians who are aware, if you ask around. Today, the more likely danger seems to be treating the ordinary pain of being human as a Prozac deficiency. Unless you hold Eli Lilly stock, the same cautions would seem appropriate.

You of course recognize that I am describing sort of an ideal, but there is literature put out by Alcoholics Anonymous itself on this topic. Sometimes it helps to give A.A.s A.A. literature, not scholarly literature. So write to G.S.O.: they put out some very good pamphlets. One, as I recall, summarizes a couple of talks that Bill Wilson gave on this topic, because it is a recurring concern. So my most practical suggestion is to get in touch with G.S.O., but look in on your local service office too. A.A. itself has some good literature on this.

Question: I heard that in the Los Angeles area in the 30's and 40's they were trying to treat alcoholism with an essentially spiritual program, that they came up with something called religious psychology?

[EK]: I may not have much on that directly, but let me offer what I do know. The first attempt to start A.A. in Los Angeles was by some compassionate social workers who knew some drunks. They got the Big Book and tried to start A.A., but of course they really could not. Today, some would call them "clueless," but I think that is a bit cruel: they certainly were compassionate, caring people and they did everything they possibly could.

About "an essentially spiritual program," most of the early A.A.s I've talked with knew about Richard Peabody's 1931 book, *The Common Sense of Drinking*, and said that it "had everything A.A. had except the spiritual." And that was the book that just about all professionals used, at least until Strecker and Chambers *Alcohol: One Man's Meat* came out in 1938. The Strecker and Chambers book, incidentally, was published in January and had to go into a second printing in March; contrast that with the slow initial sales of the A.A. Big Book, which took almost two years to sell out its first printing of less that 5,000 copies.

[BREAK]

PART TWO: The Spirituality of Imperfection

The previous segment, on the history of Alcoholics Anonymous, was sort of an updating and fleshing-out of the story I told in *Not-God*. Now, following your suggestions, I would like to offer some glossing thoughts about what I have called *The Spirituality of Imperfection*.

What I hope to do in this segment is to go beyond that book to the wider topic of spirituality and therapy. Yes, there is a perfectionistic tradition within spirituality. But it is not the whole story. Let's begin where some people see a problem, that place in Scripture where Jesus says, "Be perfect as your heavenly Father is perfect." As the context makes clear – it has to do with the *breadth* of the Father's love – the Greek word here translated as "perfect" means *complete*. (Besides Matthew 5:48, check out the use of the same word in Matthew 19:21 and John 17:23.) What Jesus is saying here is that our love should be complete in the sense of extending to everyone, as the heavenly Father's love extends to everyone. The perfectionist tradition within spirituality does not rest on that quotation, though it is often used erroneously.

The wider tradition of a spirituality of imperfection, though evident in the New Testament, is first developed explicitly in the desert spirituality of the late second century. My hero is Macarius, who had the first clear

125

vision of spirituality as a journey, a vision similar to that presented by Father Pat last evening. This vision sees spirituality as the kind of journey represented in the old pilgrimage idea. It is not a straight-line: You don't get on a turnpike or you don't get on an airplane. This is a journey on foot, and it involves wandering and uncertainty.

Macarius was an outspoken opponent of the recovery-porn of the third century. The motto they were chanting at those proto-pseudo Twelve-step meetings ran: "Off with the old man, on with the new." And that drove Macarius up the cave wall. In his understanding, there is no such "once and for all." Yes, we are "made new," but it is not as simple as donning or doffing an item of clothing. Rather, the spiritual journey is one of a constant falling down and getting up again, a building something up only to have it knocked down and having to build up again. This is the spirituality of imperfection. It is not "Everyday and every way I am getting better and better," because it just does not work that way. Besides, as Macarius loved to point out, if all we did was make progress, we would become conceited, and conceit is the ultimate downfall of Christians. (Perhaps the same is true of alcoholics?) The journey we are on is a pilgrimage on which we wake up some mornings and realize we are not as far ahead as we were a while before, and that is okay, so long as we realize it and are ready and determined to do something about it. It is a pilgrimage journey, it is a wandering journey, it is a day-at-a-time journey, which is what the word *journey* means, after all.

That, I think, is also very evidently the spirituality of Alcoholics Anonymous, a spirituality of imperfection, of falling down and getting up again. I am not talking here of slips and relapse, or at least not of that only. What is essential to this spirituality is an awareness of the dark side, an awareness rooted in the experience of tragedy. It was this spirituality that the early members of Alcoholics Anonymous rediscovered, and it is a spirituality at polar opposite from the bland, have-a-nice-day, smiley-button, huggy mindlessness that enthusiasts of the so-called "new age" purvey as spirituality. Tragedy, like alcoholism, can be denied . . . for a time. But when it can no longer be denied, when powerlessness and unmanageability rub against noses ground into the gutter, then something else is needed, something deeper and darker and richer and fuller. If you

126

will forgive an effort to build on a homely image of Monsignor Ronald Knox, what we need at such moments is not the encouraging prim smile of the distant aunt of an established church or the flouncy exuberance of the empty-headed adolescent doxy of the fad spirituality of the moment: we need our own very earthy mother who, in pain, brought us, crying, into this land of both joys and tears and who knows the reality of our sufferings as well as our joys.

Alcoholics Anonymous came into being during the cultural trauma of the Great Depression, and A.A. could not have come out of any American era other than the 1930's. That was the decade when this culture hit bottom. Read the discussion of Step One in the *Twelve and Twelve*. There Bill describes what it was like to be a drunk during the Depression. The imagery "completely bankrupt" is economic, and that is the true language of this culture. Coming out of this context, Alcoholics Anonymous recaptured in very American terms the ancient tradition of powerlessness, of limitation.

This is a tradition of *spirituality*, not of "therapy." The two are distinct, after all. Difference, of course, does not imply that one is better than the other. No, both are good: in fact, most of us need both. However, to confuse the two is to harm both. In saying that spirituality and therapy are different, I am not saying they are absolutely distinct. They are related: It is not like apples and bird baths; it is more like apples and oranges. There are likenesses between them, but they are different. And when we lose the distinction . . . when you try to eat an orange like you eat an apple, you are going to get a sticky wet face and a bitter taste in your mouth.

If, on the other hand, we make the distinction, acknowledge the difference, we can better utilize both spirituality and therapy. Therapy seeks to find explanations that will enable a person to grow to greater control of his or her life in the expectation that such empowerment will enhance self-esteem. Although it may be and indeed usually is humane, therapy is also scientific. Among other things, it can appropriately be both taught and bought. Spirituality, on the other hand, begins in an awe that recognizes the reality of mystery, not the least of which is the mystery of one's own paradoxical being – the reality that one is capable of evil as well as good, good as well as evil. And we are not only "capable": we *do* both good and evil, though neither perfectly, so so much for our "control." Also, because awe, mystery, and paradox fall outside the scientific paradigm, spirituality produces no experts. Those who attempt to traffic in spirituality are by that very fact revealed to be charlatans.

Let me tell you my favorite story in the area of medical economics. Like so many penetrating stories, it comes to us from the Hasidim:

A rich Hasid comes to the rabbi and says, "Rabbi, I have been blessed by G-d in so many ways. I have great wealth. I have all the goods of the world. But I am nevertheless miserable and unhappy. Rabbi, can you help me?"

And the rabbi says, "Yes, I think I can. Here come with me." And the rabbi goes across the room to the window and says, "Look out the window and tell me what you see."

The Hasid looks out the street below and says, "I see people. I see people walking by."

The rabbi says, "Ah, yes, good. Now come over here to the other side of the room. Look into that mirror and tell me what you see."

And the Hasid goes over to the mirror and says, "Why it is a mirror, Rabbi. I look into it and I see myself."

And the rabbi says, "Yes, very good. Now notice that in the window there is glass and in the mirror there is glass. But as soon as a little silver is added you cease to see others and see only yourself."

Scientific therapy involves a specialized body of knowledge, mastered by study, possessed by professionals who justly ask payment for their expertise. That is not all that it is but it is that: amateur therapy is a problem and an abuse. And all of you recognize that. That is why those of you who are therapists work on your credentialing and take courses. Spirituality, on the contrary, involves wisdom gained by experience and generally made available in relationships of reciprocity, such as friendship, which by definition cannot be sold. Some realities are changed in their very nature when they become market entities, objects of commerce. Our culture is not ready to admit that. However, as economist Joan Robinson observed some fifty years ago, "Bought sex is not the same." Neither is bought friendship.

Spirituality offers *images to understand* life and how it is changed. Therapy offers *techniques to change* life. The Serenity Prayer captures this. We need the courage to change what can be changed. We also need the serenity to accept that which cannot be changed and the wisdom to know the difference. Those moved by spirituality have usually thought in terms not of "having changed" but of having *been* changed. This is one way of recognizing a spiritual change. Those who have undergone a true *metanoia* know that *they* have not changed, they *have been* changed. They tried to change themselves for a long time, but it did not work. And then, suddenly, somehow, through a process of letting go, they discover themselves as changed. The ancient Pietist axiom, "Let go and let God," reflects this sense. You will find many rich modern expressions in the writings of Anthony deMello.

To be a sober alcoholic, like being a saved sinner, signals embrace of a paradox that recognizes the enduring reality of tragedy as well as of comedy. Neither of these play a large part in most therapies. Therapy is thin, usually healthily lean; the therapies purveyed in the books found in the recovery section of book stores are emaciated. Modern therapies seem all to insist that "I'm okay, you're okay." Spirituality suggests that I am not "okay," and you are not "okay"; but hey, that's alright. In the words of the Nobel Prize winning Mexican poet Octavio Paz, "North Americans consider the world something that can be perfected. We consider it something that can be redeemed."

Both real spirituality and genuine therapy, then, exclude the so-called Recovery Movement. That movement has to do with selling things more than with any kind of healing. The recovery movement is a good example of what happens when spirituality and therapy get confused. We end up with neither, and into that vacuum flows whatever is in cultural ascendancy – in our time, greed.

Spirituality advises and enables not self-enhancement but a commitment that is necessarily to something outside of and larger than our "selves." The main problem with the word co-dependence is that no one knows what it means. If you doubt that, read Frank Troise's lead article in the 1995 *Alcoholism Treatment Quarterly*, in which he deconstructs Cermak's conceptualization of "codependency" as personality disorder. I realize that there are other understandings of co-dependence, and I trust Father Marty will address their constructive and healthy use. But the way I hear this word used over three-quarters of the time (and I do keep track), is as a synonym for compassion and caring. The current tendency of people who present themselves as "recovering" to insist that there is something "sick" about compassion and caring and generosity should awaken concern in all of us.

Why? Let me suggest two reasons, the first cultural and *post factum*, the second theological and having to do with the nature of spirituality. Leon Wurmser, a psychiatrist who studied shame long before it became fashionable fad, pointed out that "Shameless cultures start seeing no shame attached to the most shameless exhibitionism and flaunting of even gross sexuality and instead find shameful things like compassion and caring and gentleness." I fear that what Wurmser predicted, thirteen years ago, has overtaken much of the crowd that flaunts its commitment to eradicating "co-dependence."

Spirituality points us outside ourselves. The main task of any spirituality is to put us in touch with reality beyond . . . beyond the self. The book *Alcoholics Anonymous*, in the chapter promising "There Is A Solution," insists that "Our very lives, as ex-problem drinkers, depend upon our constant thought of others and how we may help meet their needs." Try dropping that as a "True or False" on your average recovery movement enthusiast or CoDA member. "Our very lives . . . depend upon our constant thought of others and how we may help meet their needs." That does not deny that I have needs. But central to any spirituality is attention to that which is beyond the self. All art, religion, and love are connected to the quest to transcend the self without claiming to escape the narrow prison of self.

Varieties of A.A. and "Real A.A."

As said earlier, if I were today to write a book on Alcoholics Anonymous, I would title it *Varieties of the A.A. Experience*. The word "fundamentalist" is so often mis-applied that I will not use it, but in every community, among adherents to any ideology, there are always some who insist that the "first way" was better, that the original was best. One problem with that claim, of course, is the assumption that we *know*, from our very different context, what was "first" or "the original." But that is less a problem with Alcoholics Anonymous than it is with Christianity.

A.A.'s story does present some difficulties, but 1935 is closer to our experience than is 28 A.D. Most members of the fellowship today do not claim that "The way it was in 1935 is the way it should be." But intriguingly, many who do incline in that direction do not seem to realize how varied Alcoholics Anonymous was from – if not the very beginning – at least 1937, when the New Yorkers split off from the Oxford Group while the Akronites continued meeting in the midst of the Group at the home of T. Harry and Clarace Williams. Fortunately, we have not only the published reminiscences of such as Dr. Earl M., and the research of Niles P. published in the book *Dr. Bob and the Good Oldtimers*, but tape recordings of early members telling their stories and detailing their experience. I have recently been immersed in seven different tapes, dating from 1946 to 1968, of Marty Mann telling her story at large public gatherings.

And there is other direct evidence. Take the topic of A.A. meetings themselves. When they wrote the Big Book, they did not know there were going to be meetings as we know them. Look in the Big Book for mentions of meetings. You will find the word *meetings* once, on page 162, talking about how these people gather one night a week to provide a place to bring newcomers. Meetings developed. And the different forms of meetings: from sitting around and chatting to question and answer, then speakers, then a lead discussion. In the October 1947 *A.A. Grapevine*, the lead article asked "How do you do it?" and invited an exchange of ideas and experience about the different types of meetings found throughout A.A. Some early groups also had rules – I have already mentioned Los Angeles. It was very difficult to belong to Alcoholics Anonymous in Rochester, New York, and Little Rock, Arkansas: those two locations had the hardest nosed A.A. Jackson, Michigan, came in a close third.

In 1946, A.A.'s first Central Service Office put out a pamphlet titled "A.A. in Cleveland." Let me quote from it at length, because this is what early A.A. was like.

A.A. groups are not mentioned in the Twelve Steps, nor are hospitals, central offices, minstrel shows, clam bakes, bowling teams, softball leagues, open meetings, or many of the other activities of the movement. . . .

A.A. groups are fundamentally little bands of people who are friends and who can help each other stay sober. Each group, therefore, reflects the needs of its own members. The way a group is managed is the way its members want it to be managed for their common benefit. As a result, we have large groups, small groups, groups which have refreshments, groups which never have refreshments, groups which like long meetings, groups which like short meetings, social groups, working groups, men's groups, women's groups, groups that play cards, groups which specialize in young people and as many other varieties as there are kinds of people. . . .

Each group has its own customs, its own financial problems, and its own method of operation. As long as if follows as a group the same principles A.A. recommends for individuals – unselfishness, honesty, decency, and tolerance – it is above criticism. . . .

Because this is a large country, because the cultures of various sections and cities differ, because of chance and fate, there is no great uniformity in A.A. customs. The only national standards are the book, *Alcoholics Anonymous*, and the literature put out by The Alcoholic Foundation. The Foundation [also] tries to curb dangerous practices and to avoid unfavorable and inaccurate publicity.

(Those interested in reading the complete text may find it in Wally P., *But, For the Grace of God* (Wheeling, WV: The Bishop of Books, 1985), pp. 87ff. "The Bishop of Books," Charlie Bishop, Jr., may be reached at 46 Eureka Ave., Wheeling, WV 26003, or at Bishopbks@aol. com)

Note, by the way, in that quotation, the reflection of the Oxford Group "Four Absolutes" of "honesty, purity, unselfishness and love" – and how "purity" has become *decency* and "love," *tolerance*. Both those changes reflect some things specific to the Cleveland A.A. of the time. Subtle changes and not so subtle.

Much of what I have done and continue to do involves trying to interpret Alcoholics Anonymous to professionals. One reason why that is necessary, after sixty plus years of A.A. history, is because even groups listed in meeting books are not always "real A.A." in the sense of being Twelve-Step groups. So the question gets asked, "How do you recognize real A.A.?"

What I advise professionals is, first, that you do not make a referral to A.A. by telling somebody, "Go to A.A." or even, "There is an A.A. meeting at the Third Presbyterian Church: you should go over there." You make a referral to a person. You find some person who has the kind of sobriety you want your client to have, and you introduce the two of them to each other. Alcoholics Anonymous is a program of identification. And there are so many varieties of people that this is the only way in which to make a real referral. So you find an A.A. member who has what you want your client to have, and you let that person decide which meetings to go to and take the newcomer along.

That is the sure way of finding "real A.A." But if you want some general thoughts about how to recognize it . . . well, let me be so bold. Please note that these are not criteria, these are not rules. These come from my experience with people who have the kind of spirituality/sobriety that I want and that I hope for others to have. I invite you to shoot holes in them or to add to them if you will. What follows here is not carved in stone; it is rather simply the best I have been able to come up with thus far in thinking about this topic and trying to answer a very real question posed by some good-hearted and concerned professionals at a time when there seems to be a danger that the overflow of treatment thinking into Alcoholics Anonymous and other Twelve-Step groups will overwhelm their spirituality with psychobabble jargon.

Five generalizations from observation, then – qualities that allow recognizing genuine Twelve-Step groups, whether of A.A. or Al-Anon, or OA, for the topic here is genuine Twelve-Step groups. I have seen non-A.A. Twelve-Step groups, and I have also seen groups that though they called themselves "A.A.," do not strike me as having much to do with the Twelve Steps.

1. Language - Vocabulary: if you want therapy, seek out a therapist. Our society has seen fit, probably wisely, to license those deemed competent to "do therapy": choose from that list, and I would suggest choosing one on that list who recognizes the difference between amateur and professional therapy as well as the difference between therapy and spirituality.

But if you seek not so much therapy as a setting in which to pursue or deepen the spirituality that is sobriety, find a setting in which the vocabulary used is the vocabulary of the Twelve Steps. Does the language used at meetings speak of "defects of character" and "shortcomings", of taking one's own "moral inventory" and "becoming willing" and "humbly asking"? If so, you are probably in the right place. But if the language is about drives and narcissism and shame and inner children and teddy bears and co-dependence and being a victim, you are probably not in the right place. Twelve-Step groups use the language and vocabulary of the Twelve Steps, not of therapy. There is nothing wrong with the vocabulary of therapy. It belongs in therapy. It may belong in cocktail party conversation. It surely belongs in academic bull sessions. But in Twelve-Step meetings, what belongs is Twelve-Step language and Twelve-Step vocabulary. Listen for them. Use them.

2. Humor: The laughter that characterizes A.A. and other genuine Twelve-Step meetings is often misunderstood. Humor has been defined as "the juxtaposition of incongruity," the putting together of two things that do not belong together. Well, as human beings – this weird combination of matter and spirit, body and soul, beast and angel, phrase it how you will – we human beings are put together funny! Except we cannot see our own incongruity; just as the eye cannot see itself, its own face, the mind cannot grasp itself, its own being. Among the greatest incongruities, of course, is "sober alcoholic," and that is why that identity is so important: it signals acceptance and embrace of our incongruity and so of our humanity.

But because we cannot see our own incongruity, we need a kind of mirror, and that is what the stories told at meetings provide. What happens at meetings is that people get up and tell stories of what they used to be like, what happened, and what they are like now, and those stories hold up a mirror in which the listeners recognize their own incongruity. The laughter that takes place in an A.A. meeting is not laughter at the speaker, it is laughter at self. This is why it is so healing. Any genuine Twelve-Step meeting will have laughter, the humor that comes from the embrace of this image of imperfection.

3. Story-Style: Listen to the stories that are told. Do they "share experience, strength and hope" by telling stories that "describe in a general way what we used to be like, what happened, and what we are like now"? Or do people at those meetings instead, as one adherent told me recently, "do some of that but mostly we tell what's happening to us and how we feel about that."

Twelve-Step meetings have a story style that "describe[s] in a general way what we used to be like, what happened, and what we are like now," as it says on page 58 in the Big Book's chapter on "How It Works." Note *describe in a general way:* this is not the Geraldo show or related obscenity. But there is that emplotment, that sequential narration that is the nature of story; and that is very different from "This is what is going on, this is how I feel about this, and my self is feeling better and I got reaffirmed three times and my inner-child feels hugged." That may be marvelous, that may be wonderful. But it is not Twelve-Step.

Please be clear that I am not condemning nor saying that there is anything "wrong" with that other style. As Robert Wuthnow's book, *Sharing the Journey*, points out, it is often helpful. It may even be "spiritual," depending on what kind of stories are told. Only it is not Twelve-Step spirituality. And that is okay. The whole world does not have to be Twelve-Step. But there is the very real danger that if you do not call things by their proper name, you may lose them.

4. The Twelve Traditions: Like everything else in A.A., its Twelve Traditions come from its members' experience. The task of the Twelve Traditions has been described as "protecting the spirituality of the Steps." Some very sober members tell me that the Twelve Traditions are to the spirituality of the group what the Twelve Steps are to the spirituality of the individual. Bill Wilson attached great importance to the Traditions, as a letter he wrote to Father Dowling when he was working on the book *Twelve Steps and Twelve Traditions* makes clear. In it, Bill writes that he hopes the pieces on the Steps will "act as bait for reading" the essays on the Traditions. (The letter is reproduced in Fitzgerald's *Soul of Sponsorship*, pp. 55-56.)

Some Akron enthusiasts have claimed that Dr. Bob never approved the Traditions. Wrong. Read Bob's article in the September 1948 *A.A. Grapevine*, "The Fundamentals in Retrospect," where Bob talks about the need for the Traditions especially because of the ego of alcoholics. Bob saw the Traditions as a check on this ego. And that is why, in approaching any group that claims to be "Twelve-Step," I look especially for attitudes and practice in the areas of anonymity and being non-professional, and affiliations, and opinion on outside issues. One large function of the Twelve Traditions over time has been precisely to protect the

Twelve Steps from confusion with anything else. Note how poorly the Traditions fit any existing expression of religion OR therapy.

If you have not yet come across this in your area, by the way, let me caution you that some professionals openly admit that they attend A.A. meetings to troll for clients. Some groups read at the beginning of meetings a request that "if you are a professional at this meeting, you should be here either because you share our common problem or because you wish to learn. This is not the place for you to seek out clients for your private practice." It is also effective, in combating this practice, just to stick with the Twelve Steps, especially their language. Meetings that seem branches of bookstores or souvenir shops invite intrusion. This is not a condemnation of all such tokens: I am Catholic in my tradition, and I know the value of sacramentals. And so I do not hate teddy bears, and I do not hate holy water or trashy reproductions of the Sacred Heart. We realize that some people, and perhaps all of us at some times, need these things, and wise traditions make such aids available. But when the sacramental displaces the sacrament, when people choose a meeting because at this one you get a discount on sponsor bear, then the tail is wagging the donkey. Something has happened to priorities. "First Things First," it says somewhere.

5. Community: And lastly, the nature of the community. There is vast literature on groups today. The best of it recognizes that support groups and self-help groups, therapy and the recovery movement and spirituality, are different. One way that they are distinct is in their origins. People join Twelve-Step groups not because they "want to" but because they *have to*. This is a tough point. But I will never forget a speaker at an A.A. meeting who observed: "I did not come to A.A. to save my soul, I came here to save my ass. It was only years later I learned they were attached."

The problem with this criterion is that, seeing what some people get when they pursue what they need, other people want that. And that is okay: you could hardly stop it, nor, likely, would you want to stop it. But in any real Twelve-Step group the center of gravity will be among the ones who know that they *need*, for it is with them that the needing newcomers have to identify. If you listen to the stories, you can tell the difference.

137

The sense of "need," of course, doesn't mean some kind of fear that you are going to take a drink if you do not go to this A.A. meeting on a given night. It is just that you know that unless you are at these meetings, unless you are within this fellowship, you are going to get sick in some way or another and probably eventually will drink.

Well, that's enough, I am sure. I would like to close with a final story, but I think it more important to throw this open to your questions and discussion.

Question: What about the programs for alcoholics that are not spiritual, like Rational Recovery, for example?

[EK]: This is a difficult one to answer just now, because there has been a recent split in the Rational Recovery movement, with Jack Trimpey going one way and others going off in a different direction. I really do not know much more than that it has occurred, and that many who did not go with Trimpey object to what appears to be an effort by him to commercialize, sell for money, as least some aspects of that program.

But let me speak a bit more generically. At least some years ago, when I observed a couple of Rational Recovery groups, some people who went to RR because they could not stand the religion in A.A. did sort of graduate from Rational Recovery to A.A. What happened, I think, is that they found that RR was not enough for them, and they also discovered some A.A. group that was not objectionable to them.

I am finding something similar, by the way, in another program that does not oppose Alcoholics Anonymous but that objects to the use made of A.A. by the treatment industry. "Moderation Management," it is called, and coincidentally it began in Ann Arbor, where I now live. Simply stated, MM is for people who are problem drinkers but may not be alcoholics. In thinking this way, it follows the A.A. Big Book. MM does not advocate "controlled drinking" for alcoholics; it does say, agreeing with the Big Book rather than with treatment providers, that not everyone who has problems with alcohol is an alcoholic.

138

Moderation Management, which is a voluntary non-profit program much like early Alcoholics Anonymous, suggests guidelines for moderation. If you learn from their guidelines, and achieve moderation in drinking, fine. But a certain percentage, maybe a quarter to a third, learn from the guidelines that they cannot drink moderately, and so they move to an abstinence program, often A.A. Alan Marlatt found something similar in his program at the University of Washington, by the way. If you offer problem drinkers, young ones who would never have gone to A.A. or any abstinence program, an invitation to moderation, those who find they cannot adhere to it may choose abstinence earlier and sooner than otherwise would likely have been the case.

We all have been somewhat brain-washed by the minions of the treatment industry, so let me recall for you some things I know you have read in the book, *Alcoholics Anonymous*:

> If anyone who is showing inability to control his drinking can do the right-about-face and drink like a gentleman, our hats are off to him. Heaven knows, we have tried hard enough and long enough to drink like other people! . . . We do not like to pronounce any individual as alcoholic, but you can quickly diagnose yourself. Step over to the nearest barroom and try some controlled drinking. Try to drink and stop abruptly. Try it more than once. It will not take long for you to decide, if you are honest with yourself about it. (pp. 31-32)

Earlier, the Big Book distinguishes alcoholics from *both* "moderate drinkers [who] have little trouble in giving up liquor entirely if they have good reason for it" *and* from "a certain type of hard drinker [who] may have the habit badly enough to gradually impair him physically and mentally [and even to] cause him to die a few years before his time." Such drinkers, the Big Book notes, "if [given] a sufficiently strong reason . . . can also stop or moderate, although they may find it difficult and troublesome and may even need medical attention." (pp. 20-22)

Programs like Moderation Management try to give that "sufficiently strong reason." Historians are not prophets, but I think that with the changes going on in health-care and insurance and all that, we are already beginning to see a shift where more and more people are coming into Alcoholics Anonymous from some kind of monitored moderation program than from the treatment industry that, let's remember, is barely twenty years old in its expansive, medically oriented, phase.

Let me repeat: most moderation programs, and Moderation Management is a good example, are not trying to make alcoholics into controlled drinkers. They are trying to distinguish between alcoholics and those who can control their drinking. And what that effort is discovering is that some 25 to 40 percent of the people who come asking, "Help me to control my drinking because it seems to be getting out of control," decide, "I must be an alcoholic; it's too much effort to control my drinking, so I'd better go to A.A." And the evidence we have, though admittedly as yet only slight, suggests these individuals would not have tried A.A. at this time without that other experience.

So people are finding a different route to A.A. through these moderation programs. This is part of the change that is going on. People used to come into A.A. off the street, then people came into A.A. from treatment, and now it looks like in the future, with HMOs and the trajectory of the for-profit health-care system, most people might start coming to A.A. from these programs that aim to help people find out whether or not they can control their drinking. Admittedly, as you well know, we live in a world shaped by original sin, and so not all moderation programs have high ethical standards and are exempt from greed. But their record here is surely no worse than that of a treatment industry made up of programs that have lately devoted themselves to convincing everyone that they are addicted to something, something this particular treatment modality just happens to be able to treat, all too often at outrageous cost, especially if we compare what is offered with that first effective treatment program provided by Sister Ignatia.

But the ethical programs, and Moderation Management is one of them, make very clear that if you are an alcoholic you do not belong in them. Their thrust is: "This is not a program for alcoholics. This is a program for people who have problems but still show evidence of being able to control their drinking. This will help you to decide whether or not you can. And if you can, this program can help you do it."

Question: What you said about language and vocabulary in A.A.: what we are hearing is one facet of the variety of A.A. Isn't your criterion awfully restrictive? The fact is that today certainly more people are coming to A.A. from treatment. So the language of treatment will be in the room. Is not that yet another ordinary human development that will also be A.A.?

[EK]: It may be. My thought and feeling are that a Twelve-Step group should use, basically, the language of the Twelve Steps. Maybe that language will be glossed and commented on in these other vocabularies – yes, that is inevitable and not unwelcome: all living realities grow and change. Perhaps a parallel: certainly not every Catholic parish society is speaking today in the language of the Apostles' Creed. But there is a difference between Newman's "development of doctrine" and the kind of corruption that prefers pagan goddesses to Jesus Christ.

My concern is not theology or therapy but their practice by amateurs. Any profession has a body of knowledge and of skills that are to be learned. I respect most professionals who show that accomplishment. I have no problem when professionals use even the terms "co-dependence," or "denial." But when "denial" becomes a synonym for "You disagree with me" and "co-dependence" a slightly less vulgar way of calling someone a naive ass, we are not dealing with professionals, or at least with the kind of professionals who merit respect. Yes, as far as A.A. is concerned, people coming from different backgrounds will bring a different language. But I still think that in a Twelve-Step group one should hear at least occasional references to the Twelve Steps. Maybe it is only a reflection of my own sickness, but I need to hear about moral inventory and making amends and defects of character – I much prefer defects of character to low, or high, self-esteem.

Question: Your "need to" and "want to" point about community: Sometimes people who have been in recovery for about ten years sort of drop out and some then come back. Is this around the question of need to and want to? Do they convince themselves after years of going to meetings that, "Well, I guess I am at a point where I do not need to any more"? I am never convinced of that any more for myself.

[EK]: Your question makes clear that I did not make clear that I was speaking of why people come in the first place – I was not clear on that, so thank you. But if that is the first question, you pose an interesting second one: what happens when that sense fades? What about people who, having once had that sense, then come to feel they no longer "need to"?

Let's start by looking at the data. Old timers in general do cut down their meeting attendance. Someone has claimed that one of the reasons A.A. stopped taking its membership survey a few years ago was that the attendance of old-timers was falling off to the point of embarrassment. I do not know whether that is true or not: since they will not release the figures, who knows? From what I do know, one factor behind why they stopped taking the survey was that the membership asked "Why are you taking it? How does it help alcoholics?" and not having a good answer to that (though I think there is one), they stopped. Never forget that Alcoholics Anonymous is run by its grass-roots members, and how can you please two million alcoholics? Before second-guessing any action taken by the people at 475 Riverside Drive, ask yourself: Can you imagine anything more difficult than having nearly two million alcoholic bosses?

But to your question: impressionistically, there does seem to be a falling off in frequency of meeting attendance over time, but that need not mean that these individuals no longer have a sense of needing to be there. The criterion that lasts over time, it seems to me, is the same: "If you have decided you want what we have," find the people who have what you want. Remember the classic criterion of spirituality? It has nothing to do with "feeling good"; it is "seeking out the company of the saints." And so people "keep coming back" so long as they find at the meetings those sources of identification that are the heart and soul of both recovery and community within Alcoholics Anonymous.

Sometimes, though, for diverse reasons – some having to do with invasions by people in treatment or by takers of illegal drugs with whom they find identification difficult – sometimes these "groups" start meeting informally, elsewhere. What began as "after the meeting at Ho-Jo's" becomes in a way "the meeting at Ho-Jo's." I wish I had more data; obviously, this is a tough phenomenon to study. But I do know that some of this is happening, and so the nature of the "attendance fall off" is not that clear.

Also, of course, one does not feel the "need" of which I spoke at every moment. It's sort of like those World Wide Web browsers – surely you are all into the new electronic age! – where near the upper left corner there is a button marked "Home"; and no matter how many links you pursue, and how lost you get, you know that there is that little button and you can click it and be back to where you started, where you are oriented. I think a lot of oldtimers use A.A. that way. Still, some also do "keep coming back" out of a dedication to "passing it on," as an expression of gratitude for what they have received. "I came to get, now I come to give," as some have explained their attendance to me when we have chatted. But I think that metaphor of "home" holds for a greater number. They may not come to meetings often, but they know the meetings are there, and that they can go to them. If they stay away too long, of course, changes can detract from the sense of "home" when they do drop by. But in both these cases – "home" and the "gratitude gang" – I think there is a very real sense of "need" that hangs on.

It's lunch time! Thank you very much for your courteous attention and for your challenging questions. And I am grateful to you for this opportunity to share many of these ideas-in-the-rough with you. Keep in touch: I need to keep hearing your own "experience, strength, and hope."

REFERENCES

For the reader's convenience, here is the bibliographic information on books mentioned in the preceding presentation:

Fitzgerald, Robert. The Soul of Sponsorship: The Friendship of Fr. Ed Dowling, S.J. and Bill Wilson, in Letters. Center City MN; Hazelden; 1995.

Darrah, Mary C. Sister Ignatia: Angel of Alcoholics Anonymous. Chicago; Loyola University Press; 1992.

Wing, Nell. Grateful to Have Been There: My 42 Years with Bill and Lois, and the Evolution of Alcoholics Anonymous. Park Ridge, IL; Parkside Publishing Corp.; 1992.

P., Wally. But, For the Grace of God . . . How Intergroups and Central Offices Carried the Message of Alcoholics Anonymous is the 1940s. Wheeling, WV; The Bishop of Books; 1995.

Mercadante, Linda A. Victims and Sinners: Spiritual Roots of Addiction and Recovery. Louisville, Kentucky; Westminster - John Knox Press; 1996.

Peabody, Richard R. The Common Sense of Drinking. Boston; Little, Brown, and Co.; 1931.

Strecker, Edward A. and Chambers, Francis T. Jr. Alcohol One Man's Meat. New York; Macmillan; 1938.

[Anonymous]. Dr. Bob and the Good Oldtimers A Biography, With Recollections of Early A.A. in the Midwest. New York; Alcoholics Anonymous World Services, Inc.; 1980.

Originally titled simply "Twelve-Step Programs," this piece was requested by Peter H. VanNess, editor of the Spirituality and the Secular Quest *volume (#22) of* World Spirituality: An Encyclopedic History of the Religious Quest, *General Editor Ewert Cousins, New York: Crossroad, 1996. It is a bit more free-wheeling than most of my other presentations, in part because of being directed to a wider audience that evidence suggested held many misconceptions about Twelve-Step programs and specifically Alcoholics Anonymous.*

Whatever Happened to Twelve-Step Programs?

Some time in 1990, reported *New York Times* religion writer Peter Steinfels, a cleric showing his church to a visitor confided: "There is more spirituality in this building on Tuesday evenings in the basement than on Sunday mornings in the sanctuary."[1] What went on in that and countless other church basements on weekday evenings were meetings of Alcoholics Anonymous and other groups, often termed "Twelve-Step groups" because derived from or in some way imitative of A.A. Even though not all such meetings take place in church basements, there is a problem with this modern version of "upstairs-downstairs." As the decade of the nineties unfolded, many challenged its insight. What had won grudging respect as an effective way of making available time-tested spiritual insight came increasingly to be criticized as a form of New Age religion or mocked as a manifestation of psychologizing fads.[2] Where, then, do Twelve-Step programs fit in a study of spirituality and the secular quest?

The term *Twelve-Step Programs* denotes groups of people who seek to put into practice the "Twelve Steps" formulated and introduced by Alcoholics Anonymous between 1935 and 1939. The term also connotes to many the plethora of therapeutic-spiritual hybrids that have more recently sprung up in the wake of the "human potential" or "New Age" movements. Because some of these present themselves, or are perceived to be, manifestations of Twelve-Step insight, we must begin with a distinction. The distinction is between those programs and groups that emphasize putting into practice the literal Twelve Steps, and those other programs and groups that focus their language and practice elsewhere, whether the source of that different thrust be esoteric or psychological.

That distinction is rarely so precise in mushy reality. Not even all gatherings listed as meetings of Alcoholics Anonymous, for example, fall into the first category. Practice, not labels, must guide. What actually occurs within any program or group is more important than how that reality is named. The line between the Twelve-Step and apparently related approaches may be blurry, but the differences are real. More importantly, because the difference is, at bottom, between, on the one hand, a modern reformulation of classic spiritual insight, and, on the other, a classic denial of traditional spirituality, the real story is **how** the one engendered the other.

There is a help for exploring that story, for distinguishing between genuine Twelve-Step programs and other ventures sometimes confused with them. Programs imbued with the spirit of the Twelve Steps are also Twelve-Tradition programs, adhering to the Twelve Traditions also originally set forth by Alcoholics Anonymous. The Twelve Steps shape the spirituality of participants in groups that set forth such programs; the Twelve Traditions shape the groups, making them apt vehicles for conveying Twelve-Step spirituality. After an exploration of the Twelve Steps, then, we shall examine also the significance of the Twelve Traditions.

The Twelve Steps
Any understanding of Twelve-Step programs must rest on some knowledge of the Steps as originally set forth by Alcoholics Anonymous. A.A.'s Twelve Steps begin with the word, "We," which remains implicit at the beginning of each Step. The less important reason for the 'We' is its implication of community, a facet we shall explore later. More significant to A.A.'s earliest members was their presentation of these Steps not as prescription, but as description: "Here are the Steps we took, which are suggested as a program of recovery"; so begins the actual listing of the Twelve Steps in the book *Alcoholics Anonymous*. The Steps do not set rules; they relate experience.

A.A.'s First Step reads: "We admitted we were powerless over alcohol – that our lives had become unmanageable." In commenting on this Step, A.A. co-founder Bill Wilson spoke of "absolute humiliation" and "utter defeat": "The principle that we shall find no enduring strength until we first admit complete defeat is the main taproot from which our whole society has sprung and flowered."[3] This understanding recaptured an ancient insight: classic vocabulary speaks of "emptying" (κενωσις) and of crying "out of the depths." Alcoholics Anonymous finds the beginning of recovery from alcoholism in the process of "hitting bottom." The admission of limitation, and, specifically, of the insufficiency of self-control – this is the beginning of Twelve-Step spirituality.

Despite the prominence of the word *believe* in the second of the Twelve Steps – "Came to believe that a Power greater than ourselves could restore us to sanity" – the stories told within Twelve-Step programs reveal that this Step deals less with faith than with **hope**. The point of the Second Step, according to co-founder Wilson's expatiation in *Twelve Steps and Twelve Traditions*, is encouragement to open-mindedness to new possibilities. The Second Step's "sanity" signifies the openness that makes possible "an optimal relationship between what one truly is and everything that is," an openness to both the inner and the outer dimensions of spirituality. The "Power greater than ourselves" need not be personalized: the point of this Step is the simple acknowledgment that one's self is not God, not the center of the universe, not "everything that is." Psychiatrists studying the Twelve Steps have found here a check on narcissism.[4] Step Two attests that even if the First Step seemed an act of despair, its very desperation contains the seed of hope.

The admission of failure plus the perception of hope opens the door to "surrender," although that classic term is eschewed in the A.A. texts.[5] "Made a decision to turn our will and our lives over to the care of God *as we understood Him*," reads the Third Step; the italicized phrase is a late addition insisted on by the more secular (in their own terms, the more agnostically-inclined) among A.A.'s earliest members. The literature on this Step portrays the alcoholic as "an extreme example of self-will run riot," insisting that "selfishness – self-centeredness . . . is the root of our troubles." Members of Alcoholics Anonymous caution each other against demanding to be "in the driver's seat." The attempt to control – their own feelings, other people – is what gets alcoholics into trouble. Wariness of claims to control, then, hallmarks sobriety, which A.A. members understand as far more than the mere dryness of "putting the cork in the bottle." As a true practice, A.A.'s "sobriety" consists in **living** the Twelve Steps. Such sobriety is a synonym for spirituality, even for what others term sanctity.

The next six Steps may conveniently be examined as three pairs. These concern self-knowledge, dealing with one's failings, and making restitution for harm done. "4. Made a searching and fearless moral inventory of ourselves. 5. Admitted to God, to ourselves and to another human being the exact nature of our wrongs." Some form of the word *honesty* appears three times in the brief paragraph that opens the "How It Works" chapter of the book, *Alcoholics Anonymous*. Although the modern term *denial* does not appear in A.A. literature, cautions against "self-deception" and "self-delusion" are frequent. A.A.'s inventory reflects the traditional practice of the *examen*, but the word 'inventory' emphasizes survey of the positive as well as the negative, assets as well as liabilities. The **admission**, in addition to its quiet reminder of Step One, captures some of the values of the practices of confession and reconciliation. "This feeling of being at one with God and man, this emerging from isolation," is how Wilson described them in concluding his explication of Step Five.[6]

Some see in Steps Six and Seven the very heart of the Twelve-Step program. "6. Were entirely ready to have God remove all these defects of character. 7. Humbly asked Him to remove our shortcomings." Both Steps conspicuously divert attention from any particular disability (such as alcoholic drinking) to the living of life. More deeply, both strengthen awareness of the individual's inability to exert control, thus reinforcing the surrender of all claims to be "in the driver's seat." In this spirituality, one seeks less to change oneself than to be open to being changed. Steps Six and Seven direct attention to one's own role in the difficulties one experiences, without imposing with that recognition the kind of obligation that wilts resolve. Being "entirely ready" and "humbly asking," however, are not quietist abdications, as anyone who tries to practice these Steps will discover.

"8. Made a list of all persons we had harmed, and became willing to make amends to them all. 9. Made direct amends to such people wherever possible, except when to do so would injure them or others." The practice of making amends has a second and less obvious meaning. Face-to-face candor fosters the honesty that is so central to sobriety. Steps Eight and Nine carry the Fourth and Fifth Steps deeper. Here, in a less protected setting, honesty with others invites even greater honesty with oneself. Also, in a deepening of the "inventory" image of those earlier Steps, the insistence on amends conveys the classic spiritual vision of an ordered universe. There exists a "right order," and one who has disturbed it by wrongdoing has the responsibility to set it right.

Members of Alcoholics Anonymous sometimes refer to the final three of the Twelve Steps as "the maintenance Steps." Step Ten sets that tone by recapitulating Steps Four through Nine: "Continued to take personal inventory and when we were wrong promptly admitted it." Twelve-Step spirituality is not a once-and-for-all spirituality. Again there comes the reminder that one does not attain sobriety/spirituality in solitary isolation: to "admit" something requires an-other to admit it to. Those who seek sobriety need others, and those who associate with persons seeking sobriety will discover that they are needed.

Step Eleven opens other classic themes: "Sought through prayer and meditation to improve our conscious contact with God *as we understood Him*, praying only for knowledge of His will for us and the power to carry that out." The traditional disciplines of "prayer and meditation" are presented as means "to improve." As the A.A. "Big Book" says, "We claim spiritual progress rather than spiritual perfection."[7] For those who live the Twelve Steps, "progress" is like Alasdair MacIntyre's conception of a practice, something midway between the pure perfection of being saved and the pure pragmatism of not-drinking.[8] The use of the word *improve* assumes a "contact" already present; the specification "conscious" is also important. Both are noted when members discuss this Step. Finally, consistent with the recognition that spirituality involves mystery and miracle rather than magic, the purpose of prayer is presented not as an attempt to control God, but as an expression of deference to divine reality.

149

Almost as well-known as A.A.'s First Step is its Twelfth: "Having had a spiritual awakening as the result of these steps, we tried to carry this message to alcoholics, and to practice these principles in all our affairs." The Step has three noteworthy parts. First, as with Step Eleven's "conscious contact," "a spiritual awakening" is not promised or encouraged but assumed, and it occurs "as the result of these steps." The word *awakening* was preferred to *experience* because the latter seemed "too religious," but early confusions led to the addition of an Appendix on "Spiritual Experience" in the second (March 1941) printing of the book *Alcoholics Anonymous*. Presenting spiritual awakening or experience as "the personality change sufficient to bring about recovery from alcoholism," the Appendix notes that it "has manifested itself among us in many different forms," but most often in "what the psychologist William James calls the 'educational variety' because they develop slowly over a period of time."[9]

The second part emphasizes "carrying this message"; note the specification of *this* message and the restriction of its constituency "to alcoholics." Derivative programs have had to vary this last phrase, but it is essential to Twelve-Step spirituality that the target be limited. To aim – implicitly or explicitly – at the whole human race is to miss the point and therefore the meaning of the Steps themselves. Accepting limitation is as essential to the spirituality of the program as it is to that of the individual, as A.A.'s Fifth and Tenth Traditions remind.[10]

Last comes the phrase Bill Wilson intended to use as the title of his book on A.A. spirituality, a work begun but never completed: "To practice these principles in all our affairs."[11] Note that as with "carrying this message," "practicing these principles" is something that "we *tried to*" do. A.A. wisdom recognizes a successful Twelfth-Step call to be one on which the caller does not drink: someone "powerless over alcohol" does not define success in terms of any ability to control another's drinking. Finally, as if to underline what became clear in Steps 4, 5, 6, 7, 8, and 10, there is the reminder that spirituality cannot be partial. By its nature, what is spiritual cannot be partly so, and thus its practice must be "in *all* our affairs." Nor is this only a traditional understanding as VanNess's "Introduction" to this volume makes clear. Such embracing inclusivity –

this sense of necessarily dealing with *wholes* – characterizes all expressions of spirituality, religious or secular.

The ideas and practices contained in these Twelve Steps are not new. The Twelve Steps of Alcoholics Anonymous represent – re-present, make present again – insights embedded in the classic spiritual traditions of the "Peoples of the Book." Those richer traditions do contain far more: as Wilson loved to remind, "A.A. is but a kindergarten of the spirit." A.A.'s earliest members rediscovered that thread of the ancient wisdom that has been called "The Spirituality of Imperfection."[12] In introducing the story of how they accomplished this rediscovery, and of the significance of their achievement, two facets of the first presentation of the Twelve Steps merit brief attention.

The book *Alcoholics Anonymous* presents the Twelve Steps in a chapter titled, "How It Works." That "how" is descriptive rather than analytic. What the chapter and the Steps promise, and deliver, is not the kind of technical explanation that allows for precise manipulation and controlled studies, but a simple description of how A.A.'s earliest members, obsessive-compulsive drinkers all, had been able to live constructively and even happily without drinking alcohol. Secondly, the Steps do tell *how* rather than "why." They do not explore causality. Instead, Twelve-Step spirituality brings a phenomenological approach to reflection on experience. It achieves this not least by remaining descriptive – for example, by encouraging the inventorying of self rather than the blaming of others. The vocabulary of the Steps attends to *one's own* "unmanageability," insanity, wrongs, shortcomings, defects of character. It lists the persons that *I* have harmed, not those who may have harmed me. Close by the Twelve Steps in the A.A. Big Book comes the reminder: "Resentment is the 'number one' offender. It destroys more alcoholics than anything else."[13] Twelve-Step spirituality does not perceive alcoholics as victims. Description, not ascription, is the task of the Steps.

The Story of the Twelve Steps

The Twelve Steps were formulated by Alcoholics Anonymous, which came into existence between 1935 and 1939. Although the early members of Alcoholics Anonymous developed these Steps from their own experience, broader forces shaped their interpretation of that experience. The story of that shaping is the story of the Twelve-Step program, the story of a spirituality conveyed precisely by the telling of stories. In telling their own story, the early members of Alcoholics Anonymous presented its program as deriving from "medicine, religion, and our own experience." Proximately, A.A. came into being out of what was at the time termed "The Oxford Group." That group's animus as well as its vision of itself seems best conveyed by both its first and its later names: the "The First Century Christian Fellowship" and "Moral Re-Armament."[14]

A.A.'s connection with the Oxford Group began when, sometime in 1931, Dr. Carl Jung told an alcoholic American that his only hope of cure lay in finding "a religious experience." Jung's patient, a businessman who never affiliated with Alcoholics Anonymous, joined the Oxford Group and eventually carried its (and Jung's) message to an alcoholic friend who in turn brought that message in late 1934 to his former drinking buddy, William Griffith Wilson.[15]

Wilson resisted the religious elements in his friend Ebby's news. Some weeks later, though, during his fourth hospitalized detoxification, Bill experienced the kind of spiritual awakening classically described by William James in *The Varieties of Religious Experience*, a book that the Oxford Group encouraged Wilson and those who followed him to read. In that book and in his physician's confirmation of the change Bill sensed in himself, he found both validation of his recent experience and a theologically-styled understanding of the "deflation at depth" that well described the experience of the middle-class alcoholic of that era.

At both Towns Hospital where he had been detoxified, and at a mission run by Calvary Episcopal Church, then the virtual headquarters of the Oxford Group, Wilson's early efforts to share his discovery proved fruitless. Then in May 1935, on a business trip to Akron, Ohio, Wilson found himself again obsessed with the desire to drink alcohol, a craving he had not experienced over the preceding five months. Reaching an Oxford Group member via the hotel church directory, Bill was invited to meet an alcoholic surgeon, Dr. Robert Holbrook Smith. When they met the next day, Wilson, somewhat awed at approaching "a man of science," told

Smith not of his spiritual "hot flash" nor his understanding of alcoholism as some kind of malady, but of his own experience of drinking and trying to not drink and especially of his own need, now, to talk to another alcoholic so that he would not drink this day.

Dr. Bob, who had been attending the Oxford Group for over two years as "a student of the spiritual" but who had nevertheless continued his alcoholic imbibing, heard in Bill's story both understanding and hope. Some weeks later, traveling to a medical convention in Atlantic City, Smith went on one last binge. Then on June 10, 1935, Dr. Bob Smith had his last drink – a bottle of beer given him by Wilson to steady his hand sufficiently to allow him to perform surgery. Members of Alcoholics Anonymous regard that date on which their second co-founder achieved sobriety as the birthday of their fellowship, the first Twelve-Step program.

"The alcoholic squadron" grew slowly within the Oxford Group until 1937 when the New York contingent left those auspices as too demanding, "too religious." In Akron, the connection lasted until 1939: separation occurred partly because of the discomfort of some Catholic alcoholics who deemed the Oxford Group "too Protestant." During this time, members spoke of their "word-of-mouth, twenty-four hour program." The Oxford Group used much popular religious literature, but none of it offered special instructions for alcoholics. By early 1938 many of the alcoholics felt the need to set down in writing what they had learned, and the decision was made to produce a book. In the course of drafting that book, eventually titled *Alcoholics Anonymous*, Bill Wilson one afternoon, in an "anything but spiritual mood," set out to scratch down "what we called 'the word-of--mouth program.' Though subject to considerable variation, it all boiled down into a pretty consistent procedure . . . ."[16]

Outlining that procedure, Wilson felt "that the program was still not definite enough." Seeking to be "more explicit," to leave "not a single loophole through which the rationalizing alcoholic could wriggle out," he decided that "our six chunks of truth should be broken up into smaller pieces . . . the better to get the distant reader over the barrel, and at the same time . . . to broaden and deepen the spiritual implications of our whole presentation." After scribbling for "perhaps half an hour," Bill paused at what seemed a stopping point to number the new steps. "They added up to twelve. Somehow this number seemed significant. Without any special rhyme or reason I connected them with the twelve apostles." Except for a few very minor changes, these are the Twelve Steps that come down to us.[17]

"Spiritual rather than religious"

The changes made to Wilson's first draft – replacing the word "God" in Step Two with "Power greater than ourselves," the addition of "as we understood Him" after the word "God" in Steps Three and Eleven, and the deletion of the phrase "on our knees" in Step Six – were forced by those members who found the original version "too religious." The early members of Alcoholics Anonymous liked to present "medicine and religion" as the source of their insights, claiming William James and Carl Jung as quasi-founders of their program, but the most important contribution to Alcoholics Anonymous of both Carl Jung and William James, as well as of the Oxford Group, was their openness to unconventional spirituality. This is expressed within not only Alcoholics Anonymous but virtually all other Twelve-Step groups in their presentation of their program as "spiritual rather than religious."[18]

The claim of A.A. (and derivative programs) to be "spiritual rather than religious" convinces few at first hearing. It is, after all, hardly original: most new religions begin by denying that they are new and/ or that they are religions. Twelve-Step programs, however, do come by the claim honestly, for they share the main motivation behind the assertion – the attempt to appeal to those alienated by what they think of as "religion." Most of the earliest targets – and members – of Alcoholics Anonymous had been raised in conventional religion but had abandoned its practice during their drinking years. Feeling condemned by practitioners of religion, they avoided religious settings. Still, many, their sober stories revealed, experienced a kind of shame over not being good enough for those realities. For many, but not all, such individuals, A.A.'s "kindergarten of the spirit" led to recommitment to formal religion.[19]

Later candidates for Twelve-Step programs brought different experiences and attitudes. Most came less versed in conventional religion but more alienated from it. For many of these, "spiritual rather than religious" served as a shibboleth permitting initial investigation. Also, for a time in 1970s and 1980s, the term 'spirituality' bore a positive connotation among especially those young people whose experimentation with chemical use led them to Twelve-Step settings.[20] There is another facet to the claim, "spiritual rather than religious." Spoken by an individual, it can signal a choice of the private that rejects the communal. One can seek spirituality by oneself, but religion is never a merely personal affair. As the word suggests, religion binds people to other people. At least one aspect of spiritual life can be found in solitude.[21]

This tendency was balanced within Alcoholics Anonymous itself by locating "the root of our troubles" in "self-centeredness" and discovering the importance of "fellowship" to its program. Some have reproached Twelve-Step groups for focusing attention inward. The criticism has validity, although it tends to ignore the very real distinction between "self-help" and "mutual-aid" – a difference as important as that between professional assistance and self-help. Genuine Twelve-Step groups are "self-help" in the sense that professionals as professionals have no role in them. On the other hand, emphasis on unmanageability, admitting fault, making amends, and relying on a "Power greater than ourselves" creates a setting of "mutual aid" rather than one of bootstrapping "self-help." The invitation is to outreach and connection.[22]

How do adherents to Twelve-Step programs understand "spiritual rather than religious"? Twelve-Step programs do offer a vision classically termed "religious." But expressions of religion historically seem to involve: (1) doctrines, which require belief; (2) rules, which command or prohibit actions; (3) and an institutional authority, which formulates the doctrines and enforces the rules; (4) worship and ritual, which express reverence for the professed source of all of the above, are also characteristic of religion.

Twelve-Step programs require none of these. Must members believe in God? Fifty plus years of A.A. experience suggests that the only belief necessary to sobriety is that one's self is not God, an admission that members who term themselves atheist or agnostic readily make. The only rule likely to be heard around Alcoholics Anonymous runs, "Don't drink and go to meetings" – far from imposing commandments for anyone inclined to claim membership. Authority? "Great suffering and great love are A.A.'s disciplinarians; we need no others. . . . We simply leave it to John Barleycorn." Groups do develop routines, in which outsiders may discern something similar to ritual, but one finds no semblance of worship.[23]

The concept of worship raises another point. Many associations, and not least religious societies, reveal a tendency to fall into a kind of self-worship – a conviction that "we" are somehow better than all the heathen "they"s. For members of Alcoholics Anonymous, the culture still sufficiently stigmatizes alcoholics so that anonymity continues to serve the purposes that begot its practice. Early A.A. members cherished anonymity because it protected them, attracted new recruits, and guarded the fellowship against the vagaries of some members. They soon discovered an even more important value, recognizing anonymity as a "spiritual ten-strike" because it restrained tendencies to grandiosity. Programs and groups that do not take anonymity seriously, that claim to be "Twelve-Step" without also being "Twelve-Tradition," thus lose what the Twelfth Tradition calls "the spiritual foundation." One benefit of the backlash against Twelve-Step programs may be a revival of that awareness.[24]

Spiritual rather than Material: The Experience of Addiction

More important than the "spiritual rather than religious" contrast proclaimed by Twelve-Step rhetoric is the spiritual-as-other-than-material distinction lived out in Twelve-Step practice. That the first Twelve-Step program was Alcoholics Anonymous is no accident. The tradition out of which the Twelve Steps grew saw the greatest threat to "the spiritual" not in "the material," but in the tendency to confuse the material with the spiritual – a confusion reified in the inability to recognize **enough**, the precise condition that renders alcoholism such an apt metaphor for that confusion.

Dr. Carl Jung's presentation of alcoholism as an instance of *spiritus contra spiritum* – spirits warring against the spiritual – aptly captured that sense.[25] This vision posits the distinction between the spiritual and the material as fundamental: the very word 'spiritual' onomatopoeically conveys that it is other-than-material. Like breath or breeze, the spiritual is experienced in its effects but not directly seen. It can never be owned, bought, or sold. This distinction, though, implies no condemnation of the material. The incarnational insight of mainline western spirituality recognizes material reality as a vehicle for the spiritual – as reality to be rejoiced in, but also to be respected – for it bears a potential for danger not least because of the power of its connection with the spiritual.

The attitude to beverage alcohol held by most members of Alcoholics Anonymous, especially in the context of A.A.'s 1930s origins, affords a useful illustration. Locating alcoholism in the alcoholic rather than in the alcohol, in the human being rather than in the bottle, displeased Prohibitionists even as it mollified the alcoholic beverage industry, but neither was the intention of early A.A. members. They were rather reflecting the classic spiritual insight that "sin" resided not in creation but in what people did with it. Some members even describe their alcoholism as a kind of *felix culpa*, expressing gratitude even for being alcoholic, because, as they see it, only the depths of their alcoholism made it possible for them to find the heights of serene sobriety.

Materialism has another facet, as the ongoing story of Twelve-Step programs attests: there lurks always the danger of another kind of confusion of the spiritual with the material, the peril that an expression of spirituality will itself become commodity – an item of commerce, a vehicle for greed. Early Alcoholics Anonymous was not immune to this tendency. Wilson located the beginning of the fellowship's "group conscience" in members' opposition to what they saw as the danger of his "selling the program" if he accepted a proffered employment opportunity in the hospital where he had been detoxified. Among many such pulls towards entrepreneurial endeavors, A.A.'s early experience hammered out what became its traditions of singleness of purpose, non-involvement in outside enterprises, and self-support. By establishing these traditions A.A. avoided the trap of becoming itself a commodity.[26]

But among some groups too glibly labelled "Twelve-Step," programs that ignore the Twelve Traditions, matters developed differently. Often shaped by professional therapies for addictions ever more broadly conceived, these in time formed what came to be called the "Recovery Movement." Although that term may include programs that remain true to Twelve-Step insight, most movement groups, as the term suggests, show little respect for or even awareness of the Twelve Traditions. The story of how Twelve-Step programs gave rise to such groups affords a modern example of how a secular spirituality, like a religious spirituality, can cease to be spiritual when it becomes a commodity.

The Commodification of the Twelve Steps

Because of A.A.'s centrality in the story of Twelve-Step programs, the process by which recovery programs became commodities is best seen within the history of Alcoholics Anonymous. That development may be outlined in three phases: 1935-1955, 1956-1976, 1977-present. From the time of A.A.'s conception in 1935 through its self-proclaimed "Coming of Age" in 1955, members sought cultural acceptance, pursuing this goal as a way of reaching more alcoholics. Paths tried but not taken included affiliating with the National Council for Education on Alcoholism and sacrificing anonymity for the sake of promotion. In both cases, grass-roots member reactions shaped what by 1950 became the Traditions of nonaffiliation with outside enterprises and anonymity as a "spiritual foundation." Most A.A. members found acceptance best attained by emphasizing their program's respectful connections with medicine and religion, professions at the time viewed as altruistic.

Largely because it carefully eschewed being mistaken for either therapy or theology, Alcoholics Anonymous not only attained the cooperation of medical and religious professionals but avoided being co-opted by either group. It achieved this by (largely implicitly) playing the one off against the other. Echoes of a science vs. religion debate still resonated in the 1940s, and while that led some in each camp – medicine and religion – to write off Alcoholics Anonymous as belonging to the opposition, it enabled A.A. itself to fend off a too smothering an embrace by either group. Members remained aware of their debts to both.

1955 marks a turning point because not only did A.A. itself celebrate its "Coming of Age," but that twentieth anniversary gathering was honored by a message from U.S. President Dwight Eisenhower, who echoed the praise accorded Alcoholics Anonymous by the American Public Health Association, which had earlier bestowed upon A.A. its Lasker Award.

During its second twenty years, from 1956 to 1976, Alcoholics Anonymous developed organizational stability, smoothly handling what could have been a major hazard to continuity – the death in 1971 of longer-lived co-founder Bill Wilson. This period also witnessed a shift from the organization being merely accepted to being positively valued. In a world that sought the personal salvation of peace of mind from advice columnists and religious popularizers, endorsement by such luminaries brought considerable prominence. Alcoholics Anonymous passed the test. The high point of Twelve-Step program respectability likely occurred in 1976-1977, when Presidential spouse Betty Ford and actors Jason Robards and Mary Tyler Moore – though carefully saying nothing about A.A. affiliation – spoke openly of their alcoholism in a vocabulary that listeners understood reflected the Twelve-Step way of life.[27]

The period after 1977 brought the developments that require distinguishing between those programs and groups that focus on living the Twelve Steps, and programs and groups that, though they may have adopted some Twelve-Step elements, actually oriented their practice elsewhere. One reason for the respect accorded A.A. by the professions of medicine and religion was the fellowship's acceptance of its own limitations. Claiming to be neither medicine nor religion, A.A. threatened neither. But the acceptance of its own limitations as a fellowship – an acceptance that aptly paralleled the individual alcoholic's acceptance of the limitation implicit in the admission, "I am an alcoholic," – bore ambiguous fruit. On the one hand, it was the reason why other Twelve-Step groups formed: Alcoholics Anonymous members claimed no competence in anything other than their own alcoholism. On the other hand, this awareness, to which so many other groups owed their inspiration, did not always attract their imitation.

As the example of A.A.'s first offspring, Al-Anon (a Twelve-Step program for spouses and others who love an alcoholic) attested as early as the 1950s, the Twelve-Step way of life could be helpfully applied to difficulties other than alcoholism. In that decade and the next, groups of people stigmatized for other obsessive-compulsive behaviors, notably gamblers and over-eaters, quietly adopted and adapted for their own conditions the Twelve Steps – and the Twelve Traditions – set forth by Alcoholics Anonymous. Each group applied the program to its own particular disability, recognizing that though the Twelve Steps make available a way of life livable by all, entry into that way of life comes only through the doorway of a specifically experienced powerlessness. In the 1970s, two complicatedly related changes occurred, changes that eventually affected not only A.A.'s offspring and imitators, but also the way people understood the term *Twelve-Step program*. The two changes concerned the notions of alcoholism-as-disability and alcohol-as-drug.

Under the umbrella afforded by civil rights legislation, the "Hughes Act" of 1970 and additional laws passed in 1973 and 1978 sought to aid alcoholics by moving public policy, if not attitudes, toward understanding alcoholism as a disability meriting the same consideration as others. These acts broadened and in some cases mandated opportunities for treatment, and a new industry soon sprang into being. Early A.A. had made use of "drying out" facilities. Following Dr. Bob Smith's example, members from the beginning sought hospital admission for the medical detoxification of those who needed such care. Over time, halfway houses emerged for the more severely impaired, and a few treatment settings developed – usually carefully nonmedical – staffed and supported by members of Alcoholics Anonymous who undertook these efforts largely for the sake of their own sobriety, as a part of their Twelfth-Step work.

When the new laws broadened funding for treatment, a slow evolution in practice became a mad race for money. What had been largely a labor of love – and in some settings remained so – became in others mainly a way of making money, as wider cultural awareness and legislatively mandated insurance coverage combined to create a fruit ripe for plucking. Critics pointed out that the consistent bane of spirituality, greed, seemed to guide many who now clothed their projects in Twelve-Step language. A.A. applied the pragmatic phrase "whatever works" to staying away from the first drink. Some of the new treatment providers applied the maxim to developing new "products" and manipulating diagnoses. Before long,

160

some who worked in treatment found themselves queried more often about "the bottom line" than about "quality sobriety." Many of the most effective, those most experienced in spiritual service, moved to other settings or even other fields. Before long also, some funders of care – governments, companies, insurers – began to suspect that they were being defrauded. Reacting against the abuses, some began to view all recovery programs as rip-offs, rejecting anything that smacked of the Twelve-Step programs with which they associated this experience.[28]

The second significant 1970s occurrence was the recrudescence of American twentieth-century "reefer madness" – the discovery of apparently rampant use of psychoactive chemicals, or in the common shorthand, "drugs." Medical historian David Musto has termed addiction "The American Disease." When drugs are mentioned, few think of ethyl alcohol, but, using the concept of "chemical dependency," many in the treatment industry labored to change that understanding to meet the reality that public opinion (and funding sources) showed more concern over drug addiction than over alcohol abuse. Recognition of the relationship between the two had been present in Alcoholics Anonymous since at least 1944, when an alcoholic physician, interned in the federal facility at Lexington, Kentucky, wrote to *The Grapevine* proposing a "Hopheads Corner" within Alcoholics Anonymous, for members also addicted to "other chemicals." This understanding served well for over three decades. Narcotics Anonymous was begun, in Lexington, by A.A. members reaching out to their fellow drug addicts who were not alcoholics.[29]

The exigencies of treatment – and the realities of funding – changed perceptions as well as practices. Recognizing that treatment did not cure addiction, for what "cure" took place occurred in the ongoing practice that was recovery, some treatment providers began encouraging their ever broader population of clients to attend A.A. meetings, even if they were not alcoholics. Another new and different population arrived as judges increasingly began to sentence drunk driving offenders to attendance at Alcoholics Anonymous meetings.

Individual groups in A.A.'s decentralized fellowship reacted variously. Some agreed, some refused, to sign (preferably initial) court attendance slips. Some began meetings with the request that those who had no desire to stop drinking leave or remain silent, and/or that those who had problems other than alcohol speak only of their alcohol-related difficulties in this setting. Others held closed (for admitted alcoholics only) and open (to anyone interested) meetings in different rooms in the same building, referring newcomers to the latter. Still other groups divided, some members leaving to found a new group either more public or more private than the setting that had provoked their departure. A.A.'s General Service Office, drawing on the experience of the groups, developed "Guidelines" for "Cooperating with Court, A.S.A.P. and Similar Programs"; most legal authorities were happy to work within them.[30] Although similar guidelines were suggested for treatment settings, cooperation proved more difficult in this more complex area. Some professionals who worked with alcoholics and addicts had entered the rapidly expanding field hastily and lacked real knowledge of Twelve-Step programs. Sometimes they made inappropriate referrals. To meet that problem, which increased as the multiplication of addictions and treatments swelled the number of Recovery Movement candidates, other professionals, as well as the victims themselves, formed new groups.

Many of these groups, especially those concerned with what came to be called "process addictions," tried to cling to the Twelve-Step style, but their actual practice often moved away from Twelve-Step insight. Cut off from the Twelve Traditions, some programs adopted professional ideology, rejecting the telling of stories of "experience, strength, and hope" for the satisfactions of analyzing the past in the categories of therapy. Others seemed to foster visions of self-as-victim, attracting criticism that added tar to the already forming backlash against anything that smacked of "Twelve-Step." As more than one observer noted, some of the new groups offered less a Twelve-Step program than a ready-made market for pushers of "recovery" paraphernalia.[31]

By the 1990s, the situation seemed hopelessly confused. On the one hand, the term "Twelve-Step" came laden with connotations of self-pity, narcissism, and greed. On the other hand, many continued to find in various Twelve-Step programs vehicles for a spirituality that even outsiders recognized as real. "If you have decided you want what we have," runs A.A.'s introduction to the Twelve Steps. One description of spirituality suggests that it is that which, when I see it in another, I want some of it, and if I get it, my participation in it enhances rather than diminishes that other's own participation and joy in it. Another description, noting the frequent use of the words 'insight' and 'vision' in speaking of spirituality, suggests that it involves not so much seeing different things as seeing things differently – the ability to recognize in reality more than that which can be owned or coveted.

Both descriptions well fit A.A.'s understanding of sobriety, the Twelve-Step mark of spiritual well-being. Such a reality will always be a mystery, a paradox, and not least because it comes in different forms. The very variety of Twelve-Step programs and their members, no less than the variety of saints revered by tradition, reminds that there is no one way to be spiritual. This is perhaps the key insight mediated by the actual experience of the first Twelve-Step program, Alcoholics Anonymous.

Twelve-Step Spirituality

Variety and paradox: Twelve-Step programs came into being in Akron, Ohio, when a visiting New York hustler sought out a local alcoholic physician. Although Akron remained a hub of A.A. activity, New York soon became the new fellowship's main center. Differences between Akron and New York A.A. appeared early on, as opinions varied about the word 'God' in the Steps and the use of the Oxford Group "Four Absolutes." The differing emphases were passed on as the young fellowship spread, but they remained largely latent until later decades brought the wider mobility of a more numerous membership and the gaudier borrowings of the Twelve-Step mantle. The chief difference, from the beginning, as the examples suggest, concerned how members understood "the spiritual."

Although some observers interpreted this divergence in terms of the stereotypes of urban sophistication vs. heartland wholesomeness, members in both regions reflected each view. The distinction was more accurately between those perhaps best termed the "transcendentally inclined," who viewed the spiritual as somehow *other* and whose vocabulary tended to echo that of traditional theology, and the "immanentists," for whom the spiritual pervades all reality, and whose vocabulary, although less common in the 1940s and 1950s, fits far better both ancient mystical traditions and recent cultural fashions.[32]

For the first forty years of the history of Twelve-Step programs, both these approaches were evident, each respectful of the other. That balancing of the two visions, which was an important factor in shaping the Twelve-Step insight, can be studied in Bill Wilson's *A.A. Grapevine* articles. Whether because of Wilson's loss or, more likely, because of the impact of what have been termed the "Culture Wars," mutual respect and balancing compromise between the transcendent and immanent spiritual approaches, as well as between therapeutic and spiritual emphases, began in the late 1970s to give way to increasing polarization among programs claiming the Twelve-Step mantle. These divisions, though, ignore the essence of Twelve-Step spirituality, which involves finding a way of living with incongruity, a way to embrace paradox.[33]

The Paradox of Twelve-Step Spirituality

The story of Twelve-Step programs suggests that a spirituality, to be recognized as genuine in a secular age, must enable the bridging of difference, the embrace of paradox. Twelve-Step spirituality began with the then-revolutionary discovery that "sober" and "alcoholic" could be both/and rather than either-or. Similarly, so long as they bridged medicine and religion without claiming to be either, so long as they mediated both transcendent and immanent spiritual understandings, Twelve-Step programs helped participants to attain some kind of spirituality and were acknowledged as effective even by many who did not participate in them.

When some imitators deviated from that Twelve-Step insight to become either a form of therapy or a mode of New Age religion, they lost respect not least because they lost effectiveness. There is nothing wrong – indeed, there is much right – with both therapy and religion accurately labeled, but it abuses both to present either as the other, or to recognize insufficiently their distinction from one another. The Twelve Traditions protect the Twelve Steps from such confusion of spirituality or religion with therapy. They do this by implanting an acceptance of limitation, which encourages respect for difference. These complementary attitudes clear a space within which the realities of paradox may be lived. Programs that ignore the Traditions tend to reject paradox; most seem also to slip away from first the vocabulary, and then the practice, of the Twelve Steps.

Twelve-Step spirituality began not only in the admission of "powerlessness" and "unmanageability" but in the acceptance and embrace of the paradoxical identity "sober alcoholic." In finding in *paradox* a key to spirituality, Twelve-Step programs reclaimed a tradition perhaps too glibly dismissed in an era intolerant of mystery and mistrustful of anything that cannot be explained and controlled. Twelve-Step programs offer an arena for, and a way of, living with the paradoxes embodied in one's own life. To be a "sober alcoholic" – a term originally shocking that has become overfamiliar and even banal – is to accept that one lives not only with but *in* paradox.

Twelve-Step programs offer a spirituality of paradox. The stories told at meetings evidence that and how these programs inculcate experiences of release, gratitude, humility, tolerance, and forgiveness. Each involves paradox. Release's freedom comes only to those who "let go." The vision that is gratitude – the recognition of how generously one has received – is given only to those who give of themselves. Humility accepts that living humanely, like being a "sober alcoholic," involves accepting the reality of being both/and rather than claiming or demanding to be either-or. Tolerance of others' weaknesses flows from confronting one's own flaws. The ability to forgive comes only out of the experience of being forgiven. These experiences, paradoxes all, hallmark and even constitute Twelve-Step spirituality.

Living in paradox involves accepting the tragic as well as the joyous. "The chiefest sanctity of a temple is that it is a place to which people go to weep in common," Unamuno wrote. Twelve-Step programs provide such temples. An age that views all suffering as merely evil and a culture frustrated by ambiguity and dominated by a technology intolerant of paradox find such temples threatening, as some criticisms of Twelve-Step groups make clear. Yet weeping is not moaning – a distinction sometimes ignored. In theological terms, what the critics protest is the seeming promise of "cheap grace" or, in a more secular vocabulary, "soft science": the point is the same. Just as bought love ceases to be love, so too do spirituality that can be sold and science that can be merchandised lose their unique natures. Those who glibly explain mystery and who confuse miracle with magic merit challenge. Such tendencies lurk in all, and perhaps especially in those who are spiritual. Twelve-Step experience suggests that only those who recognize that they themselves have *both* wept in tragedy *and* moaned in self-pity have standing to point out that difference to others.[34]

Twelve-Step Spirituality as Metaphor

A spirituality that embraces paradox will be sensitive to metaphor. Twelve-Step programs have significantly influenced the metaphors in which twentieth-century people understand deviant behaviors. Examining these metaphors thus illumines both the rise and the apparent decline of Twelve-Step programs as vehicles of spirituality. The medicalization of deviance marks a main characteristic of advancing modernity: those who act contrary to social norms come to be thought of as "sick" rather than as "sinners." Twelve-Step programs played a two-phased role in this development, not only advancing that change but advancing beyond it.

First, although it is not true that Alcoholics Anonymous teaches that alcoholism is a disease, for such teaching would violate A.A.'s Tradition on "outside issues," their experience led many A.A. members, and others, to move from the moral toward a medical model of alcoholism and other addictions. Secondly, however, in its presentation of the alcoholic as suffering from physical, mental, emotional, and spiritual disability – and especially in its emphasis on spiritual issues – the Twelve-Step approach broadened the medical model in a holistic direction.

Groups untrammeled by A.A.'s Twelve Traditions even more avidly promoted medical explanations of their deviant behaviors. In doing so, some abandoned holistic understanding for legal advantage. How we speak shapes how we think, and so the shift from the language of common experience to the vocabulary of professional therapy had larger ramifications. The Twelve Steps made available in modern terms an ancient spiritual tradition – the core Greco-Judaeo-Christian insights that shaped Western civilization. A.A.'s early imitators – Al-Anon, Gamblers Anonymous – hewed close to that tradition, adapting it as necessary, but retaining such insights of the classic spirituality as the centrality of the danger of pride, the embrace of imperfection and a delight in paradox.

The shift from the Twelve Steps to therapy can be seen as early as Charles Dederick's founding of Synanon in 1958. Synanon and other programs for users of illegal drugs usually presented themselves honestly, as something other than Twelve-Step programs. They claimed to go beyond the Twelve-Step approach; Dederick, for example, opined that comparing A.A. to Synanon was like comparing a rowboat to an airplane.[35] Some of these non-Twelve-Step programs hew closer to Twelve-Step practice than do some newer phenomena that present themselves as Twelve-Step programs. Many (but not all) "adult children" and "codependency" associations, for example, run directly contrary to Twelve-Step insight. The reliance on a literature produced by quasi-professionals has led to preferring the vocabulary of therapy to the language of spirituality and to analyzing the past in ways more redolent of 1930s psychotherapies than of any recognizable tradition of spirituality.

Twelve-Step programs are, of course, not the only kind of spirituality – not even the only kind of recovery spirituality. Openness to paradox does not mean that Twelve-Step spirituality lacks a distinctive character. A.A. literature delineates a spirituality conveyed by the telling of stories of "experience, strength and hope" – stories that "disclose in a general way what we used to be like, what happened, and what we are like now." It is on this basis that the Twelve Steps are presented, as the very next sentence of "How It Works" invites: "If you have decided you want what we have and are willing to go to any length to get it – then you are ready to take certain steps." Groups that center their practice on "sharing what things are like and how we feel about that" do not offer the same program. They may provide great therapeutic benefits and even valid spiritual consolation, but the change from "we" to "things" and the shift from deciding and willing to feeling: these are not unsubstantial variations.

Individualism and Community

Two final topics deepen insight into the workings of Twelve-Step programs and aid in distinguishing Twelve-Step spirituality from ersatz imitators. Twelve-Step programs both subvert and foster *individualism*. The resulting ambiguous relationship to *community* is resolved by the way members understand their participation in these programs.

The Great Depression of the 1930s marked the nadir of the deepest American faith – confidence in individual autonomy, in the power of each individual to be "the master of my fate, the captain of my soul." The decade that gave rise to industrial unionism understood that acknowledging a need for others need not signal weakness or aberration.

The "we"-ness of the admission of individual powerlessness, the insistence on needing others implicit in the Fifth, Ninth, Tenth, and Twelfth Steps, the fellowship of the meetings that even the A.A. Big Book did not anticipate: these subverted the ideology of radical individualism and the patterns of thinking that sustained it. Personal situations as well as social conditions attested that the old individualistic ideology was no longer tenable. A.A.'s revolutionary contribution was not medical diagnosis of the "disease" of alcoholism but its insistence that the most important reality in the life of any alcoholic, sobriety, could not be attained alone. One needed an-other, whether that "other" was understood as other people or as some kind of more remote Higher Power. If "the root of our troubles" is "self-centeredness," its uprooting begins with the acknowledgment that there *is* a "power greater than ourselves."

Yet such an understanding, even as it ostensibly subverts individualism, appeals to a specifically Protestant "Higher Power." Contact with that "Power greater" is unmediated: Alcoholics Anonymous is neither a church nor a people. A.A.'s Twelve-Step approach thus undermined individualism in a very individualistic way. An opening to community emerges in the Twelve Traditions, but the Traditions protect community very gingerly. The First Tradition recognizes its importance by reminding that "Our common welfare should come first; personal recovery depends upon A.A. unity." The Third Tradition enshrines A.A.'s powerlessness to restrict its own community by establishing that "The only requirement for

A.A. membership is a desire to stop drinking" – an internal reality almost impossible to gainsay.

What about the larger community? Do Twelve-Step programs deflect people from responsibility, from working to change conditions that cause suffering? Twelve-Step insight does incline toward the strategy of improving reality outside self by first improving the reality of one's self, as opposed to an approach that seeks to improve self by changing outside reality. But in a way of life that embraces paradox, this is a matter of both/and, not either-or. The Serenity Prayer, so cherished by A.A. members, asks: "Grant me the serenity to accept the things I cannot change, the courage to change the things I can, and the wisdom to know the difference." Criticisms along this line assume that basing affiliation on awareness of a shared flaw will discourage social action. Such an assumption ignores history: many movements committed to changing the world have "founded their sense of internal community on an ideology of common sinfulness and weakness."[36]

"An ideology of common sinfulness and weakness" implies something more about the cohesion of community, offering another useful way of distinguishing Twelve-Step programs from imitators that have abandoned the vision of those Steps. What is the basis on which an individual takes part? Does one join this group and participate in its program because one needs to, or because one "wants to" do so? In the community created by and within Twelve-Step programs, one participates not because one wants to, but because one *needs to*. Early A.A. members, for example, saw the choices available to the actively drinking alcoholic to be "abstinence, insanity, or death," and their experience suggested that at least some alcoholics were able to abstain only within the fellowship of Alcoholics Anonymous.

This distinction between the style of community created by Twelve-Step programs composed of those who *need to* belong, and the "self-help" mode of "sharing and caring" groups available for those who *want to* join them, returns us to the core of Twelve-Step spirituality, the sense of powerlessness. Alcoholics are not the only ones who "hit bottom," and so here again we find not some clean-cut either-or but instead a slippery spectrum of both/and. Any group that styles itself "Twelve-Step" or "self-help" will likely contain some individuals who profess that they are there by choice, and others who attest that they are present out of necessity. It nevertheless remains true that the more closely any program adheres to A.A.'s original Steps and Traditions, the more numerous will be those who say they participate not because they want to, but because they have to.

Twelve-Step programs and their offspring rehearse in capsule form a common process in the history of spiritual insight. There may be no Second Law of Spiritual Thermodynamics that leads inevitably to the entropy of the Sheilaism described in Robert Bellah's *Habits of the Heart*; but at least within the mainstream tradition of which Twelve-Step programs are a part, it is a common phenomenon that the sense that one is being drawn to or compelled by some larger reality becomes for later generations the judgment that one chooses and decides for oneself.[37] Programs that remain true to the Twelve Steps and Twelve Traditions seem able to retain a traditional qualification of the individualism inherent in the tradition: awareness that one needs others for one's own very survival substantially limits any sense of absolute individual autonomy.

Final Reflections

Several themes recur in the story of Twelve-Step programs, inviting thought. One wonders, for example, whether it is preferable to be "sick" or to be a "sinner." As R.D. Laing noted concerning the term *mental illness*, changing the name of a reality is less likely to change our understanding of that reality than it is to change our understanding of the name. An age acutely sensitive to pain has, ironically, multiplied stigmata.

Second, must the broadening of a spiritual insight lead inevitably to its loss? Oxford Group historian Walter Houston Clark thought that this eventually happened to the Oxford Group, suggesting that A.A.'s departure from that organization's auspices had allowed it to avoid a similar fate. The new program's insistent singleness of purpose in accepting the limitation of dealing only with alcoholics reflected awareness of the danger. As Bill Wilson later summed up: "Most of all, the Oxford Group taught us what *not* to do."[38] Spiritualities always exist in some material context. In time, the core Twelve-Step insight of accepting limitation became attenuated not only in imitators but even within the A.A. fellowship itself, as the very decentralization that preserved it from professionalization became the avenue for its corruption by commodification. Many both within and outside of A.A. resist this trend, and so this part of the story continues, albeit differently in diverse Twelve-Step settings.

Finally, it is fitting in an age of language theory that the uses and misuses of metaphor – and specifically of addiction as metaphor – summarize the story of the spirituality of Twelve-Step programs. From A.A. members' recognition of their own experience in Carl Jung's portrayal of alcoholism as a warring of *spiritus contra spiritum*, to the vision that sees virtually every activity as some kind of addiction, there runs a tortuous but real trail.

Twelve-Step programs have to do with spirituality because they have to do with addiction. Only when it is recognized that addiction is *more than* metaphor can addiction *as* metaphor work. Because those who have experienced actual addiction know its reality, they can translate that metaphor. The traditional spirituality of the Western world, from which the insight of the Twelve-Step programs derives, recognized *materialism* – the fixation on quantity, on *more* – as the ultimate expression of the core sin of self-centeredness. Related to this sin is the claim to be oneself the center of the universe or God. Perhaps only a culture capable of questioning its own materialism can produce and sustain individuals who find in Twelve-Step programs a vehicle of spirituality.

NOTES

1. Peter Steinfels, "Clerics wonder whether religion can learn lessons from recovery programs for addicts," *The New York Times*, April 28 1990.

2. Wendy Kaminer, *I'm Dysfunctional, You're Dysfunctional* (Reading, Mass.: Addison-Wesley, 1992); Charles J. Sykes, *A Nation of Victims* (New York: St. Martin's, 1992).

3. Bill W[ilson], *Twelve Steps and Twelve Traditions* (New York: A.A. World Services, 1953), 21-22.

4. John E. Mack, "Alcoholism, A.A., and the Governance of the Self," in *Dynamic Approaches to the Understanding and Treatment of Alcoholism*, eds. Norman E. Zinberg, and Margaret H. Bean (New York: Free Press, 1981), 128-162; Edward J. Khantzian and John E. Mack, "Alcoholics Anonymous and Contemporary Psychodynamic Theory," in *Recent Developments in Alcoholism*: vol. 7 of *Treatment Research*, ed. Marc Galanter (New York: Plenum Press, 1989), 67-89.

5. For an analysis of A.A. in these terms, see the writings of Harry M. Tiebout, especially "Therapeutic Mechanisms of Alcoholics Anonymous," *American Journal of Psychiatry* 100 (1944): 468-473; "The Act of Surrender in the Therapeutic Process," *Quarterly Journal of Studies on* 10 (1949): 48-58; "Surrender vs. Compliance in Therapy," *Quarterly Journal of Studies on Alcohol*, 14 (1953): 58-68; and "The Ego Factor in Surrender in Alcoholism," *Quarterly Journal of Studies on Alcohol*, 15 (1954): 610-621.

6. W[ilson], *Twelve Steps and Twelve Traditions*, 63.

7. A.A. members affectionately refer to the book, *Alcoholics Anonymous*, as the "Big Book." The term originated when those who produced it, hoping to convince depression-era drunks that the $3.50 book was worth purchasing, asked its printer to "use the heaviest paper he could find," so that the book would be literally weighty. World War II rules on paper use required changing to more economical stock, but the name stuck.

8. Alasdair MacIntyre, *After Virtue* (Notre Dame, Ind.: Univ. of Notre Dame, 1981), chap. 14; also see the editor's "Introduction" to this volume.

9. *Alcoholics Anonymous* (New York: A.A. World Services, 1976), 569.

10. According to Wilson's explanation of why Alcoholics Anonymous left the Oxford Group, this acceptance of limitation was the reason why A.A. came into being: "The Oxford Group wanted to save the world. I only wanted to save the drunks." Wilson (New

York) to McGhee B., 30 October 1940). A.A.'s Fifth Tradition is: "Each group has but one primary purpose -- to carry its message to the alcoholic who still suffers;" and its Tenth Tradition reads: "Alcoholics Anonymous has no opinion on outside issues; hence the A.A. name ought never be drawn into public controversy."

11. For the story of this effort, and its traces, see: Ernest Kurtz and Katherine Ketcham, *The Spirituality of Imperfection* (New York: Bantam, 1992), 130-131.

12. *Ibid.*; Kurtz and Ketcham directly explore Twelve-Step spirituality. For the wider context, see: Simon Tugwell, *Ways of Imperfection* (Springfield, Ill.: Templegate, 1985).

13. *Alcoholics Anonymous*, 64.

14. Walter Houston Clark, *The Oxford Group: Its History and Significance* (New York: Bookman Associates, 1952), 35.

15. Ernest Kurtz, *Not-God: A History of Alcoholics Anonymous* (Center City, Minn.: Hazelden, 1979); this is the most fully documented presentation of A.A.'s history. It should be supplemented with two A.A. publications, *Alcoholics Anonymous Comes of Age* (New York: A.A.W.S., 1957) and *Pass It On* (New York: A.A.W.S., 1984); also by Bill Pittman, *A.A.: The Way It Began* (Seattle, Wash.: Glen Abbey Books, 1988).

16. *Alcoholics Anonymous Comes of Age*, 160-161.

17. For the original version of the Twelve Steps, with a more detailed discussion of the changes, see: Kurtz, *Not-God*, 70-71.

18. In 1961 Wilson wrote to Jung telling the Swiss psychiatrist of his role in A.A.'s origins. Jung's reply indicated familiarity with Alcoholics Anonymous and offered a directly spiritual understanding of alcoholism and recovery from it. This correspondence, slightly edited, appears in *The A.A. Grapevine* issues of January 1963 and 1968 and in *The Language of the Heart* (New York: A.A. Grapevine, Inc., 1988), 276-281.

19. The stories in the first and second editions of *Alcoholics Anonymous* attest to this; Wilson himself had an unconventional religious upbringing and never affiliated with any denomination.

20. Aldous Huxley, *Moksha* (Los Angeles: J.P. Tarcher, 1977).

21. The problem was stated by St. Basil who noted that "the defect of the solitary life was that it provided no opportunity to practice the virtues of humility and patience or to perform the practical works of mercy -- 'If you live alone, whose feet will you wash?'"; Clifford Hugh Lawrence, *Medieval Monasticism: Forms of Religious Life in Western Europe in the Middle Ages* (London: Longman, 1989 [1984]), 10.

22.   Most A.A. members strenuously deny that their program is one of "self-help"; the usual comment runs: "Self-help . . . we tried that, and it didn't work; that's why we're a God-help program."

Some recent imitators, wandering from Twelve-Step insight, can seem to foster self-centeredness by suggesting that involvements with others are their adherents' problem.   The emblem of "Co-Dependents Anonymous, Inc." that appears on its literature, "To Thine Own Self Be True," illustrates the point – perhaps especially for those aware of the line's context in *Hamlet*. The other words on the emblem are "Discovery, Recovery, Self, Respect [Self-Respect?]". Compare this with the terms on the A.A. emblem imitated: "Recovery, Unity, Service." A.A. specifies its "Third Legacy" as "Service," and in 1965 made a commitment to "The Declaration," which pledges: "I Am Responsible."

23. *Alcoholics Anonymous Comes of Age*, 120; W[ilson], *Twelve Steps and Twelve Traditions*, 178; also Kurtz, *Not-God*, 108.

The language and practice of some A.A. groups has led to the formation of "Rational Recovery" groups and "Secular Organizations for Sobriety"; see James Christopher, *How to Stay Sober: Recovery Without Religion* (Buffalo, N.Y.: Prometheus Books, 1988). Such groups, which do not claim to offer a Twelve-Step program, have thus far drawn few members; on atheists and agnostics and the Twelve Steps, see: Jon R. Weinberg, *A.A.: An Interpretation for the Nonbeliever* (Center City, Minn.: Hazelden, 1975).

24. Wilson, "Our Anonymity Is Both Inspiration and Safety," *A.A. Grapevine* (March 1946) and "Why Alcoholics Anonymous is Anonymous," *A.A. Grapevine* (January 1955); both are reprinted in *The Language of the Heart*, 16-20, 209-218.

25. The letter from Jung (Zurich) to Wilson, 30 January 1961, has been frequently reproduced, e.g.: *The Language of the Heart: Bill W.'s Grapevine Writings* (New York: A.A. Grapevine, Inc., 1988), 280-281.

26. W[ilson], *Twelve Steps and Twelve Traditions*, 140-142; The traditions referred to here are 5, 6, and 7: "5. Each group has but one primary purpose --to carry its message to the alcoholic who still suffers. 6. An A.A. group ought never endorse, finance, or lend the A.A. name to any related facility or outside enterprise, lest problems of money, property, and prestige divert us from our primary purpose. 7. Every A.A. group ought to be fully self-supporting, declining outside contributions."

27. Betty Ford, *The Times of My Life* (New York: Harper & Row, 1978).

28. See, for example: Stanton Peele, *The Diseasing of America: Addiction Treatment Out of Control* (Lexington, Mass.: Lexington Books, 1989).

29. Letter from "Doc N.," *The Grapevine*, 1. 3 (August 1944); see also the letter from "Doc M." of Shelby, N.C., in the following issue.

30.   There are fifteen sets of such "Guidelines": lists and order forms for all A.A. literature may be obtained from A.A. World Services, Inc., 475 Riverside Drive, New York, N.Y. 10115; "A.S.A.P." = Alcohol Safety Action Programs, which were eepecially popular among police forces in this era.

31. The literature is vast, but a good beginning would include Tadeusz Gierymski and Terence Williams, "Codependency," *Journal of Psychoactive Drugs* 18:1 (1986), 7-13; William R. Miller, "Adult Cousins of Alcoholics," *Psychology of Addictive Behaviors* 1:1 (1987), 74-76; Edith S. Lisansky Gomberg, "On Terms Used and Abused: The Concept of 'Codependency,'" Edith S. Lisansky Gomberg (ed.), *Current Issues in Alcohol/Drug Studies* (New York: Haworth, 1989), 113-132; Rick A. Myer *et al.*, "Co-dependency: An Examination of Underlying Assumptions," *Journal of Mental Health Counseling*, 13:4 (1991) 449-458.
     Robin Room, "Alcoholics Anonymous as a Social Movement," Barbara S. McCrady and William R. Miller (eds.), *Research on Alcoholics Anonymous: Opportunities and Alternatives* (New Brunswick, N.J.: Rutgers Center for Alcohol Studies, 1993), 167-187; this text specifically delineates conflicts between "the ideology of codependence" and the Twelve-Step vision. For the more popular perception, see: Alison Humes, "The Culting of Codependency," *7 Days*, November 1, 1989; and for a literature review, see: Carol LeMasters, "Reading Codependency," *Christianity and Crisis* (June 18, 1990), 200-203.

32. The distribution of ideas in early A.A. can be seen in the stories printed in the first edition of *Alcoholics Anonymous*; on the affinity with traditional mysticism, see: Bernard McGinn, *The Foundations of Mysticism* (New York: Crossroad, 1991).

33. Wilson's *A.A. Grapevine* articles have been collected and published in the book, *The Language of the Heart*. On recent events, see: James Davison Hunter, *Culture Wars: The Struggle to Define America* (New York: Basic Books, 1991); and Robert Wuthnow, *The Restructuring of American Religion* (Princeton, N.J., Princeton University Press, 1988).

34. Miguel d'Unamuno, *The Tragic Sense of Life* (New York: Dover Publications, 1954 [1921]), 17; the final point is illustrated in many *A.A. Grapevine* stories, see: "Ginger" in the February 1992 issue (vol. 48, no. 9), 50-53.

35. Lewis Yablonsky, *The Tunnel Back: Synanon* (New York: Macmillan Co., 1965), 49-55.

36. The final quotation is from: Robin Room, "Healing Ourselves and Our Planet" (Paper presented at the 18th Annual Alcohol Epidemiology Symposium of the Kettil Bruun Society for Social and Epidemiological Research on Alcohol, Toronto, June 1-5, 1992).; see also: Frank Riessman and Timothy Bay, "The Politics of Self-Help," *Social Policy* 23:2 (1992), 28-38.

37. One of the women the authors interviewed named her private faith 'Sheilaism' after herself; it included a belief in God and an intention to love and care for herself and others. See: Robert N. Bellah *et al.*, *Habits of the Heart* (Berkeley: University of California Press, 1985), 221, 235.

38. *Alcoholics Anonymous Comes of Age* (New York: A.A. World Services, 1957), 74-75.

From the beginning of my study of the fellowship and program of Alcoholics Anonymous, my main purpose has been not to tell AA's story to its members but to introduce its reality to academic and other professionals. I am gratified that A.A. members recognize their story in my research. But my chief aim has been and remains to offer accurate knowledge of a very important reality that is too often ignored or misunderstood.

The following article was my first attempt to further that goal after the publication of Not-God: A History of Alcoholics Anonymous. Invited by the editor of the Journal of Studies on Alcohol, I attempted a tour de force for the academic mind, "piling it on" with 125 references from very diverse fields. I apologize to the general reader for the complexities of this piece, though I also invite you to enjoy with me this blatantly grandiose effort to get the attention of those who look down on Alcoholics Anonymous.

This article was also the first place I presented for wide distribution my ideas on shame, which were soon taken up by others and distorted beyond all recognition. For both reasons, then, this is both a humbling and a satisfying re-reading for me.

Why A.A. Works:

The Intellectual Significance of Alcoholics Anonymous

It is time to take Alcoholics Anonymous seriously. A.A. members, of course, do take their program seriously; and, as A.A.'s 50th birthday nears, virtually all professionals in the field of alcoholism treatment esteem the fellowship and its contributions (1-8). Few deny A.A.'s therapeutic success and consequent social significance, but that is not the point at issue.

Each passing year reveals ever more clearly that A.A. is also a phenomenon of unique *intellectual* significance, yet this kind of respect is rarely accorded it – especially by professionals (3, 5, 9, 10). A.A. itself, with its axiomatic injunction "Utilize, Don't Analyze" and its inherent wariness of grandiose claims, manifestly contributes to this disregard. Yet it would seem that professionals, trained in intellectual analysis for the benefit of society, abdicate responsibility, when they refuse or neglect this task.

In what follows I propose that A.A. has an intellectual significance that is inappropriate and even unconscionable to ignore. That significance derives from A.A.'s participation and place in the larger social history of ideas. Its importance to professionals flows from the fact that awareness and of sensitivity to this historical context can shed useful light on why A.A. has proved such an effective help for so many people.

Three awarenesses undergird this intuition of A.A.'s intellectual significance and invite its analysis: the nature of its origins and sources, the profound parallels that exist between the A.A. insight and the animus of existentialist philosophy, and the readiness with which its ideas have infused other social phenomena (11-14). Concerning the first, little requires rehearsal here: most readers will already be familiar with A.A.'s incorporation of the philosophy and psychology of William James, with its debt to Carl Jung and William Duncan Silkworth, and with the style of the wisdom mediated to A.A. by the Oxford Group.[1] For those lacking this familiarity, a brief resume of A.A. history will follow shortly.

The second awareness – that of the profound resonances and the affinities of orientation between A.A. and the philosophies of existence – furnishes the framework for the analysis that follows. The task of clarifying this perception, then, must be the responsibility of this paper as a whole. One introductory, context setting observation is nevertheless appropriate, not least because it also sheds light on the intellectual significance of A.A.'s impact on other social phenomena. A.A. is not generally accorded intellectual respectability because its core insistence on essential limitation and on mutuality as preferable to objectivity reveal it

---

[1] There are four main sources (15-18) that analyze the origins and history of A.A. Most of the references will be to my own work (17) since it is indexed and contains full citations to primary and other secondary sources.

to be a counter-Enlightenment phenomenon antithetical to the central assumptions of self-styled "modernity." Especially in America, the philosophies of existence have labored under a similar handicap (17, *pp. 165-171;* 19, *pp. 23-41;* 20).

Both then, are outcasts; and therefore their attractiveness to human outcasts – to the wrecked flotsam and the discarded jetsam of contemporary society – should neither surprise nor repel. It should rather, indeed, inspire serious intellectual investigation, especially in an era when historians strive to penetrate "inner history" by studying the oppressed and seek to describe reality "from the bottom up."[2] Non-elites, ordinary people, can be studied not only statistically: penetrating to their ideas, as evidenced by the history of such phenomena as A.A., can also open the door to an exciting and respectful new confluence of "popular culture" and "intellectual history." Ideas – interpretations of reality – have a social history that is not necessarily the monopoly of the elite. That history can be studied, and it merits study, as this investigation hopes to demonstrate.

To be fruitful, such a study must delve into the implications of A.A.'s core ideas of essential limitation and shared mutuality. The analysis that follows is therefore twofold: an exploration of A.A.'s focus on essential limitation that will illuminate the process by which its fellowship and program work; and an examination of the interpersonal mutuality infusing that process that will clarify the nature as well as the style of how Alcoholics Anonymous heals.[3]

The History

Before embarking on that analysis, I shall briefly review A.A.'s early history as it relates to this investigation. The usual birth date assigned A.A. is 1935, but A.A.'s origins and the development of its insight were

---

[2]For recent statements of the problem, and the hope, see Barzun (21), Handlin (22), Schlesinger (23) and Degler (24).

[3]In the original version of this article, here and elsewhere I used the term "A.A. therapy"; given the history detailed in some of the previous articles, I soon became disenchanted with that formulation, and so I have changed it in this reprinting to reflect more accurately my meaning in the present context.

179

more complex than that simple date might indicate. A.A. proximately came into being out of the Oxford Group, an evangelically styled attempt to recapture the pietist insight of primitive Christianity. From the Oxford Group, A.A. inherited – not always without change – much of its tone, style and practice, as well as many of its enduring problems (17, *pp.44-52*; 18, *pp. 2134-2139*).

In late 1934, a temporarily abstinent Oxford Group member, Edwin Thatcher, approached the then-drinking individual who would found A.A., William Griffith Wilson, with his message of "salvation." Thatcher was an enthusiastic and uncritical Oxford Grouper, yet his message embodied more than the Group's simple pietism. He had been led to salvation from his alcoholism within the Group, but by an individual whose own alcoholism had been treated by the noted Swiss psychiatrist, Carl Jung. Thus a Jungian insight and emphasis infused his presentation when he told the story of his cure to Bill Wilson (17, *pp. 8-9*).

Despite Thatcher's visit, Wilson continued to drink. Yet he found that he had been touched and profoundly affected by the realization of how "in the kinship of common suffering," one alcoholic could talk to another. Shortly after, Wilson – undergoing his fourth and final hospital detoxification – connected what his physician had told him of the hopelessness of his alcoholic condition not only with what Thatcher had told him of Oxford Group principles and Jung's insight, but with what he himself had discovered in William James's *Varieties of Religious Experience.* For during his hospitalization, Wilson underwent a "spiritual experience" that brought him vivid conviction about the unity of these diversely derived insights. Wilson left the hospital in December 1934, and proceeded to try to share his new knowledge with other alcoholics – to no avail, although he himself remained sober. His wanting to work with alcoholics made no impression on those with whom he worked (17, *pp. 17-23*).

In May of 1935, Wilson traveled to Akron, Ohio, on business. The business purpose of his visit failed, and the recently sobered promoter found himself again overwhelmed by the obsessive-compulsive craving for alcoholic oblivion that he had so confidently thought he had overcome.

In desperation, Wilson sought out another alcoholic – one to whom he could talk for his own sake, rather than to "save." By way of an Oxford Group connection, Wilson located Dr. Robert Holbrook Smith, whose attaining of sobriety a month later both made him "co-founder" and marked in hindsight A.A.'s formal birth (17, *pp. 27-33*).

It took several years – two in New York City and four in Akron – for the new fellowship to break away from the Oxford Group. In both cases, it was the religiosity of the Group that impelled separation. Finally, in 1939, the book *Alcoholics Anonymous* was published, and a group of alcoholics met as "Alcoholics Anonymous" in a new city (Cleveland, Ohio), without direct connection to Wilson or Smith, and without any Oxford Group affiliation (17, *pp. 39-52, 68-82*).

A.A. borrowed and learned from diverse sources – William James and the Oxford Group, Carl Jung and William Duncan Silkworth. Its own continuing experience also significantly shaped the development of A.A.'s thought. The concepts embodied in both terms of its name best briefly clarify that insight. The alcoholic, in the A.A. understanding, is one who finds himself or herself in an utterly hopeless situation: obsessively-compulsively addicted to alcohol, he by definition must drink alcohol and so destroy himself. Although alcoholism is conceptualized by A.A. as by others as "disease" or "malady," the alcoholic does not *have* alcoholism – he *is* an "alcoholic." Therefore he cannot do what others, non-alcoholics, do with joyful impunity: non-obsessively-compulsively drink alcohol. Contained in the term "alcoholic," then, are the implications of utterly hopeless helplessness and essential personal limitation 17, *pp. 22-23, 194-196*).

Anonymity implies, first, others: one cannot be "anonymous" to oneself. Through its own experience, A.A. learned that the necessity of "deflation at depth" and of some experience of "conversion" – as its sources referred to the process – implied something about the alcoholic's human need for others. It was this second lesson that A.A. in its program and practice developed into its guiding insight, the core of its contribution. For from its own experience, A.A. learned that alcoholics, in their own weakness and limitation, needed others precisely in *their* weakness and limitation. Only by giving could the alcoholic get – sobriety: only by exposing vulnerability could the alcoholic find healing. Thus developed A.A.'s therapeutic dynamic, the shared honesty of mutual vulnerability openly acknowledged (17, *pp. 214-215, 221-224*).

Elsewhere (17), I have summarized and explored A.A.'s fundamental insight, within the context of the history of religious ideas, under the heading of human not-God-ness. This concept will be clarified and set in its philosophical context by what follows, but it seems apt to conclude this introduction of A.A. to those unfamiliar with it by quoting from that summary:

> "Not-God" means first "You are not God," the message of the A.A. program. . . . The fundamental and first message of Alcoholics Anonymous to its members is that they are not infinite, not absolute, not God. Every alcoholic's problem had *first* been, according to this insight, claiming God-like powers, especially that of *control*. But the alcoholic at least, the message insists, is *not* in control, even of himself; and the first step towards recovery from alcoholism must be the admission and acceptance of this fact that is so blatantly obvious to others but so tenaciously denied by the obsessive-compulsive drinker.
>
> But Alcoholics Anonymous is *fellowship* as well as *program*, and thus there is a second side to its message of not-God-ness. Because the alcoholic is not God, not absolute, not infinite, he or she is essentially limited. Yet from this limitation – from the alcoholic's *acceptance* of personal limitation – arises the beginning of healing and wholeness. . . To be an alcoholic within Alcoholics Anonymous is not only to accept oneself as not God; it implies also affirmation of one's connectedness with other alcoholics. . . . The invitation to make such a connection with others and the awareness of the necessity of doing so arise from the alcoholic's acceptance of limitation. Thus, this second message that affirms limitation is well conveyed by the hyphenated phrase, "not-God."
>
> The form "not-God" reminds that affirmation is rooted in negation, that the alcoholic's acceptance of self as human is founded in his rejection of any claim to be more than human. And the hyphen – a connecting mark – reminds of the need for connectedness with other alcoholics that A.A. as fellowship lives out and enables (*pp. 3-4*).

"Not-God" is a theological term, even if not exclusively a religious concept. One reason behind its choice is the affinity of orientation and timing between the birth of A.A. and the dawning in America of "neo-orthodox" religious thought: 1934 has been called the *annus mirabilis* of American religious history (17, *p. 180)*. But that Depression decade witnessed more than a theological shift. The middle third of the 20th century also marked the rise to maturity of the philosophies of existence, the beginnings of the broad diffusion and deep appropriation of existential-ist insight. Because all phenomena are affected by their "climate of opinion," this aspect of A.A.'s historical context also merits study (25, *p.216)*.

The co-founders and early members of A.A. were neither theologians nor philosophers: indeed, most were unsophisticated intellectually. Yet these individuals came to terms with their alcoholism, and they formulated a set of ideas and practices for treating it, in a specific intellectual context. This paper will attempt to delineate and to explicate that environment of ideas. It will also suggest that alcoholism and specifically the fellowship and program of A.A. hold a special place within it: alcoholism, because it is a metaphor for the postmodern "Age of Limits"; A.A., because it makes available the wisdom of that metaphor (17, *pp.200-202)*.

Finitude and the Concept of Essential Limitation

"We admitted that we were powerless over alcohol – that our lives had become unmanageable." A.A. addresses itself not to alcoholism, but to the alcoholic. The First Step of the A.A. program focuses upon the alcoholic as one who is essentially limited. The acknowledgment "I am an alcoholic" that is inherent in the admission of powerlessness over alcohol accepts as first truth human essential limitation, personal fundamental finitude, at least for the alcoholic.

What is this human finitude, the explicit acceptance of which A.A. requires in its First Step? It is, among other things, the first insight of existentialist philosophy, which explains human finitude as the presence of a *not* in the very being of any human individual.[4] Finitude concerns limitations – what one *cannot* do and *cannot* be. Fundamental finitude is not, however, the mere sum of human limitations. Rather, the fact of finitude is the core of human be-ing. At that core, positive and negative existence interpenetrate. This means that human strength coincides with human pathos, human vision with human blindness, human truth with human untruth, human being with human nonbeing. If we do not understand human finitude, human being itself escapes us (19, *p. 290*).

The first theme of all philosophies of existence posits that human be-ing is limited being: *the limitation of being* marks the starting point of all existentialist thought. The A.A. member who comes to accept and to speak his identity within A.A. by saying, "My name is . . . and I am an alcoholic," attains this understanding and embraces the existentialist insight into the human condition: "Man is his finitude (19, *p. 111;* 36; 37).

Guided by A.A., alcoholics come to understand finitude, to discern the existential meaning of "nothingness," in two ways. Some, confronted with the dire choice of abstinence, insanity or death, by reflecting on those possibilities become aware of the reality of the fact that some absolute limitation has become absolutely inevitable. They thus attain the consciousness described by Sartre: "Consciousness is a being, the nature of which is to be conscious of the nothingness of its being" (36, *p. 86*).

This perception engenders "dread" – the *Angst* of Heidegger, the *angoisse* of Sartre, the "anxiety" or "anguish" of translators who, unwilling to resort to foreign-language italics, struggle to retain the term's root. The concept lies in that etymological root: the ancient Indo-European ANGH expresses onomatopoeically the sense of constricted narrowness, the

---

[4] Because of the obscurity of many existentialist writers, especially Heidegger (28), and because as historian rather than philosopher I claim no mastery over their writings, I rely heavily on secondary sources (19, 29-35) in the analysis that follows. Citations will be to the philosophers of existence themselves when a direct quotation is used or when an interpretation is my own. In those cases where I am aware of drawing an interpretation from a secondary source, the citation will be to that source, although responsibility for the interpretation and its application of course remains mine.

tightening and the choking that existentialist insight posits as the essential human condition. This sense of dread arises from the rub finitude, the realization of one's own possible nothingness (19, *p. 226*).

For others, the experience is more Kierkegaardian: their anguish arises from the sense of nothingness engendered by the alcoholic experience itself – the gnawing through unspecifiable sense of the meaningless, treadmill-like quality of repetitively insatiable addiction. These discover "nothingness" within their own hearts. Kierkegaard asked, "What effect does nothing produce? It begets dread" (38, *p. 38*) A person experiences dread rather than fear when he cannot say "what is it that bothers" – a frustrated feeling of vacuity not uncommon among alcoholics wrestling with their addiction. It is an experience that lies at the core of the existential perception.

> I cannot say what it is that bothers me in the case of dread. In fact, if one were to ask me what bothers me, I would probably say "Nothing." In saying that I do not mean that I am bothered at all, but that there is no *thing* that bothers me. What bothers me is my existence. . . . Heidegger asks quite seriously this question: What is this "nothingness" (*Nichts*) about which one has such a dreading anxiety? What is the existential meaning of "Nothingness"? (30, *pp. 116-117*).

The alcoholic who knows the experience of alcoholism within himself knows the meaning of Heidegger's question. Sartre's core existential insight conveys the same point in another way, yet again in a way with which all alcoholics can readily identify: the ultimate freedom is to say "No" (19, *p. 241*; 36, *pp. 619ff.*).

The existential meaning of "Nothingness"; the ultimate freedom as saying "No"; these ideas bespeak finitude – the essential limitation of human be-ing (30, *p.31*). A.A. teaches in several ways the fundamental insight that the first truth of alcoholic human be-ing is essential limitation, and that therefore the first requirement for recovery of humanity is acceptance of essential limitation.

A.A. achieves this first by suggesting that fundamental finitude, essential limitation, is the definition of the alcoholic condition. This is the deep meaning of A.A.'s concept of the "alcoholic" and emphasis on avoiding "the first drink." The two are related. The "alcoholic," A.A. teaches, is one who cannot drink any alcohol safely. There is an essential "not" an inherent limitation – in the very concept of "alcoholic." This *not* is an essential rather than an accidental limitation, because it applies to the first drink. The gropings of the active alcoholic who suspects that he is in trouble are familiar – the staunch efforts to stop drinking before drunkenness, the tortured attempts to determine what is "my limit": two drinks? four beers? only with meals? A.A., in teaching that "the first drink gets the alcoholic drunk," inculcates that the alcoholic does not *have* a limit, he *is* limited – and this is the meaning of "essential limitation."

Even more striking, perhaps, because so often misunderstood, is how A.A. inculcates this truth by applying the insight to itself. At its very birth, A.A. departed Oxford Group auspices because the Group, with its heritage of Christian perfectionism as revealed in its emphasis on "The Four Absolutes," seemed both to demand and to claim too much (17, *pp. 212, 242*). Because of this intuition that – at least for alcoholics – the problem of the Oxford Group was that it claimed to do too much, A.A. focused attention on its own limitation. As Wilson phrased it in his briefest explanation of why his followers abandoned the Oxford Group: "The Oxford Group wanted to save the world, and I only wanted to save drunks."[5] Thus, A.A.'s claim that its fellowship and program are "spiritual rather than religious" involves not so much a rejection of religion as a profession of the acceptance of limitation.

A sensitivity to this deeper meaning of A.A.'s exemplary application to itself of the acceptance of essential limitation can shed light on something about A.A. that some professionals at time find puzzling. "Why does not A.A. *as* A.A. welcome all addicted people, alcoholic or not, into its fellowship? Why are alcoholics so exclusive?"

Some individual A.A. groups, of course, do welcome at their meetings dually addicted or generically "chemically dependent" people. Yet A.A.

---

[5] [Wilson, W.] Memorandum to our writing team. [1954] [Unpublished manuscript in the A.A. archives, p. 21.]

as A.A. does not because it cannot and still remain A.A. By accepting the limitation of its "primary purpose to carry its message to the alcoholic" (15, p. 106; 27, pp. 150-154), A.A. deepens its witness to and drives home the centrality of the acceptance of essential limitation as first principle.

The fact of fundamental finitude and the need to accept this essential limitation pervade the program as well as the fellowship of A.A. They are clear in the oft-repeated A.A. mottoes, "First Things First" and "One Day at a Time." The emphasis upon accepting limitation infuses A.A.'s own description of "How It Works," from the "Rarely" that opens that key fifth chapter of its "Big Book" through the "tried to" that lies at the heart of its Twelfth Step to its concluding qualification of its promise as "progress rather than perfection" (26, pp. 58-60).

Honest acceptance of essential limitation is therefore the core of Alcoholics Anonymous. That honesty thus becomes both the price and the reward, both the process and the purpose, of the A.A. member's First Step acceptance of himself or herself as "powerless over alcohol." In a way suggestive of the psychoanalytic contract, A.A. has intuited the existential truth that accepting the reality of self-as-feared may be an essential precondition of finding the reality of self-as-is (39).

Truth, Knowledge and "Objectivity"
Such an insight is termed "existential" because it fits well the philosophies' of existence understanding of truth as *aleitheia* – an unveiling, or disclosure, of a reality essentially beyond human control. According to this understanding, the pursuit of truth is not manipulative – is not the attempt to seize upon the correct tool that will allow grasping reality in order to control it. To search for truth means rather to find the right perspective – the point of view that will allow the phenomenon to reveal itself. As Heidegger, following Husserl, insisted: the "phenomenon" is by definition that which shows, discloses, itself (19, pp.213-216; 30, pp. 34ff.; 31, pp.25-46).

Modern thought, even that rigorously Enlightenment-positivistic, is no stranger to this proposition that it is the hidden that is "real." The sense that identifies the hidden with the real pervades modern science as well as modern literature. But modern science, as commonly understood, is inherently technological, imbued with an intrinsic imperative to control. Its practitioners and imitators thus too readily lapse into perverting the search for all truth into a mere quest for some means of manipulation. Control, especially absolute control, requires new tools rather than a different perspective (34; 40, *p. 58*; 41, *pp. 61ff.*; 42; 43, *p. 168*).

Humane thinkers, those who study human phenomena, existentialist thought reminds, must eschew the imperative of control. Human beings, as human, are neither mere tools nor mere objects – for what is an "object" but another potential tool? The subject-object dualism that derives from Descartes has immeasurably increased human knowledge and control of things. Applied to persons, however, as the experience of A.A. within the field of alcoholism testifies, it is not only sadly lacking, but tragically destructive. Subject-object dualism, with its demand for "objectivity," regards the attainment of truth as an act of conquest rather than of revelation. The dualistic style and approach thus do violence to human values. Treating persons as things can only increase alienation. Such an approach thus fuels rather than cures alcoholism (17, *pp. 325-326*; 44).

According to the insight of Alcoholics Anonymous, the pressures of alienation and the ache of loneliness that so bedevil modern humankind and not least the alcoholic arise not from the sense of limitation, but from the refusal to accept essential limitation. Imbued with this intuition, A.A., like the philosophies of existence, suggests striving for holistic rather than manipulative insight. A.A. furnishes a correct perspective rather than a controlling – and therefore potentially destructive – tool. For Kierkegaard and the existentialists, such a "correct perspective" on human finitude involved fear and trembling and dread: it was a perspective attained by standing on the brink of "the sickness unto death" that is despair. For A.A. members, it is the perspective achieved by "hitting bottom" (38, 45, 46).

"We do not come to know a (human) phenomenon by conquering and subduing it, but rather by letting it be what it is" (19, p. 214). Acceptance of this limitation marks for existentialist thinkers the beginning of sanity; for members of A.A. it signals the first step to sobriety. And acceptance of this insight invites deeper exploration of the affinity between the philosophies of existence and A.A.

From *Aleitheia* to *Gelassenheit*: the Wholeness of Limitation

The first intuition of Alcoholics Anonymous – that the alcoholic begins recovery by accepting the personal reality of essential limitation – is bound up with a larger insight: that there is a wholeness in that limitation. In one sense, the wholeness of limitation is but a corollary of essential limitation, of human finitude as ultimate fact. Yet, from a more profound perspective, it is the wholeness of limitation that is central, for only this insight can enable true acceptance of limitation. Under this heading, the wholeness of limitation, I shall examine four topics central to A.A.'s pragmatic, existential effectiveness: "letting go," the nature of the human condition, limited control, and limited dependence.

The philosophies of existence insist that we do not know reality by conquering and subduing it (which changes the reality), but rather by letting it be what it is (31, *pp. 51-54*). At the very least, such knowledge of reality-as-it-is must precede any attempt at control that will destroy the reality as it is. "Letting it be what it is" – the *Gelassenheit* of the philosophies of existence – came naturally to A.A. from its Pietist heritage. A.A.'s Oxford Group origins imbued it with the instinct expressed in the ancient adage, "Let go and let God" (17, *pp. 179-180*). And it is important to note that, at least within A.A., this maxim mandates much more than mere Quietist resignation. Recovery from alcoholism does not come about by irresponsible passivity. But how, then, and why, does "letting go" bring healing?

Strikingly, both A.A. with its injunction to "let go" and the philosophies of existence in their recommendation of *Gelassenheit* reflect modern therapeutic insight as well as recapture ancient wisdom. "Letting go" and *Gelassenheit* heal the dis-ease engendered by the attempt to will what cannot be willed because they mark operative acceptance of the wholeness of limitation and therefore effective embrace of the reality of the human condition.

"The attempt to will what cannot be willed": the alcoholic, in A.A.'s understanding, cannot will to not-drink any more than an insomniac can will to fall asleep. As Farber (47, 48) has delineated in his analysis of the modern era as "The Age of Disordered Will," there exist two different realms in which human will operates, and confusion of these realms issues in self-defeating frustration. In some matters, the human will can choose to possess certain objects: this is the realm of "utilitarian" or "technical" will. In other cases, however, the human will can choose only to move in a certain direction: in this second realm of "existential will," one can choose only orientation and means. Problems arise when one attempts to apply the will of the first realm – the utilitarian will that chooses *objects* – to those portions of life that, because they are directions or *orientations*, wilt or even vanish under such coercion. These problems are compounded when, in a repetitive vicious cycle, one attempts to solve them by the use of chemicals, thus again and on a deeper level seeking to apply the utilitarian will to the realm of existential orientation (49).

Let me try to clarify by offering a few examples (some again suggested by Farber) in addition to falling asleep and not drinking (47, *p.*7). One can will knowledge, but not (directly) wisdom; submission, but not humility; self-assertion, but not courage; congratulations, but not admiration; physical nearness, but not emotional intimacy; dryness, but not sobriety. In each case, indeed, any attempt directly to will the second renders its actual attainment all the less likely. Some matters, and among them the more significant in human experience, are attained only by letting them – and ourselves – be; and that is the promise of *Gelassenheit*.

Nor is this the lonely insight of Farber, A.A. members and existential-ist philosophers. Experience with diverse patients and problems has in recent years prompted therapists of many persuasions to seek to place a similar brake on the quest for technological control, to recommend acceptance rather than activity: "It is generally believed that activity and mastery are virtually synonymous. . . . But certain kinds of achievement require a kind of controlled passivity, a mastery of our fear of passivity and helplessness (50, *p. 50*). Some psychiatrists have built on the research of Edward Bibring, which they interpret as demonstrating that it is precisely excessive tenacity in clinging to ambitious, adolescent goals that renders individuals most vulnerable to the overwhelming failure that depression represents. "It is the contrast of our goals with our own awareness of our helplessness to achieve them which is likely to produce depression. It is this exaggerated disparity which destroys one's confidence" (51, *p. 159*).

In addition to being "existential" and "modern," this insight concerning *Gelassenheit* and "letting go" has a uniquely American therapeutic foundation in the thought of William James and in the practice of Harry Stack Sullivan, both of which influenced A.A.'s development. James (52) insisted that the surrender of "pretensions" is essential to sane self-esteem: "[Self-feeling] is determined by the ratio of our actualities to our supposed potentialities. . . : thus,

$$\text{self-esteem} = \frac{\text{SUCCESS}}{\text{PRETENSIONS}}$$

One can increase self-esteem by adding to success, but a more radically effective enhancement results from damping pretensions. Precisely this difference of understanding concerning how to achieve self-acceptance, indeed, led A.A. to reject the Oxford Group's emphasis on its "Four Absolutes" and therefore to depart its auspices (17, *pp. 50-51, 242-243*).

According to Sullivan (53, *p. 206*), the first step to psychological cure occurs when a patient learns that more security may come from abandoning some security-seeking behavior than could ever be achieved by it. Such surrender is therapeutic not only because the act itself adds to one's security, but especially because it allows and invites confrontation with those other anxiety producing situations that the patient had formerly attempted to escape or to deny by the behavior (54, *pp. 542ff.*). Sullivan's description of the first step to cure captures precisely the first psychological gain attained by the alcoholic who stops drinking alcohol. Abandoning alcohol, allows, as accepting self as "alcoholic" leads, the A.A. member to confront self as-feared, thus enabling him to find the reality of self-as-is.

The A.A. Vision of the Human Condition

The understanding that finds a kind of wholeness in essential limitation echoes ancient wisdom. According to this tradition, to be human is to be caught in a middle, to contain a contradiction. Human be-

191

ing is essentially limited, yet human beings yearn – need – to transcend that limitation. This vision gave rise to the ancient dichotomy between body and soul, an image for the human as the conjunction of the limited and the infinite. It is an understanding that has haunted many thinkers. It is also a vision worth exploring; first, to understand the nature of the human as limited but whole, whole although limited; second, to begin to fathom how this condition of wholeness in limitation can be transcended.

Within the history of western thought, Pascal (and before him Augustine) founded their philosophies on the insight that to be human is to occupy a middle position in the universe, a position between the infinitesimal and the infinite (55, *pp. 88-94*; 56). To be human is to be an All in relation to nothingness, a Nothingness in relation to the All. This middle position of humanity is the final and dominant fact of the human condition. It is also a perfect image of the significance of the finitude of human existence (57, *pp. 203-219*).

One of Pascal's aphorisms clarifies the meaning of that finitude and invites an appreciation of the significance of the contradiction inherent in this middle position and thus in the human condition: "He who would be an angel becomes a beast" (55, *p. 242*). As *both* angel and beast, the human can be *only neither*. Centuries later the American philosopher George Santayana (58) used the same image to make its complementary point in a different way: "It is necessary to become a beast if one is ever to become a spirit" (*p. 230*).

Together, these understandings and their point – as both angel and beast, one cannot be only either – embrace A.A.'s core perception and process. In the A.A. understanding that can be heard, paraphrased, at any A.A. meeting, the alcoholic drank in the attempt or claim to be one *or* the other, angel *or* beast: the essence of sobriety resides in the acceptance that one is both – that because one can be only both, the effort to be only either is doomed to frustration and failure.

This vision posits an essential incongruity at the core of the human condition. Both the perennial theme and its inherent incongruity have been explored in detail by Ernest Becker, who, in his study *The Denial of*

Death (59), strikingly captured this understanding of the human condition in a way that both clarifies the point here and deepens appreciation of one often misunderstood facet of A.A. Becker suggested that to be human is to be "a god who shits" (*p. 58*).

Humor derives from the perception of the juxtaposition of incongruity. When the incongruity is inherent, essential, there can be no more healing – whole-ing – experience than the laughter that marks acceptance of it. Such laughter characterizes A.A. meetings because those gatherings so well reveal the incongruity of the human condition, the humor of being human. Within Alcoholics Anonymous, humor and laughter are never at others as objects, but at the contradictions within self revealed by the human experience of others. A.A. humor and A.A. laughter express appreciation of the insights into self garnered from the experience of others with whom one identifies. They thus witness to A.A. members' acceptance of the paradoxical nature of the human condition as essentially limited but inherently striving for the unlimited.

In attempting and claiming to attain transcendence by their use of alcohol, alcoholics come to touch – even to wallow in – the depth of their own finitude. Recognizing the incongruity between that endeavor and its result frees from both. Such humor is neither veiled aggression nor mere compensation: it rather manifests the central animus of A.A.'s theory of personality and of human nature (60, *pp, 94-96, 145-147*). The human as beast-angel, as not-God, means that the essence of being human resides in the human condition's conjunction of infinite thirst with essentially limited capacity. Acceptance of this reality comes easily to the alcoholic who understands her alcoholism: the phenomenon of alcoholism replicates the essence of the human condition.

Limited Control and Limited Dependence
A final facet of A.A.'s focus on the wholeness of limitation may help to clarify further. A.A. understands the alcoholic as an "all or nothing person" (17, *p. 229*). Sartre (61) well captured the alcoholic's essence: "They want to exist all at once and right away" (*p. 333*). The futility of this attempt manifests itself especially in two areas: control and dependence.

In the A.A. understanding, the drinking alcoholic drinks alcohol in an effort to achieve control – absolute control over his feelings and environment; yet his drinking itself is absolutely out of control. Similarly, the drinking alcoholic denies all dependence. She drinks in an attempt to deny dependence upon others, upon anything outside herself; but her dependence upon alcohol itself has become absolute. The alcoholic's problem, then, involves the demand for absolute control and the claim to be absolutely independent. A.A. attacks this double problem in a twofold way. First, the alcoholic is confronted with the facts that, so far as alcohol is concerned, he is absolutely out of control and absolutely dependent. Then, when this reality contained in the very concept "alcoholic" has been accepted by the admission of "powerlessness over alcohol," A.A. prescribes *limited* control and *limited* dependence.

The emphasis on control as limited, as neither absolute nor to be abdicated, pervades the A.A. program. "You can do something, but not everything" runs the constant implicit, and at times explicit, message. A.A. members are warned against promising "never to drink again." They learn, rather, "not to take the first drink, one day at a time." They learn to pick the telephone rather than the bottle. They are encouraged to attend A.A. meetings, which they can do, rather than to avoid all contact with alcohol, which they cannot do. The A.A. sense of limited control is admirably summed up in the famed "Serenity Prayer": "God grant me the serenity to accept the things I cannot change, the courage to change the things I can, and the wisdom to know the difference" (15, *p. 196)*.

The "can" and "cannot" of the Serenity Prayer inculcate the concepts of limited control and limited dependence. They also clarify the depth of the affinity of orientation shared by A.A. insight and existentialist thought. In the A.A. understanding, alcoholism is an obsessive-compulsive malady; the active alcoholic is one who must drink, who *cannot* not-drink (26, *p. 24)*. Therefore the alcoholic who joins the A.A. fellowship and embraces its program does not thereby surrender her freedom to drink; rather, she gains the freedom to not-drink – no small liberation for one obsessively-compulsively addicted to alcohol. Within A.A., the passage from "mere dryness" to "true sobriety" consists precisely in the change of perception – perspective – by which the A.A. member moves from interpreting his situation as the prohibition, "I cannot drink," to understanding its deeper reality as the joyous affirmation, "I *can* not-drink."

The alcoholic who finds sobriety in A.A. by accepting the goal of limited control thus discovers in his very being the fundamental existentialist insight: "The essential freedom, the ultimate freedom that cannot be taken from a man, is to say No" (19, *p. 241*). This sense of wholeness in limitation, this embrace of fundamental finitude, suggests further another, complementary goal: limited dependence.

The modern, post-Enlightenment mind tends to view all dependence (but especially essential dependence) as humiliating and dehumanizing. Its goal of autonomy leads modern thought to define full humanity as the overcoming of all dependencies, maturity as the effective denial of dependence itself (62, 63). Many current therapies, unlike A.A., are imbued with this assumption of modernity: their interpretation, diagnosing alcoholism, is to proclaim that the alcoholic's problem is "dependence on alcohol" (2, 64-68).

A.A.'s longer-wisdomed insight does not contradict this interpretation. Indeed, Alcoholics Anonymous agrees with and accepts the diagnosis; but, untrammeled by the assumptions of post-Enlightenment modernity, freed by its affinity with the existentialist impulse, A.A. locates the definition's deeper truth by shifting its implicit emphasis, interpreting the experience of its members as revealing that the alcoholic's problem is not "*dependence* on alcohol," but "dependence on *alcohol*." To be human, to be essentially limited, A.A. insists, is to be essentially dependent. The alcoholic's choice – the human choice – lies not between dependence and independence, but between that upon which one will acknowledge dependence – a less than human substance such as alcohol within oneself, or a more than individual reality that remains essentially outside – beyond – the self (17, *pp. 125-126, 210-217*).

The limited dependence sought by Alcoholics Anonymous merits further explication, but that inquiry is best forwarded by turning to the next topic, in which it is implicitly contained: the transcendence of essential limitation enabled by the human need for others.

Transcending Limitation

"Outside – beyond – the self"; "the human need for others"; the acknowledgment of essential limitation, even conjoined with the acceptance of a wholeness in limitation, are not in themselves the whole story of A.A. healing. Because of human middleness, because of the contradictory sense of being inherently pulled both to more and to less, resting in limitation proves unsatisfying to the human mind and spirit. To be fully human, one must not only accept limitation: one must also somehow go beyond it. Yet because there is a wholeness in its limitation, the need of the human situation is for a transcendence of essential limitation that does not claim or attempt to escape that limitation. The problem comes down to this: how is it possible to "go beyond" without embarking on some claim to ultimacy, without becoming ensnared in some other treadmill-like, addictive quest for "more" that will eventuate in yet another essentially futile attempt to achieve qualitative change by the mere piling up of quantities of anything? (30, *p. 68*; 69; 70, *pp. 179-182*).

The need for human transcendence – for getting beyond, outside of, one's own limited self – inspires much art, most religion, and all love. It is also a theme of the philosophies of existence, perhaps best appreciated in the "baffled transcendence" that haunts Kafka's world (33, *pp. 142ff.*; 34, *p. 63*). As existentialist, this theme derives from the philosophy of Edmund Husserl, who emphasized the intentionality of consciousness. Husserl saw consciousness as "essentially referential:" to be conscious is always to be conscious *of* something. Because consciousness thus inherently points beyond itself, it necessarily involves a self-transcendence. Martin Heidegger exhibited a similar understanding in his suggestion that the very meaning of "existence" denotes "to stand outside oneself, to be beyond oneself" (30, *p. 45*; 31, *pp. 46-54*; 72, *p. 78*; 73, *p. 26*; 74).

The self-transcendence, the getting outside of oneself and therefore beyond the condition of essential limitation that is taught and enabled by Alcoholics Anonymous, involves embracing a new relationship with others. A.A.'s insight proposes that if these others also accept their own essential limitation, a self-transcending relationship with them is not only possible but inevitable. It is a necessary corollary of accepted personal essential limitation that each needs "other", that to be fully human is to

196

need human others. Some existentialist thinkers have found in this realization only tragedy. Sartre lamented that, because one is essentially limited, " to be conscious of another means to be conscious of what one is not" (75, *p. 318*). But this insight of A.A. reminds that "the other" is also essentially limited, and therefore that to be conscious of that "other" also invites consciousness of what one *is* (69, *p. 271*; 70, *p. 173*).

Within human relationships, relationships between those essentially limited, the model for interaction is not Kierkegaard's "either-or" but a dialectical mutuality (76-78). It is the claim to be God to another or the demand to possess God in another that imposes the "either-or" approach; Kierkegaard's point, indeed, was that only for and with God is "either-or" appropriate. When neither is "God," when neither claims or demands infinite fullness, the mutual acceptance of essential limitation opens to the possibility of a relationship of mutual enrichment, to a give-and-take exchange between two beings "congenial" to each other. (73, *p. 92*) Accepting mutual essential limitation enables living out a dialectical relationship of congeniality that defines creatively the human need for others.

The "need for others" is, of course, A.A.'s most famous facet (79). Usually, those outside A.A. regard it condescendingly; it is interpreted away as "the substituting of a social dependence for a drug dependence" (10, *p.232*); or as "accepting the emotional immaturity of alcoholics and supplying a crutch for it" (9). Yet some observers have also recognized positive aspects in the need for others that is taught by A.A. One psychiatrist (80) has located the reason for A.A.'s success in this approach, which – as opposed to some mere disease concept of alcoholism – inculcates in the alcoholic and many who would help him the "understanding that human involvement is needed" (*p. 58*). Another profound student of Alcoholics Anonymous (81) has noted concerning research on personality changes within A.A. that "if any one trend stands out . . , it is the [constructive] modification of self-other attitudes and perceptions" (*p. 218*).

A.A. does not, of course, stand alone as a modern expression of the insight that to be human is to need others (69, *p. 271*; 70, *pp. 173-174*).

Yet the specific company in which it stands by reason of its therapeutic philosophy clarifies A.A.'s place within the history of ideas. Contemporaneous with A.A.'s development, the American psychiatrist Harry Stack Sullivan (82), in formulating his "theory of interpersonal relations," made three points concerning the therapeutic need for others. Sullivan saw anxiety as a result of and defense against insecurity, noted that this insecurity was always associated with other persons, and proposed that anxiety and insecurity had this association because their root source was continuing deprivation in personal relations. More recently, the existential analyst R.D. Laing (83) perhaps most pithily stated the point, and in a way that illuminates the Sartrian lamentation noted above; "Every relationship implies a definition of self by other and other by self" (*p. 86*) Humanistic psychology has consistently emphasized that "being with" another rather than "holding back" from others need not involve any loss of self, any diminution of identity; it can rather open to the enrichment of the essentially limited self (51, *p. 172*; 60, *p. 241*; 84-87).

All these insights and emphases are related to the deeper philosophical stance that expresses itself most clearly in the philosophies of existence: the root rejection of Cartesian dualism. Descartes's *cogito* establishes a world of subject-object (34, *pp.111-116*). Thus "spectatorship" – observation of, rather than interaction with – becomes the first relationship (43, *pp, 213 ff.*) This objectification has come to characterize not only the positivistic sciences such as physics but, less helpfully, what are called the "social sciences"; it also permeates most usual modern therapeutic approaches (88-96). Other persons become, as for Freud (97), objects that provide or withhold the satisfaction of needs or, as for Lasswell (98), the embodiment of roles, thus limiting personal relations to some version of indulgent, deprivational or indifferent; or, following Ruth Benedict's (99) extension of Freudian insight, other persons become an audience that gives or withholds approbation or ridicule. The demand for "objectivity" thus renders others a "they" who are necessarily apart from and over against the person seeking involvement with them (60, *pp.153-155*).

Accepting persons as ends-in-themselves, the Kantian imperative, is impossible in a Cartesian world. Such acceptance becomes possible only in a world-view that transcends the subject-object dichotomy – a world in which human relationships can be reciprocal and mutual. The philosophies of existence seek to portray such a world. Heidegger distinguished between things that were *Zuhanden*, ready-at-hand to be *used* according to some purpose given them by oneself, and being – reality – that was *Vorhanden* or present-at-hand. The *Vorhanden* is the world as given, as present: consciousness must simply comprehend (30, *pp. 198-199*; 74, *pp. 27-39*).

The intimacy enabled by the human need for others requires comprehending the paradox that essentially limited human beings are always **both** *Vorhanden* and *Zuhanden* to each other. Each person is ready-at-hand, however, only according to his or her presence-at-hand. Between two persons conscious of their essential finitude, there arises a complementary mutuality; each is to the other according to the needs of both. Such relationships of intimacy and mutuality open the way for the self to expand beyond its own limitations in depth of feeling, understanding and insight. One's own identity is not weakened but strengthened by the meaning one has as a person for others as unique individuals (60, *pp. 159-160*; 83, *p. 82*; 86, *p. 42*).

To achieve such intimacy and mutuality requires risk: one must trust oneself as person to others as persons, instead of regarding them (or self) as object, role-embodier or audience (60, *p. 239*). A.A. members achieve such relationships of intimacy and mutuality by deriving their awareness of their need for others from the fundamental recognition that they, as alcoholics, are essentially limited. Within A.A., this realization is not merely privative, the recognition of a lack: the need for others bridges to a positive existence by way of identity as "an alcoholic." A.A. members accept themselves and each other not only as essentially limited but as whole in their limitation: they find, that is, a positive identity in their essential limitation. They thus realize that other human beings, and most patently other alcoholics – the others most needed by alcoholics, the others gathered together within A.A. – are clearly essentially limited; and therefore there is an essential limitation on how those others are needed. The first thing known about these others is that they also need others: thus the foundation for mutuality is established.

How Mutuality Makes Whole

It is this perception and acceptance of mutuality that enables transcending the "self-centeredness" that A.A. members understand to be "the root of our troubles" (26, *p. 62*) The mutualities that A.A. teaches, enables and lives out are especially three: making a difference, honesty and dependence.

These mutualities are linked – with each other as well as with "needing others" – because both the reality and the concept of mutuality derive from the essential limitation of the human condition, from the fact of human wholeness in limitation. Both the possibility and the necessity of mutuality between persons arise from the dialectical mutuality inherent within each person, from the reality that to be human is to be both beast and angel. Because the human condition is essentially mixed, humans can be only "both"; A.A., as we have seen, interprets the phenomenon of alcoholism as testifying to the impossibility of being only "either." Thus, A.A. teaches that the relationship between the polarities of human life is necessarily dialectical and mutual, is never "either-or."

In a dialectical relationship, a relatedness of mutuality such as that inhering in the essential human condition, each element subsists both from and for the other; a person cannot have one without the other because one does not exist without the other. And because one can have only *both*, one's possession of *each* is intrinsically limited. The apparent contradictions inherent in being human thus present not alternatives to be chosen between, but paradoxes to be transcended by synthesis. A.A.'s message is that such transcendence requires "others"; for, because to-be-human is to be "both," a human individual can be neither "either" nor "only."

All this has been, no doubt, painfully abstract: the concept of the dialectic can be excruciatingly elusive (77; 78; 100, *pp.228-240*). Yet this thinking can be clarified and concretized: such indeed is one role of the mutualities taught by and lived out within A.A. I turn, then, to an examination of these mutualities: that between the giving and getting of making a difference; that between honesty with self and honesty with others; and that between human dependence and personal independence.

Making a Difference

The ability to make a difference is a deeply basic human need; indeed, Alcoholics Anonymous founded its fellowship upon this vital need. At A.A.'s very beginning, when co-founders Bill Wilson and Dr. Bob Smith approached the bedside of the alcoholic who was to become "A.A. Number Three," it was their implicit appeal to Bill D.'s need to give that opened his mind and laid the solid foundation for what would become the essential hallmark of the A.A. approach. Wilson and Smith told this first "man on the bed" that they were talking to him for their own sakes far more than for his. Bill D. believed them, and therefore he listened: "All the other people that had talked to me wanted to help me, and my pride prevented me from listening to them, and caused only resentment on my part, but if I would be a real stinker if I did not listen to a couple of fellows for a short time, if that would cure them" (26, p. 185).

Many later therapists have shared the same insight. It became the special theme of the existential phenomenologist of psychotherapy, R.D. Laing (83), who criticized the more classic therapeutic approach as defective precisely because of the model its therapist presents: "A prototype of the other as giver but not receiver, unresponsive or impervious, tends to generate in self a sense of failure. . . . Frustration becomes despair when the person begins to question his own capacity to 'mean' anything to anyone" (pp. 84-85) In such situations,"the person experiences, not the absence of the presence of the other, but the absence of his own presence as other for the other" (p. 138).

Laing is of course exceptional and even eccentric (by "modern" standards), a thinker whose explorations carried him beyond the mainstream of psychoanalytic thought (101). More classically, a similar understanding has been propounded by the anti-positivist Freudians, W.R.D. Fairbairn, Michael Balint and Harry Guntrip, who emphasize that "the patient's need to regress" arises not in pursuit of "'satisfactions' of so-called instinctive needs, but rather in search of 'Recognition' as a 'Person'" (102, p. ix). Developing what has been called "personal relationship therapy," these thinkers also reflect another tradition: the Eriksonian and ego-psychology insight that "a sense of self and trust of the self require . . . a feeling of efficacy" (51, p. 88; 73, p. 26; 103, 104).

The concept of mutuality – as the example of making a difference by getting *and* giving clarifies – entails two reciprocal modes: one both gets by giving and gives by getting. Andras Angyal (105) captured this conjunction of the need to give and the need to receive as these are found and expressed within A.A. "We ourselves want to be needed. We do not only have needs, we are also strongly motivated by neededness... We are motivated to search not only for what we lack and need but also for that for which we are needed, for what is wanted from us" (*p. 120*).

Honesty: with Self and with Others

The second mutuality taught by and put into practice within A.A. involves honesty. One lesson of A.A.'s experience is that there exists an essential mutuality between honesty with self and honesty with others: both may be present or both may be absent, but neither can exist without the other. Most A.A. members come to their understanding of the necessary mutuality between honesty with self and with others precisely from their personal experience of the inevitable mutuality of dishonesty with self and others.

As with the mutuality of making a difference, of giving and getting, the mutuality involved in honesty and dishonesty with self and others is not a unique discovery of A.A. Again Laing, perhaps because of his openness to dialectical thinking, has provocatively explored this insight: "Those who deceive themselves are obliged to deceive others. It is impossible for me to maintain a false picture of myself unless I falsify your picture of yourself and me" (83, *p. 143*). And: "It is a form of self-deception to suppose that one can say one thing and think another" (73, *p. 18*).

A profound description of the process underlying this mutuality has been offered by Leslie Farber, who pointed out that as any human individual becomes aware of the absolute separateness of his being from all others, he feels in this discovery both pleasure and terror (106, *p. 196*). Sometimes, out of terror, a person will dissimulate in his presentation of himself to others in a effort to quell the pain of separateness by winning approval and acceptance. To the extent that he does so, and succeeds, he will experience a queer, unnamable apprehension, becoming trapped in an uneasy state that he finds both painful and corrupting.

202

Having traced this familiar picture, Farber rejects its usual interpretation, which sees such pain and corruption as the consequences of low self-esteem and interprets the fear of others as the cause of continuing dishonesty. He suggests rather that, once the habit of such dishonesty begins to harden, the crucial source of such a person's pain *is* his corruption. Whether from unwillingness or inability to tell the truth about who he is, such an individual knows himself in his heart to be faking. "Not merely is he ashamed of having and harboring a secret, unlovely, illegitimate self. The spiritual burden of not appearing as the person he 'is,' or not 'being' the person he appears to be – the extended and deliberate confusion of seeming and being – is by and large intolerable if held in direct view." Despairing of attaining the integrity he craves, the person turns to grasp at its illusion: since he cannot make public his private self, he commands his private self to conform to the public one. This choice beguiles to a loss of truth – not so much "telling" it, but knowing it. "There are some things it is both impossible to do and at the same time to impersonate oneself doing. Speaking truthfully is one of them" (106, *pp. 197-198*).

Anyone who has listened attentively at A.A. meetings will, I trust, find that pattern familiar and its interpretation convincing. A.A. members learn deeply, then, the mutuality between honesty with self and honesty with others: the necessity of avoiding self-deception if they are to be honest with others, and at the same time the necessity of honesty with others if they are to avoid self-deception. Living this paradoxical insight, indeed, is one of the most profound yet also most clear messages of A.A. as both fellowship and program. (26, *pp. 58, 73-74;* 27, *pp. 57-59*).

In the A.A. understanding, self-centeredness – the self-deception involved in the denial of essential limitation – radically underlies all of the alcoholic's troubles. The A.A. program and fellowship cut through this root by encouraging and enabling the disclosure of the truth of finitude. This disclosure is not so much explicitly required as it is implicitly inherent in the very concept of "Alcoholics Anonymous." As such, it is the only disclosure necessary: the acceptance of essential limitation enables its revelation, as the revelation of essential limitation enables its acceptance.

The mutuality of honesty thus not only clarifies the dialectical nature of human experience both within self and between selves; it also links the understanding of truth as disclosure with the human need for others. Because of the necessity of honesty for sobriety (a prerequisite that A.A. strongly emphasizes), the A.A. member readily learns that because to be human is to be "both," he can be neither "either" nor "only." A.A.'s very existence, as well as its emphasis on attendance at its meetings, both continually testify that progressive discovery of self – continuing honesty with self – requires others with whom one can be honest.

Dependence and Independence

Both mutualities already examined – making a difference and honesty – flow into the third mutuality inherent in A.A.: that between dependence and independence. As with the earlier mutualities, A.A.'s insight into the reciprocity of dependence-independence derives from its central focus on the reality of essential limitation as constitutive of the human condition. It is because the human is somehow the juncture of the infinite and the limited that human dependence and human independence must be mutually related, not only between people but within each person.

Mutuality means that each enables and fulfills the other. To speak of a mutuality between human dependence and human independence, then, is to point out not only that both are necessary within human experience, but also that each becomes fully human and thus humanizing only by connection with the other. Like the other mutualities that reflect the mixed human condition of beast-angel from which they derive, the mutuality between dependence and independence furnishes another example of the paradox of the necessity of both, the impossibility of either, that inheres in the human condition as essentially limited but whole in that limitation.

The usual modern point of view, infused by Cartesian and post-Enlightenment philosophical assumptions, tends to interpret dependence and independence as contradictory rather than as mutually enhancing: its goal of absolute independence is not unrelated to its ideal of absolute objectivity. The philosophies of existence, however, suggest a postmodern understanding founded upon a different insight. As Sartre (107, *p. 6)* phrased the observation even while deploring its actuality: "To Be is to belong to someone."

Recent psychoanalytic thought clarifies this reality and its basis in the nature of human infancy – the prolonged period of initial dependency and total helplessness that all humans experience. The irony of human development is that "part of the uniqueness that makes us transcendent rests in the miserable, extended, helpless state in which we are born and remain for so long – untoward in the extreme, and unparalleled in the animal kingdom" (108, *p. 3*). The deep irony is developmental, yet dependence is not only a part of each individual's personal ancient history. Rather, because of the continuing impact of that history – a history in some sense recapitulated in the very cycles of human life such as eating and sleeping – the periodic need for dependence recurs, intertwined with the equally essential need for independence.

For reasons within the history of psychological thought, the study of continuing human dependence has not found a central place in any theory of human development (108, *pp. 12ff.*). Recently, however, this surprising lacuna has begun to be filled. At least one school of analytic psychiatry has achieved rare success by building on the fundamental insight: "Dependence versus independence is the basic neurotic conflict" (102, *p. 116*). According to Donald Winnicott (102), one leader of this school of thought, for the truly mature person "dependence or independence do not become conflicting issues, rather they are complementary" (*p. 115*). In a deeply perceptive essay (109), "The Capacity To Be Alone," Winnicott carefully describes the development of the "basic ego-relatedness" that makes for mature human existence; he also touches on the paradox involved in both this maturity and its development. One matures from the "experience . . . of being alone, as an infant and small child, in the presence of mother. Thus, the basis of the capacity to be alone is a paradox; it is the experience of being alone while someone else is present."

Such experiences build "ontological security." For the individual whose own being becomes secured in this experiential sense, relatedness with others is potentially gratifying and fulfilling. The "ontologically insecure person," on the contrary, is preoccupied with preserving rather than fulfilling self: he has become obsessed with the task of preventing himself from losing himself. Such an ontologically insecure person reaches out to others in self-seeking dependency, out of the same needs that drive the alcoholic or addict to seek chemical relief. Ontological insecurity undermines any possibility of true mutuality (10, *pp. 1-2*; 73, *pp. 42ff.*; 101, *pp. 1-12*).

The ontologically secure person, on the other hand, like the truly sober A.A. member, comes to understand that one whose wholeness consists in essential limitation cannot be either wholly dependent or wholly independent – that to be human is to be both independent and dependent, and because both, neither totally. One can be only both; one cannot be only either; and because one can have only both, one's possession of each is intrinsically limited. Because, for human being, reality is essentially bound up with limitation, one achieves true independence only by acknowledging real dependence. Similarly, one can be dependent in a truly human way only by also exercising real independence (110).

Although any image must limp, because things can never adequately mirror human reality, in a sense one "charges batteries" by dependence, thus enabling independent operation. The reverse of the analogy proves equally true: being dependent without exercising independence is like overcharging a battery rarely used – destructive to both the self and the source. The weakness of the analogy, of course, lies in its implicit "either-or" sequence. In human reality, dependence and independence do not much alternate as reciprocate – simultaneously mutually concur.

A.A., both in its suggestion of a "Higher Power" and in the dynamic of its meetings, invites and enables the living out of this mutuality between human dependence and personal independence. The First Step of the A.A. program establishes the foundation for this understanding: only by acknowledging continuing dependence upon alcohol does the A.A. member achieve the continuing independence of freedom from addiction to alcohol. This mutuality between dependence and independence also clarifies (because it also undergirds) A.A.'s emphasis on limited control and limited dependence, topics explored earlier. These are, we now see more clearly, not two separate concepts, but obverse sides of the one coin of essential human limitation. Because of essential limitation, to be fully human requires the acknowledgment of both limited control and limited dependence; and it is the embrace of each that enables the attainment of its apparent opposite.

The exploration of the mutualities taught and enabled by A.A. thus reveal the richness of its simple emphasis on the alcoholic's human need for others. One A.A. cliché refers to its program as "a simple program for complex people." A.A.'s program is "simple," but insofar as that program embraces and inculcates the wisdom of dialectical thinking about the human condition, it is anything but simplistic. The need-for-others taught by A.A., perhaps its most misunderstood facet, merits more careful and more respectful attention than most scholars and most professionals have thus far been willing to give it. For example A.A.'s experience seems to suggest that dialectical analysis of relationships between people must be founded in awareness of the dialectic inherent within each person because of the essentially mixed nature of the human condition.

Alcoholics Anonymous as Therapy for Shame[6]
Fruitful as further exploration of such an insight might prove in deepening appreciation of A.A.'s intellectual significance, the dialectical nature of the mutuality taught by A.A. offers only a partial answer to our initial question: *Why* Alcoholics Anonymous works. A more direct and practical answer arises from A.A.'s illumination and treatment of yet another apparently simple facet of human being. A.A. works and also has intellectual significance, because it is – uniquely – a way of healing shame.

I have analyzed elsewhere (39), more directly than is feasible in the present article, the nature and modalities of how Alcoholics Anonymous heals shame. Here, in what follows, it is most appropriate to undergird that more popular treatment by suggesting how A.A.'s affinity of orienta-

---

[6] Although the analysis, interpretation, and organization to follow – and especially their application to Alcoholics Anonymous – are my own, in formulating these ideas I have drawn heavily on Lynd (60), Piers and Singer (111), Lewis (112), Edwards (113), and Schneider (114).

tion with the philosophies of existence peculiarly fits it for that culturally significant task.

Although existentialist thinkers themselves tend to use the term "guilt" preceded by the adjective "existential" or "ontic" for the reality that I here name "shame," a consistent case can be made for the more ancient word (30, *p. 176*; 72; 73; 83; 115). I shall make that case presently.

Everyone recognizes that shame differs from guilt. The usual understanding of this difference runs as follows: guilt is primarily internal, shame primarily external. Guilt, or self-reproach, is rooted in the internalization of values, notably parental values; shame is based on disapproval coming from outside, from others. Guilt, a failure to live up to one's own picture of oneself (based on parental values), is contrasted with shame, a reaction to actual or feared criticism by other people. Guilt, then, derives from something that one does; shame, from something about oneself that is seen (60, *p. 21*).

It has been pointed out (60) that "this distinction between guilt as response to standards that have been internalized and shame as response to criticism or ridicule by others" involves several important assumptions for example, that shame does not exist apart from the scorn of others, expressed or imagined; that there is a basic (Cartesian) separation between oneself and others; that others are related to oneself as audience (*p. 21*). The usual distinction thus tends to regard both others and oneself as instruments, remaining external to each other. From others, one should seek approval, indulgence, contributions to one's pleasure. For others, one should do the right thing, meet appropriate standards, fulfill the designated social roles. One must never lose sight of what others will think of what one does - and how what they think will affect oneself. Appraisal tends to be always present; measuring, weighing, counting (60, *p. 236*).

A further discrimination is therefore needed. At first blush, it would seem to involve some differentiation within guilt; for example, one that develops Freud's distinction between "true guilt" and "guilty fear" (51, *pp. 118-124*; 60, *p. 22*; 112, *p. 95*). Two problems, however, at once arise in the wake of such attempts: the confusion engendered by the introduction of such terms as "true" and "fear," and the obfuscation caused by masking the relationship of this phenomenon to "others." In what follows, then, I choose to retain the word "shame," but to argue for a different, broader understanding of the term. Two reasons impel this choice. In the first place, it is not idiosyncratic: at least two writers, one a competent literary scholar (60) and the other a respected psychoanalytic researcher (112), have already suggested thus reconceptualizing the distinction between shame and guilt. Secondly and more significantly, the term *shame* invites retention because "others" remain essential to this understanding – as, however, the solution rather than the problem.

The distinction itself, fortunately, is clearer than the terminological problem involved in sustaining it. It is the distinction between transgression and failure, between violating some boundary and falling short of some goal – regardless of the source of the boundary or the goal. The following schema may clarify:

	GUILT	SHAME
Results From:	A violation, a transgression. The exercise of power, control.	A failure, a falling short. The lack of power, control.
Results In:	Feelings of wrongdoing. Sense of wickedness: "I am not good."	Feeling of inadequacy. Sense of worthlessness: "I am no good."

This understanding of the distinction between shame and guilt thus builds on the concept of *boundaries*, and specifically of the two kinds of boundaries familiar, for example, to aficionados of American football: side-lines and goal-lines. In this understanding guilt arises from the violation (transgression) of a limiting boundary or side-line; shame occurs when a goal is not reached, is fallen short of. Guilt, thus indicates an "infraction"; shame, a literal "shortcoming" (60, *pp. 22, 51*; 111, *p. 11*).

Those familiar with recent studies of human development and narcissism may recognize in this distinction larger echoes. Keniston (116), Kohlberg and Gilligan (117) and Kilpatrick (118), for example, have called attention to the growing cultural importance of the distinction between "morals," which are specific rules of conduct set out by the community and subscribed to by the individual as part of the community, and "ethics," which are an extension of the sense of identity. When ethics are violated, one feels "not guilt but a sense of human failure, a kind of existential shame that one has not been who he thought himself to be" (118, *p. 117*). And in his penetrating and provocative study of the phenomenon of modern narcissism, Heinz Kohut (119) has developed the historical distinction between "Guilty Man" and "Tragic Man" (*pp. 132-133*). According to Kohut, "Guilty Man," largely a phenomenon of the past, lived within the pleasure principle; he attempted to satisfy his pleasure-seeking drives, and because of his success at this felt guilt. "Tragic Man," on the contrary, is a recent phenomenon who seeks to express the patterns of his nuclear self, and because of his failure at this, suffers shame.

Clearly, then, shame focuses on the self; and, specifically, upon the deficiency of self. That such "shame" is an existential experience may be clarified by comparing the negations of guilt and shame. "Guiltless" is clearly an honorific term: to be guiltless is to be free from guilt, that is, innocent, blameless. "Shameless," on the contrary, is a term of oppro-brium. To be shameless is to be insensible to oneself, insensitive to one's self: one who lacks shame is impudent, brazen, without decency (60, *p. 24*).

This evident difference between "guiltless" and "shameless" manifestly implies that guilt is bad, shame is good. The focus of in shame, as noted, is upon the deficiency of self; and to both A.A. and existentialist insight, to be fully human is to recognize and to accept this deficiency, this limitation of finitude that flows from the nature of the human condition. At least some shame is a necessary corollary of the mixed nature of being human, being both beast and angel, being "a god who shits."

The deficiency of self for which one feels shame can be either contingent or existential. "Contingent shame" – the shame of "sin" – results from falling short of an attainable goal. "Existential shame" – the shame of ANGH – is the sense of feeling to blame for finitude. A.A. treats both, for A.A. understands the source of the alcoholic's contingent shame to be his failure to confront the existential shame of the essential limitation of the human condition. Because of this priority, in what follows, "shame" unqualified refers most strictly to existential shame. Nevertheless, much of what will be said primarily concerning existential shame will be seen also to apply to contingent shame. One facet of A.A.'s genius lies in its utilization of experiences of contingent shame to bring one into contact with existential shame.

Shame contains a "not" – the not imposed by human finitude. To be human is to be aware that one's possibilities are not *all* possibilities: they are not only what one *can* be; they are also what one can *not-be*. The ability *to be* is also an ability to be not (30, *pp. 162-168*; 36, *pp. 36-59*). Thus, to be is to feel shame – to feel "to blame" for the not-ness lodged in one's essence. Why this "feeling to blame"? Because of the anomalous nature of the human as not-God, as beast-angel, as craving infinity yet essentially limited.

Shame, because it is rooted in this incongruity of the human condition, reflects also the paradox explored earlier in our delineation of A.A.'s mutualities. The necessity of mutuality derives from the vision that the human is the conjunction of the infinite and the limited. Because they contain that fusion, humans can relate only dialectically, not in either-or fashion. Confronted with a human situation, one can have only both of its polarities; one cannot have only either. "Feeling to blame for finitude" arises from the imperfection of such both-ness: neither polarity can be total so long as both are actual.

211

The Qualities of Shame

Three characteristics of shame (or better, of its occasion) aid in distinguishing shame from guilt and illuminate the nature of the *not* imposed by human finitude. The final characteristic to be discussed also hints at the nature and the process of shames' healing and will introduce a brief exploration of how Alcoholics Anonymous achieves this.

Guilt has to do with moral transgression; it results from a voluntary act, from a choice carried out; and it tends to be proportionate to the perceived gravity of the offense committed. Shame, in contrast, may be evoked by a nonmoral lapse, may arise for an involuntary event and tends to be magnified by the very triviality of its stimulus.

Shame may arise from either a moral or a nonmoral lapse. A common source of the latter kind of shame is disappointment or frustration. Aggression evokes guilt; defeat and failure give rise to shame (112, *pp. 80-82*). Especially two categories of inadequacy, of nonmoral shortcoming, induce shame; failure in love and the failure of sickness. Each, of course, has special relevance in the case of the alcoholic – one reason why A.A., if it is effective, must be understood as providing healing for shame (39).

That shame arises involuntarily – from incapacity, the failure of choice – should be clear from its very concept as outlined above. Guilt implies choice; haggling over guilt often focuses upon the question of how free was the choice, but the fact of choice is assumed. Shame, on the other hand, occurs over a falling short, a missing of the mark, a failure of powers. Involuntariness is a necessary concomitant of shame's focus upon the deficiency of self: the core of the pain in shame arises from the failure of choice, of will (60, *pp. 49ff*, 112, *p. 84*). Recall the description, above, of the "two realms of human will." A particularly insidious shame can arise in the wake of the failure of "the attempt to will what cannot be willed." A further example may also help clarify. One who commits adultery might feel both guilt and shame: guilt over violation of the marriage promise; shame at falling short of the marriage ideal. The man who finds himself sexually impotent with a woman he loves will feel predominantly shame: the question of morality does not enter, and – at least in his conscious mind – his sexual disability is anything but voluntary.

The final characteristic of shame to be examined is the apparent disproportion that renders it literally so monstrous an experience. Usually, the depth and extent of guilt correlate with the gravity of the offense. Shame, on the contrary, tends to be triggered by the most trivial of stimuli, and even to be intensified by the very insignificance of its cause. The very triviality of shame's source reveals most unmistakably the deficiency of self *as self*, rather than as violator of some abstract code (60, *pp. 40, 64, 235*). This disproportion that tends to inhere in shame serves to magnify further the experience of shame: one becomes ashamed at the very disproportion of one's reaction, and therefore ashamed of shame itself (60, *p. 42*). Perhaps because of this insatiable quality in shame over the trivial, it is upon the disproportion inherent in experiences of shame that the A.A. program fastens in turning shame to therapeutically constructive use.

How A.A. achieves this need not be detailed here for readers familiar with the dynamic underlying its Fifth Step and its practice of storytelling – with how these drive home to the alcoholic his unexceptional ordinariness (39, *pp. 25-27*). There is another way, more appropriate to the present exploration, in which the frequent pettiness of occasions of shame serves a therapeutic purpose within A.A.

Shame, Exposure and Denial

Because shame's stimulus is so often trivial, thus emphasizing shame's focus on the self, experiences of shame are experiences of exposure: they throw a flooding and searching light on what and who one is, uncovering hitherto unrecognized aspects of personality, revealing peculiarly sensitive, intimate, vulnerable aspects of the self (60, *pp. 49, 183*). Shame, then, invites the truth of *aleitheia*. Exposure to oneself lies at the heart of shame. The exposure may also be to others; but, whether others are involved or not, the significant exposure is always to one's own eyes (60, *pp. 27-28*). An incident described by Somerset Maugham in *Of Human Bondage* vividly penetrates to the essence of shame as the exposure to oneself of one's own weakness.

The protagonist Phillip, as a new boy at school, was ragged by classmates who demanded to see his clubfoot. Despite his almost obsequious desire for friendship, Philip adamantly refused to show his

213

handicap. Finally, one night, a group of boys attacked Philip in his bed, and the school bully twisted his arm until Philip stuck his leg out of the bed to let them see his deformity. The boys then laughed and left.

> "Philip . . . got his teeth in the pillow so that his sobbing should be inaudible. He was not crying for the pain they had caused him, nor for the humiliation he had suffered when they looked at his foot, but with rage at himself because, unable to stand the torture, he had put out his foot of his own accord" (120, *pp. 35-36*)

Exposure to others was less painful to Philip than the exposure to himself of his own weakness.

Alcoholism – indeed, addictive dependence upon any psychoactive chemical – often arises from and usually is connected with the effort to conceal such weakness, to prevent its exposure to oneself. The alcoholic or addict uses his chemical to hide, and especially to hide from himself. The endeavor to hide reveals that the critical problem underlying such behavior is shame (113).

Guilt moves to solving problems; shame, untreated, leads to hiding feelings. "Wanting to be absolved of guilt is not the addict's problem" (113, *p. 10*). Usually, the addicted person within himself is pleading passionately to be able to feel guilty. Guilt-oriented therapies, however sophisticated, fail because the addict or alcoholic cannot "mend his ways" or, by willing it, "grow up": he must maintain his addiction precisely to conceal his unendurable shame from himself. Any interference with his chemical dependency becomes the most primary of survival threats. In any case in which the avoidance of pain – the existential pain of shame – plays a basic part in the psychopathology, effective therapy must address itself first to the existential nature of that shame (113, *pp. 9-12*).

Alcoholics Anonymous builds on this insight. The characteristic defense of alcoholics, the defense against which the shared honesty of mutual vulnerability, the "identification" that is the core dynamic of A.A. so effectively operates, is denial (17, *pp. 60ff.*). Denial involves the hiding of a felt inadequacy of being. To get beyond this hiding, to transcend this denial, the alcoholic needs others. This is why the mutualities inherent in A.A., explored earlier, prove so efficacious. The effectiveness of these mutualities in penetrating denial testifies that, in shame, "others" are not so much the problem as the solution. This was, the reader may recall, one large reason for the attempt to preserve the term "shame" even while reshaping its concept. Having traversed that reconceptualization, another reason can now be brought to bear: continuity of analysis.

Shame, as herein explained, relates so intimately to "denial" because it results not merely from a "sense of failure," but from a sense of essential failure – the failure of existence. This understanding captures, I believe, the insight of Harry Tiebout in his early classic psychiatric exploration of the therapeutic dynamic operative in A.A. Tiebout distinguished between "compliance," which he saw as worse than useless because it obscured the obsessive-compulsive nature of alcoholism, and "surrender," which he presented as the key to the therapeutic process of recovery (121; 122). Tiebout's "compliance" may be understood as motivated by guilt; "surrender," as enabled by the alcoholic's acceptance of shame.

Denial, Tiebout realized, could continue despite acknowledgment of – and even attempts at reparation for – guilt. Guilt may even be a defense against confronting and accepting what is denied, as when the alcoholic accepts responsibility for what she has done when drinking as preferable to admitting that the drinking itself was beyond her control. Real guilt fears punishment and tries to escape it. The shamed person, on the other hand, for example the alcoholic just described, seeks and embraces punishment – even by admitting "guilt" – as a confirmation aiding denial of what is most deeply feared: her own failure of being.

Conclusion: Denial, Need and Limitation

The connection between shame and denial, elucidated by the exploration of "hiding" and by Tiebout's concept of "surrender," highlights another advantage of understanding Alcoholics Anonymous as a singularly efficacious way of dealing with shame. As its emphasis on honesty hints, A.A. understands denial – self-deception – to be so characteristic of the alcoholic that it is pathognomic of alcoholism.[7] This centrality accorded denial clarifies a further affinity between the insight of A.A. and the wisdom of the philosophies of existence.

All classic thought contains a concept of "sin," which refers less to some act than to a state of being. Yet, whether as act or as state of being, "sin" is understood to be that which isolates or alienates from reality – from the reality of nature, of others, of self. The primordial sin, as the Edenic myth of "original sin" illustrates, fuses dishonesty and pride: it denies that one is limited and thus not infinite; it claims self to be the center of the universe and thus "as God" (50).

The insight of A.A. and the philosophy of existentialist thinkers such as Sartre locate such "sin" identically: A.A. views it as a "dishonesty" rooted in "self-centeredness"; Sartre, as the *mauvaise foi* of "self-decep-tion." For both, it consists in the claim and the attempt to be other than human; for both, it involves the inauthenticity of a pretended appropria-tion of unlimitedness. To become fully human, A.A.'s "not-God," like Heidegger's *Dasein*, must avoid "sin" by accepting as first truth his own essential limitation (30, *pp. 64-70;* 34, *pp. 233-235*). Both visions indict the refusal to embrace one's own essential limitation as the root of all human evil, the source of all alienation.

In one important way, however, as we have seen, the insight of A.A. transcends even the thought of some existentialist thinkers. Sartre defined "Hell" as "other people" (32, *p. 79*). Alcoholics Anonymous understands the reality of essential limitation differently. According to A.A. insight, because of their essential limitation, human beings have needs. The denial of essential limitation usually manifests itself not directly, but in the denial of need (124, *p. 3*). The alcoholic's denial of need is twofold, his denial of his need for alcohol blends into and intertwines with his denial of his need for others. Early in the process of alcoholism, the alcoholic denies that it is his unmet, because insatiable, need for others that leads him to

---

[7] On the centrality of "denial," see Mann (123) and Kimball (124). That this perception if not the term itself extends far beyond Alcoholics Anonymous is clear from the tone as well as the content of Pattison (68) and Baekeland and Lundwall (125).

seek comfort or excitement in alcohol. "A few drinks" become more important than the people at a party, for example, as alcohol becomes a surer source of satisfaction than human interaction. Later in the process, after a few failures of "I can stop whenever I want to" (denial of the need for alcohol), the denial becomes again of the need for others: "Just let me alone – I can lick the thing by myself."

A.A. enables and promotes recovery from alcoholism by breaking through these twin denials of need. As fellowship, Alcoholics Anonymous invites the alcoholic to discover his own need for others by being the one place where the alcoholic himself is needed, and needed precisely and only as alcoholic. This leads to self-identification as "alcoholic," and thus to admission of the need for alcohol. As program, A.A. builds on the admission of the need for alcohol – "I am an alcoholic" – ever deepening awareness of one's need for others. A.A.'s twelve Steps begin with the word "We," and A.A. ever emphasizes that it is "fellowship" as well as "program." Thus the vicious circle of denial of need – for alcohol and for others – is broken and replaced by a twofold, mutually enhancing admission of need.

These admissions of need – for alcohol because one is an alcoholic, for others because one is a human being – signal both the acceptance of essential limitation and the embrace of wholeness in limitation. This acceptance and embrace heal, for acknowledging in oneself the essential connection between limitation and reality enables and promotes opening oneself to a new kind of relationship with others – a relationship of pluralism and complementarity that allows one who is essentially limited to attain true transcendence of self.[8]

Essential limitation means that there exists a necessary equation between being limited and being real. Again, the message of mutuality echoes: in any human phenomenon, limitation and reality are necessarily

---

[8] I have analyzed "pluralism" and "complementarity" and explained their implications elsewhere (17, *pp 151-152, 219-221*; 39, *pp. 47-51*). Also, see Heinemann (29, *pp. 190-202*) for a similar analysis from a very different and perhaps more profoundly existentialist insight.

present in a dialectical relationship; one can have only both, one cannot have only either. One can be only limited *and* real; one cannot be only limited or only real: to be real is to be limited, and to be limited is to be real.

This necessary dialectic is perhaps clearest in the matter of freedom.[9] It is their prime concern over the nature of human freedom that most deeply unites the insights of A.A. and existentialist philosophy. According to both insights, to be human is to be both free and unfree: although real, freedom is limited; although limited, freedom is real.

The conjunction *although* between "real" and "freedom" sums up the phenomenological insight of A.A. and of the philosophies of existence. Both, however, offer more. Alcoholics Anonymous renders practical existentialist philosophy's deepest contribution to understanding the human condition: the interpretive insight that, *because* real, freedom is limited, *because* limited, freedom is real. With freedom as with any other human phenomenon, to be real is to be limited, for limitation proves reality. To understand this is to be enabled to accept the wholeness of essential limitation and – for many, more important – to be enabled to recover from alcohol addiction.

Thus, the reason "Why A.A. Works" and "The Intellectual Significance of Alcoholics Anonymous" are one and the same. As unconscious bearer of the existentialist insight that found more explicit formulation elsewhere in its era, A.A. built upon its concept of "alcoholic" – its insight into essential limitation – an effective modality of healing for the malaise of its age, shame.

No direct influence from the philosophies of existence ever impinged upon the co-founders of Alcoholics Anonymous. Indeed, Bill Wilson and Dr. Bob Smith would probably – and correctly – have laughed had anyone ever called them "philosophers." Yet, because of their alcoholism, these

---

[9] For a profound and challenging discussion of "freedom," which uses provocatively the example of the alcoholic, see the index listings in Barrett (34), and especially p. 262.

men and their cohorts intimately knew the nature and ramifications of the illness, the dis-ease, that was their age's metaphor for the problematic reality of being human (17, *pp. 200-202*). We, today, live in a different age; yet perhaps even more profoundly, postmodern humanity still strives to survive and to flourish in an Age of Limits.

Many have found, and probably will continue to find, their survival manual in some variant of existentialist philosophy, in the wisdom of Eastern religions, in diverse efforts to "live closer to nature," and elsewhere. A.A.'s intellectual significance, then, is itself appropriately limited. A.A. suggests, for those afflicted by existential shame over their failure to be perfect, both a philosophy and a therapy that enable that shame's transcendence. Insofar as it is understood as a therapy for addiction, A.A. holds out hope, and even "cure," especially to those addicted to the Will to Power and Perfection – to those, that is, addicted to addiction itself (34, *pp. 192-201*; 47; 49). Perhaps in this lies its greatest significance, both intellectually and socially, for all of us.

REFERENCES

1. Norris, J.L. Alcoholics Anonymous and other self-help groups. Pp. 735-776. In: Tarter, R.E. and Sugerman, A.A., eds. Alcoholism: interdisciplinary approaches to an enduring problem. Reading, MA; Addison-Wesley; 1976.

2. Kissin, B. Theory and practice in the treatment of alcoholism. Pp. 1-51. In: Kissin, B. and Begleiter, H., eds. The biology of alcoholism. Vol 5. Treatment and rehabilitation of the chronic alcoholic. New York; Plenum; 1977.

3. Beigen, A. and Ghertner, S. Toward a social model: an assessment of social factors which influence problem drinking and its treatment. Pp. 197-233. In: Kissin, B. and Begleiter, H. eds. The biology of alcoholism, Vol 5. Treatment and rehabilitation of the chronic alcoholic. New york; Plenum. 1977.

4. Doroff, D.R. Group psychotherapy in alcoholism. Pp. 235-258. In: Kissin, B. and Begleiter, H., eds. The biology of alcoholism. Vol 5. Treatment and rehabilitation of the chronic alcoholic. New York; Plenum; 1977.

5 Baekeland, F. Evaluation and treatment methods in chronic alcoholism. Pp. 385-440. In: Kissin, B. and Begleiter, H., eds. The biology of alcoholism. Vol 5. Treatment and rehabilitation of the chronic alcoholic. New York; Plenum; 1977.

6. Leach, B. and Norris, J.L. Factors in the development of Alcoholics Anonymous (A.A.). Pp. 441-543. In: Kissin, B. and Begleiter, H., eds. The biology of alcoholism. Vol 5. Treatment and rehabilitation of the chronic alcoholic. New York; Plenum; 1977.

7. Zinberg, N.E. and Fraser, K.M. The role of the social setting in the prevention and treatment of alcoholism. Pp. 350-385. In: Mendelson, J.H. and Mello, N.K., eds. The diagnosis and treatment of alcoholism. New York; McGraw-Hill; 1979.

8. Corrigan, E.M. Alcoholic women in treatment. New York; Oxford University Press; 1980.

9. Chambers, F.T., Jr. Analysis and comparison of three treatment approaches for alcoholism: Antabuse, the Alcoholics Anonymous approach and psychotherapy. Br. J. Addic. 50: 29-41. 1953.

10. Peele, S. and Brodsky, A. Love and Addiction. New York; Taplinger; 1975

11. Borman, L.D., ed. Explorations in self-help and mutual aid. Evanston, IL; Northwestern University Press; 1975.

12. Caplan, G. and Killilea, M., eds. Support systems and mutual help: multidisciplinary explorations. New York; Grune & Stratton; 1976.

13. Gartner, A. and Riessman, F. Self-help in the human services. San Francisco; Jossey-Bass; 1977.

14. Lieberman, M.A. and Borman, L.D., eds. Self-help groups for coping with crisis: origins, members, processes, and impact. San Francisco; Jossey-Bass; 1979.

15. Alcoholics Anonymous. Alcoholics Anonymous comes of age. New York; Alcoholics Anonymous; 1957.

16. Thomsen, R. Bill W. New York; Harper & Row; 1975

17. Kurtz, E. Not-God: A history of Alcoholics Anonymous. Center City, MN; Hazelden Educational Services. 1979.

18. Blumberg, L. The ideology of a therapeutic social movement: Alcoholics Anonymous. J. Stud. Alc. 38: 2122-2143. 1977.

19. Barrett, W. Irrational man: a study in existential philosophy. Garden City, NY; Doubleday, 1962.

20. Kaufmann, W. The reception of existentialism in the United States. Midway: 9: 97-126; Summer 1968.

21. Barzun, J. Clio and the doctors: psycho-history, quanto-history, and history. University of Chicago Press; 1974.

22. Handlin, O. Truth in history. Cambridge; Harvard University Press; 1979.

23. Schlesinger, A.S., Jr. Intellectual history: a time for despair? J. Amer. Hist. 66: 888-893, 1980.

24. Degler, C.M. Presidential address: remaking American history. J. Amer. Hist. 67: 7-25, 1980.

25. Becker, C.L. What is still living in the political philosophy of Thomas Jefferson? In: Snyder, P.L., ed. Detachment and the writing of history: essays and letters of Carl L. Becker. Ithaca, NY; Cornell University Press; 1958. [Orig. 1944.]

26. Alcoholics Anonymous. New York; A.A. World Services; 1978. [Orig.1953.]

27. Twelve Steps and Twelve Traditions. New York. A.A. World Services; 1978. [Orig. 1953.]

28. Heidegger, M. Being and time. (Macquarrie, J. and Robinson, E., transl.) New York; Harper & Row, 1962. [Orig. 1927.]

29. Heinemann, F.H. Existentialism and the modern predicament. New York; Harper; 1953.

30. Gelven, M. A commentary on Heidegger's *Being and Time*: a section-by-section interpretation. New York; Harper & Row; 1970.

31. Vail, L.M. Heidegger and ontological difference. University park; Pennsylvania State University Press; 1972.

32. King, T.M. Sartre and the Sacred. Chicago; University of Chicago Press; 1974.

33. Kaufmann, W., ed. Existentialism from Dostoevsky to Sartre. New York; New American Library; 1975.

34. Barrett, W. The Illusion of Technique: a search for meaning in a technological civilization. Garden City, NY; Anchor; 1978.

35. Poggeler, O. Being as appropriation. Pp. 84-115. In: Murray, M., ed. Heidegger and modern philosophy: critical essays. New Haven, CT; Yale; 1978.

36. Sartre, J-P. Being and nothingness: an essay on phenomenological ontology (Barnes, H.E., transl.) New York; Washington Square Press; 1966. [Orig. 1943.]

37. Heidegger, M. What is metaphysics? Pp. 242-264. In: Kaufman, W., ed. Existential-ism from Dostoevsky to Sartre. New York; New American Library; 1975. [Orig. 1929.]

38. Kierkegaard, S.A. The concept of dread. 2nd ed. (Lowrie, W., transl.) Princeton, NJ; Princeton University Press; 1957. [Orig. 1844.]

39. Kurtz, E. Shame and Guilt: characteristics of the dependency cycle. Center City, MN; Hazelden Foundation; 1981

40. Hale, N.G., Jr. Freud and the Americans: the beginnings of psychoanalysis in the United States, 1876-1917. New York; Oxford; 1971

41. Bledstein, B.J. The culture of professionalism: the middle class and the development of higher education in America. New York; Norton; 1976.

42. Gaylin, W. What you see is the real you. The New York Times, p. 31, 7 October 1977.

43. Sennett, R. The fall of public man. New York; Knopf; 1977.

44. Clinard, M.B., ed. Anomie and deviant behavior: a discussion and critique. New York; Free Press; 1964.

45. Kierkegaard, S.A. Fear and trembling (Lowrie, W., transl.) Garden City, NY; Anchor; 1954. [Orig. 1843.]

46. Kierkegaard, S.A. The sickness unto death. In: Kierkegaard, S.A. Fear and trembling. Garden Cit, NY; 1954. [Orig. 1949.]

47. Farber, L.H. Thinking about will. Pp. 3-12. In: Lying, despair, jealousy, envy, sex, suicide, drugs, and the good life. New York; Basic Books, 1976. [Orig. 1969.]

48. Farber, L.H. Will and anxiety. Pp. 13-34 In: eodem. [Orig. 1966.]

49. Farber, L.H. Our kindly family physician, chief crazy horse. Pp. 106-119. In: eodem. [Orig. 1966.]

50. Szasz, T. The second sin. Garden City, NY; Anchor; 1973.

51. Gaylin, W. Caring. New York; Knopf; 1976.

52. James, W. Principles of Psychology. New York; Holt; 1890.

53. Sullivan, H.S. Conceptions of modern psychiatry. 2nd ed. New York; Norton; 1953 [Orig. 1940.]

54. Mullahy, P. The beginnings of modern American psychiatry: the ideas of Harry Stack Sullivan. Boston, MA; Houghton Mifflin; 1973.

55. Pascal, B. Pensées. (Krailsheimer, A.J., transl.) Harmondsworth, England; Penguin; 1966. [Orig. 1670.]

56. Augustine. The City of God. Books XIV and XIX.

57. Goldmann, L. The hidden god; a study of tragic vision in the Pensées or Pascal and the tragedies of Racine. (Thody, P., transl.) London; Routledge and Kegan Paul; 1964.

58. Santayana, G. Persons and places. 3 vols. New York; Scribners; 1944-1953.

59. Becker, E. The denial of death. New York. Free Press. 1973.

60. Lynd, H.M. On shame and the search for identity. New York; Harcourt, Brace; 1958.

61. Sartre, J-P. Portrait of an anti-semite. Pp. 329-345. In: Kaufmann, W., ed. Existentialism from Dostoevsky to Sartre; op. cit. [Orig. 1946.]

62. Kant, I. An answer to the question: what is enlightenment? Pp. 54-60. In: Reiss, H.S., ed. Kant's political writings. (Nisbet, H.B. transl.) Cambridge; Cambridge University Press; 1970. [Orig. 1784.]

63. Goldmann, L. The philosophy of the Enlightenment: the Christian burgess and the Enlightenment. (Maas, H., transl.) Cambridge, MA; M.I.T. Press, 1973.

64. Davis, D.L. Definitional issues in alcoholism. Pp. 53-73. In Tarter, R.E. and Sugerman, A.A., eds. ; op. cit.

65. Tarter, R.E. and Schneider, D.U. Models and theories of alcoholism. Pp. 75-106. In: Tarter, R.E. and Sugerman, A.A., eds.; op. cit.

66. Sugerman, A.A. and Schneider, D.U. Cognitive styes in alcoholism. Pp. 395-433. In: Tarter, R.E. and Sugerman A.A., eds.; op. cit.

67. Mendelson, J.H. and Mello, N.K. The diagnosis of alcoholism. Pp.1-18. In: Mendelson, J.H. and Mello, N.K. The diagnosis and treatment of alcoholism. New York; McGraw-Hill; 1979.

68. Pattison, E.M. The selection of treatment modalities for the alcoholic patient. Pp. 125-227. In: Mendelson, J.H. and Mello, N.K., op. cit.

69. Unger, R.M. Knowledge and politics. New York; Free Press; 1975.

70. Jaspers, K. On my philosophy. Pp. 158-189. In: Kaufmann, W., ed. op. cit.

71. Kocklemans, J.J. Edmund Husserl's phenomenological psychology: a historico-critical study. (Jager, B., transl.) Pittsburgh; Duquesne University Press; 1967.

72. Frankl, V.L. The unconscious God: psychotherapy and theology. New York; Simon & Schuster; 1975. [Orig. 1948.]

73. Laing, R.D. The divided self: an existential study in sanity and madness. London; Tavistock; 1969. [Orig. 1960.]

224

74. Goldmann, L. Lukács and Heidegger: towards a new philosophy. (Boelhower, W.Q. transl.) London; Routledge & Kegan Paul; 1977.

75. Sartre, J-P. Self-deception. Pp. 299-328 in Kaufmann, W., ed., op. cit.; [Orig. 1943.]

76. Kierkegaard, S.A. Either/or: a fragment of life. (Swenson, D.F. and Swenson, L.M., transl.) Princeton, NJ; Princeton University Press; 1944. [Orig. 1843.]

77. Stace, W.T. The philosophy of Hegel: a systematic exposition. New York; Macmillan; 1924.

78. Heiss, R. Hegel, Kierkegaard, Marx: three philosophers whose ideas changed the course of civilization. (Garside, E.B., transl.) New York; Delacorte; 1975.

79. Markey, M. Alcoholics and God. Liberty Magazine 16: 6-7, 30 September 1939.

80. Glasser, W. The Identity Society. New York; Harper & Row; 1975.

81. Maxwell, M.A. Alcoholics Anonymous: an interpretation. Pp. 211-222. In: Pittman, D.J., ed. Alcoholism; New York; Harper & Row; 1967.

82. Sullivan, H.S. The meaning of anxiety in psychiatry and life. Psychiatry 11: 1-13. 1948

83. Laing, R.D. Self and Others. 2nd ed. Harmondsworth, England. Penguin; 1971.

84. Mowrer, O.H. The new group therapy. Princeton, NJ; Van Nostrand; 1964.

85. Jourard, W.M. The transparent self. New York; Van Nostrand Reinhold; 1971.

86. Mayeroff, M. On caring. New York; Harper & Row; 1971.

87. Nouwen, H.J.M. The wounded healer: ministry in contemporary society. Garden City, NY; Doubleday; 1972.

88. Goldmann, L. The human sciences and philosophy. (White, H.V. and Anchor, R., transl.) London; Cape; 1969. [Orig. 1952.]

89. Purcell, E.A., Jr. The crisis of democratic theory: scientific materialism and the problem of value. Lexington, KY; University of Kentucky Press; 1973.

90. Furner, M.O. Advocacy and objectivity: a crisis in the professionalization of American social science, 1865-1905. Lexington, KY; Univ. of Kentucky; 1975.

91. Hawthorn, G. Enlightenment and despair: a history of sociology. Cambridge; Cambridge University Press; 1976.

92. Hollis, M. Models of man: philosophical thoughts on social action. Cambridge; Cambridge University Press; 1976.

93. Lasch, C. Haven in a heartless world: the family besieged. New York; Basic Books; 1977.

94. Boyer, P.S. Urban masses and moral order in America, 1820-1920. Cambridge, MA; Harvard University Press; 1978.

95. Fuhrman, E.R. The sociology of knowledge in America, 1883-1915. Charlottesville; University of Virginia Press; 1980.

96. Rothman, D.J. Conscience and convenience: the asylum and its alternatives in progressive America. Boston; Little, Brown; 1980.

97. Freud, S. Group psychology and the analysis of the ego. (Strachey, J., transl.) new York; Liveright; 1951. [Orig. 1921.]

98. Lasswell, H.D. Power and personality. New York; Norton; 1948.

99. Benedict, R. Patterns of culture. Boston; Houghton Mifflin; 1934.

100. Hegel, G.W.F. The phenomenology of mind. (Baille, J.B., transl.) New York; Harper & Row; 1967. [Orig. 1807.]

101. Collier, A. R.D. Laing: the philosophy and politics of psychotherapy. New York; Pantheon; 1977.

102. Guntrip, H.J.S. Psychoanalytic theory, therapy, and the self. New York; Basic Books; 1971.

103. White, R.W. Motivation reconsidered: the concept of competence. Psych. Rev. **66**: 297-333, 1959.

104. Erikson, E.H. Identity, youth, and crisis. New York; Norton; 1968

105. Angyal, A. Neurosis and treatment: a holistic theory. (Hanfmann, E. and Jones, R.M., eds.) New York; Wiley; 1965.

106 Farber, L.H. On jealousy. Pp. 180-202 . In: Lying, despair, jealousy, envy, sex, suicide, drugs, and the good life. New York; Basic Books; 1976. [Orig. 1973.]

107. Sartre, J-P. Saint Genet: actor and martyr. (Frechtman, B., transl.) New York; New American Library; 1971. [Orig. 1952.]

108. Gaylin, W. In the beginning: helpless and dependent. Pp. 3-38. In: Gaylin, W., Glasser, I., Marcus, S, and Rothman, D., eds. Doing good: the limits of benevolence. New York; Pantheon; 1978.

109. Winnicott, D.W. The capacity to be alone. Pp. 29-36. In: The maturational process and the facilitating environment. New York; International Universities Press; 1965. [Orig. 1958.]

110. Winnicott, D.W. From dependence towards independence in the development of the individual. Pp. 83-92. In: eodem.

111. Piers, G. and Singer, M.B. Shame and guilt: a psychoanalytic and a cultural study. Springfield, IL; Thomas; 1953.

112. Lewis, H.B. Shame and guilt in neurosis. New York; International Universities Press; 1971.

113. Edwards, D.G. Shame and pain and "Shut up or I'll really give you something to cry about." Clin Soc. Work J. 4: 3-13, 1976.

114. Schneider, C.D. Shame, exposure, and privacy. Boston; Beacon; 1977.

115. May, R., Angel, E. and Ellenberger, H.F., eds. Existence: a new dimension in psychiatry and psychology. New York; Basic Books; 1958.

116. Keniston, K. Morals and ethics. Am. Scholar 34: 628-632, 1965.

117. Kohlberg, L. and Gilligan, C.F. The adolescent as philosopher. Pp. 144-179, In: Kagan, J. and Coles, R., eds. Twelve to sixteen: early adolescence. New York; Norton; 1972.

118. Kilpatrick, W. Identity and intimacy. New York; Delacorte; 1975.

119. Kohut, H. The restoration of the self. New York. Int. Univ. Press; 1977.

120. Maugham, W.S. Of human bondage. Garden City, NY; Doubleday; 1936. [Orig. 1915.]

121. Tiebout, H.M. The act of surrender in the therapeutic process. Q.J. Stud. Alcohol 10: 48-58, 1963.

122. Tiebout, H.M. Surrender versus compliance in therapy. Q.J. Stud. Alcohol **14**: 58-68, 1953.

123. Mann, M. New primer on alcoholism: how people drink, how to recognize alcoholics, and what to do about them. New York; Rinehart; 1958.

124. Kimball, B.J. The alcoholic woman's mad, mad world of denial and mind games. Center City, MN; Hazelden; 1978.

125. Baekeland, F. and Lundwall, L.K. Engaging the alcoholic in treatment and keeping him there. Pp. 161-195. In: Kissin, B. and Begleiter, H., eds. The biology of alcoholism. Vol. 5. Treatment and rehabilitation of the chronic alcoholic. New York; Plenum; 1977.

During my brief tenure as Director of Research and Education at Guest House, our Development Director, Michael Goddard, asked if I could write a piece that might be carried in local newspapers to educate about alcoholism. One piece of alcohol advertising had been irritating me since my days at the University of Georgia, so I decided to have a try at taking on one of beer advertising's perennial fad inventions. Given the heaviness of the previous piece, I hope this serves as a more fitting conclusion to this collection of writings that I have so much enjoyed producing.

Here's to "Spuds"!

Prominent voices have recently complained of the Spuds McKenzie character used promotionally by a leading manufacturer of magic chemicals. Spuds, a supposedly lovable pit bull terrier, is presented as "a party animal." Advertisements portray him surrounded by buxom, bubbling sex objects. Those who protest the advertisements claim that they are designed to seduce young people, presumably especially males, into imbibing the sponsor's beverage.

Such fears are foolish. Young people are not dumb: they understand and will learn from the education afforded by the Spuds character. As a student of our culture's attitudes toward mind-altering chemical use, I respectfully suggest that it would be difficult to devise a more accurate depiction of the results of consuming the pushed product. Three obvious points stand out.

First, despite denials, Spuds McKenzie is at the very least made up as a pit bull terrier. The breed's reputation for erratic behavior and especially for unpredictable violence hardly requires comment. Yet so great is the honesty of the sponsor – or so great its confidence in the stupidity of its audience – that this trait is underlined by choosing as "Spuds" a patch-eyed specimen who looks as though he has lost a recent fight.

229

Second, in the advertisements, Spuds is clearly doped up to the point of being doped out. Sitting dazed dumb at parties seems a weird idea of being "a party animal." Can Spuds speak? Can Spuds dance? Can Spuds even blink his eyes? Apparently not – the surest evidence that, unlike some other advertising models, Spuds has indeed partaken of the sponsor's wares.

Third, there is the matter of Spuds McKenzie's companions. Although portrayed as vacuous air heads – an intriguing commentary on the sponsor's attitude toward women – these playful lasses are undeniably physically attractive. Yet Spuds remains oblivious to them and to their charms. I can imagine few hells worse than being surrounded by available sexuality and yet unable to enjoy the opportunity or even to notice it. Of course, as Shakespeare recognized, that is one inevitable outcome of partaking of Spuds' sponsor's product.

And so I disagree with those who find the Spuds McKenzie commercials misleading and dishonest. Rarely has any advertisement so accurately flaunted the consequences flowing from the use of the pushed product. If Americans, young or old, wish to sit dazed out of their minds at parties, unable to function socially or sexually, then they should know that consuming the products of the sponsor who brings them Spuds will effect that outcome.

The people who work in alcohol treatment should be grateful for Spuds. They often decry the stereotype of the skid-row alcoholic. The modern alcoholic is far better imaged by Spuds McKenzie – dazed mindless and sexless, scorned even while being fawned over.

Thank you, Anheuser-Busch, for an unprecedented example of truth in advertising.

[1988]

Credits and Permissions

The previously published works appearing herein are republished with the kind permission of the publications where they originally appeared. In some few cases, I have made minor modifications in the original terminology for the sake of consistency of vocabulary.

Kurtz, Ernest. "Research on Alcoholics Anonymous: The Historical Context." in *Research on Alcoholics Anonymous: Opportunities and Alternatives*, eds. Barbara S. McCrady, and William R. Miller, pp. 13-26. New Brunswick, NJ: Rutgers Center of Alcohol Studies, 1993.

Kurtz, Ernest. "Alcoholics Anonymous: A Phenomenon in American Religious History," in *Religion and Philosophy in the United States of America: Proceedings of the German American Conference, Paderborn, 1986*, ed. Peter Freese, vol. 2, pp. 447-462. (Essen: Verlag Die Blaue Eule, 1987).

Kurtz, Ernest. "'Spiritual Rather Than Religious': The Contribution of Alcoholics Anonymous." in *Prevention and Control / Realities and Aspirations: Volume II*, ed. R. B. Waahlberg, pp. 678-86. Oslo, Norway: National Directorate for the Prevention of Alcohol and Drug Problems, 1989.

Kurtz, Ernest. "The Spirituality of William James: A Lesson from Alcoholics Anonymous"; invited paper presented at the 98th Annual Convention of the American Psychological Association, Boston, MA, 12 August 1990.

Kurtz, Ernest. "Shame in the Eighties." *Alcoholism Treatment Quarterly* 4, #2 (1987): 1-6.

Kurtz, Ernest. "Commentary on Lay Treatment" in *Annual Review of Addictions Research and Treatment: Volume 2*, eds. James W. Langenbucher, Barbara S. McCrady, William Frankenstein, and Peter E. Nathan, 397-400. New York: Pergamon Press, 1992.

Miller, William R. and Ernest Kurtz. "Models of Alcoholism Used in Treatment: Contrasting A.A. and Other Perspectives with Which It Is Often Confused," *Journal of Studies on Alcohol* 55(2): 159-166 (1994).

Kurtz, Ernest "Spirituality and Recovery: The Historical Journey." *The N.C.C.A. Blue Book* 47 (1996): 5-29.

Kurtz, Ernest. "Twelve-Step Programs." in *Spirituality and the Secular Quest*, ed. Peter H. VanNess, pp. 277-302. World Spirituality: An Encyclopedic History of the Religious Quest, General Editor Ewert Cousins, vol. 22. New York: Crossroad, 1996.

Kurtz, Ernest. "Why A.A. Works: The Intellectual Significance of Alcoholics Anonymous." *Journal of Studies on Alcohol* 43, no. 1 (1982): 38-80.

Kurtz, Ernest. "Spuds McKenzie, party animal?" *The Michigan Catholic*, February 19, 1988; reprinted as "Is Spuds McKenzie just another 'booze hound?'" *The Daily Tribune*, Royal Oak, Michigan, March 16, 1988.

978-0-595-52099-2
0-595-52099-5

www.ingramcontent.com/pod-product-compliance
Lightning Source LLC
Chambersburg PA
CBHW030302290526
45785CB00001B/187